Labour and Love

Women's Experience of Home
and Family, 1850–1940

Labour and Love

Women's Experience of Home and Family, 1850–1940

Edited by Jane Lewis

Basil Blackwell

Copyright © Basil Blackwell Ltd 1986

First published 1986
Reprinted 1987, 1989

Basil Blackwell Ltd
108 Cowley Road, Oxford OX4 1JF, UK

Basil Blackwell Inc.
432 Park Avenue South, Suite 1503
New York, NY 10016, USA

British Library Cataloguing in Publication Data

Labour and Love: women's experience of home and family, 1850–1940.
  1. Women—Great Britain—Family relationships
  2. Family—Great Britain—History
  I. Lewis, Jane
  305.4'3   HQ1543

  ISBN 0–631–13957–5
  ISBN 0–631–13958–3 Pbk

Library of Congress Cataloging Data

Labour and love.
Bibliography: p.
Includes index.
1. Women—Great Britain—Social conditions.
2. Housewives—Great Britain—History.   3. Family—
Great Britain—History.   I. Lewis, Jane II. Title:
Labor and love.
HQ1593.L26   1985   305.4'0941   85–13529
ISBN 0–631–13957–5
ISBN 0–631–13958–3 (pbk)

Typeset by Dentset, Oxford
Printed in Great Britain by Page Bros, Norwich

For Leonore Davidoff, whose constant encouragement and support of women historians and historians of women in recent years has provided a major stimulus to history.

Contents

List of Tables   viii

Acknowledgements   viii

Notes on Contributors   x

Preface   xii

Introduction: Reconstructing Women's Experience of
Home and Family   1

Part I   Childhood

1 Mothers and Daughters in the Middle-Class Home
  c. 1870–1914   *Carol Dyhouse*   27

2 Limited Resources and Limiting Conventions:
  Working-Class Mothers and Daughters in Urban Scotland
  c. 1890–1925   *Lynn Jamieson*   49

Part II   Mothering

3 Labour and Love: Rediscovering London's Working-Class
  Mothers, 1870–1918   *Ellen Ross*   73

4 The Working-Class Wife and Mother and State Intervention,
  1870–1918   *Jane Lewis*   99

Part III   The Theory and Practice of Sex and Marriage

5 Marriage Laid Bare: Middle-Class Women and Marital Sex
  c. 1880–1914   *Lucy Bland*   123

6 Women and Reproduction c. 1860–1919   *Barbara Brookes*   149

Part IV   Compatibility and Tension in Marriage

 7 'A New Comradeship between Men and Women': Family,
Marriage and London's Women Teachers, 1870–1914
Dina M. Copelman   175

 8 Marriage Relations, Money and Domestic Violence in
Working-Class Liverpool, 1919–39   *Pat Ayers* and
Jan Lambertz   195

Part V   The Family Economy

 9 'Women's Strategies', 1890–1940   *Elizabeth A.M. Roberts*   223

10 Marital Status, Work and Kinship, 1850–1930
Diana Gittins   249

Index   268

List of Tables

3.1 Fertility rates for some London Boroughs, 1880–1934
3.2 Average annual infant mortality in London, 1901–3
9.1 Percentages of married women in work, 1890–1940
9.2 Average contributions of married women in York to weekly
family income in the 1890's

Acknowledgements

The editor would like to express her gratitude to the following for permission to reproduce illustrations on: p.26 BBC Hulton Picture Library: p.48 People's Palace, Glasgow Museums: p.72 Local History Library at Swiss Cottage Library: p.98 Salvation Army, photograph courtesy of the London History Workshop: p.122 reproduced by kind permission of Dr Sarah Pearson and University College London: p.148 International Planned Parenthood Federation: p.174 Greater London Record Office: p.194 The Punch Book of Women's Rights: p.222 Salvation Army, photograph courtesy of the London History Workshop: p.248 Dartington Rural Archive.

Notes on Contributors

Pat Ayers grew up in Liverpool, and is completing a dissertation at the University of Liverpool on the inter-war working-class women's economy in the city.

Lucy Bland teaches women's studies and sociology in higher and adult education. She is a member of the Birmingham Feminist History Group and although trained in sociology and anthropology, she is undertaking historical research into female sexuality which will be published by the Women's Press. She is the author of several articles including, 'Purity, Motherhood, Pleasures or Threat? Definitions of Female Sexuality, 1900–1970' in Sue Cartledge and Joanna Ryan (eds) *Sex and Love* (Women's Press, 1983).

Barbara Brookes is a historian who teaches at the University of Otago in New Zealand. She is an active feminist and has pursued research on women in the USA and Britain. She is currently teaching women's history and preparing a book on the history of the legal theory and social practice of abortion in England.

Dina M. Copelman is an assistant professor at the University of Missouri, Columbia. She completed a doctoral dissertation on London elementary-school teachers at Princeton University in 1985. Currently she is revising her dissertation and starting another project tentatively entitled 'The Cultures of Feminism', on women, culture and politics in the Edwardian period in Britain.

Carol Dyhouse teaches in the Education Area at the University of Sussex. Her research interests are in the social history of women in nineteenth- and twentieth-century England, and in women's education. Her published work includes *Girls Growing Up in Late Victorian and Edwardian England* (Routledge and Kegan Paul, 1981) and various articles on women's history and the history of educational provision for girls.

Diana Gittins is the author of *Fair Sex: Family Size and Structure 1900–1939* (Hutchinson, 1982) and *The Family in Question: Changing Households and Familiar Ideologies* (Macmillan, 1985). She has contributed to various journals, including *New Society, Oral History* and *Victorian Studies*. She was a lecturer in sociology until 1984 and is now working on a novel. She lives in Devon with her daughter.

Lynn Jamieson is a lecturer in the Department of Sociology at Edinburgh University. Her main research interests are in primary relations, Scottish oral history and sexuality. She is currently seeking funding, with Dr Caroline Bamford, for a project on 'family' and friendship relationships of sixteen year olds. She has been active in the Campaign for Nuclear Disarmament since 1980 and is at present the vice-chairman of Scottish CND.

Jan Lambertz currently studies at the Technical University of Berlin and researches the history of child abuse. She was born in Detroit and lived in Liverpool from 1981 to 1983.

Jane Lewis teaches in the Social Administration Department at the London School of Economics. She is the author of *The Politics of Motherhood* (Croom Helm, 1980) and *Women in England: Sexual Divisions and Social Change, 1870–1950* (Wheatsheaf, 1984), and the editor of *Women's Welfare/Women's Rights* (Croom Helm, 1983).

Elizabeth A.M. Roberts is a research fellow in the Centre for North-West Regional Studies, University of Lancaster, and an adult education tutor. She is particularly interested in oral history and her book *A Woman's Place: An Oral History of Working Class Women, 1890–1940* was published by Basil Blackwell in 1984.

Ellen Ross is an associate professor of Women's Studies at Ramapo College in New Jersey. She is at work on a book, *Wives and Mothers in Working Class London, 1870–1918*, which expands some of the themes explored in her contribution to this volume.

Preface

This book has been conceived and developed alongside its companion volume, *Unequal Opportunites. Women's Employment in England 1800–1918* (edited by Angela V. John). Together the volumes form a central axis around which some of the major issues facing women over a period of 150 years can be approached. In order to examine these issues in detail we have separated them into two books, one focusing on employment and the other on domesticity. At the same time we recognize that there can be no real distinction between the two and that work, if not always waged work, warrants as much attention in the volume on domesticity as in that on employment. By the same token, the structure of the labour force and attitudes towards women workers can only properly be appreciated by considering ideas about sexuality, childbearing and childraising. The hierarchies of domination and subordination within the home, as well as the support systems within and beyond it, require analysis alongside the workings of industrial capitalism. Thus the volumes are mutually dependent and are intended to be read in conjunction with each other, as in the words of the final essay in this book:

> Understanding women's position in society necessitates an understanding of the often complicated ways in which work, marriage and kinship are woven together in a perplexing intricate tapestry.

Angela V. John
Jane Lewis

The editor would like to thank Barbara Meredith for her expert help in preparing the manuscript; our editor at Blackwell's, Sue Corbett, for her patience and encouragement; and, not least, the commitment of the contributors to the project.

Introduction: Reconstructing Women's Experience of Home and Family

Jane Lewis

Women's position in the family has been a central issue to feminist analysis of the nature of and reasons for sexual inequality during the past fifteen years. Anthropologists in particular have pointed out that in pre-industrial and industrial, pre-state and non-state societies and in most cultures, women's lives have been taken up largely with the domestic, that is the reproductive, the affective and the familial, and the kinds of labour that attached most easily thereto.[1] The world of paid employment and public office has been dominated by men and occupies but a secondary position in women's lives. Thus, for example, while during the period covered by this book the wages (if not the earnings) of Lancashire women textile workers were equal to those of men, home and family were always regarded as women's primary responsibility. During the late-nineteenth and early twentieth centuries, the expansion of jobs, especially in the retailing, clerical and teaching fields, employed increasing numbers of single women in the middle as well as the working class, while local government and, to a much lesser extent national, politics absorbed the attention of a minority of women.[2] Thus women made substantial progress in moving into the public sphere during the period, but the role of men within the home showed little change. Indeed, studies show that working wives still continue to do most of the cooking, housework and child-care for their families.[3]

Whereas nineteenth-century feminists concentrated for the most part on removing the barriers to women's entry into the public sphere, especially on opening the professions to women, recent feminist analysis has stressed the way in which inequalities in the domestic world structure inequalities in the public sphere. As the

Iren provement

American anthropologist, Michelle Rosaldo, argued in 1974, if the public is ever to belong to more than an elite of women, men must participate equally in the maintenance and caring work of the household.[4] The recognition that what happens in the private world of the family must be linked to the wider social and political system means that the family can no longer be treated as a separate category for analysis and the dependent variable, 'adapting' to changes in the world of work or in state policy.

In an effort to conceptualize the structure of inequality that encompasses both public and private life, feminist scholars have developed a number of analyses to account for the male domination that ensures that whatever women do is valued less than what men do. In this they have avoided resorting to the natural biologistic explanations favoured by nineteenth-century scientists and by many writers today, particularly perhaps in the field of economics. Darwinistic Victorian science proposed that psychological and cultural differences between men and women – such as women's stereotypically greater tenderness, generosity and intuition – derived from male and female biology. Herbert Spencer believed that the more highly developed the society the greater would be the differentiation in sex roles. Social scientists and medical doctors believed that women's individual evolution was arrested earlier than men's to permit the conservation of their energies for reproduction. It thus followed that young women should be protected from the strain of school examinations and confined as much as possible to the home.[5] Darwinistic ideas like these no longer hold, but it is still argued that because women will naturally choose marriage and motherhood (which is assumed to include the work of child-raising as well as childbearing), this means that they will choose to invest less in education and job training and will seek part-time work, near home, which is in the main low paid and of low status.[6] In this analysis, it is still biology that makes the domestic the natural world of women.

Most nineteenth-century feminists accepted women's responsibilities for home and children and believed that women had to make a choice between work, and marriage and motherhood. Their claim was for equality with men in the public world on men's terms, with no special consideration or provision for women as mothers and no suggestion that men might share the work of caring and domestic labour in the home. More recent feminist thinking has questioned the 'naturalness' of the domestic sexual division of labour, for while reproduction and lactation have provided a functional basis for the identification of a domestic sphere, it does not necessarily follow that women should also raise children and take responsibility for managing home and family life. This is in fact to conflate manifestation (in this case, maternity) with capacity (for biological reproduction). It is in any case important to remember that despite the fact of male domination, the boundary between public and private has varied over time and that the range of individual variability is also high (for example, not all women mother). Nineteenth and early twentieth-century working-class women experienced a much less severe separation between productive and reproductive work than did middle-class women, because they were much more likely to be engaged in paid employment before marriage and when the family economy demanded it thereafter.

To any outside observer, women's position in the family appears to have undergone dramatic changes between 1850 and 1940. The average family size, for example, dropped from six children in the late nineteenth century to two by 1940, the decrease coming earlier for middle-class than for working-class women. In the first decade of this century, 55 per cent of women had three or more children and 25 per cent more than five, but by the 1940s these figures were 30 per cent and 5 per cent respectively. At the same time, more infants survived. At the beginning of the century, the infant mortality rate was still well over 150 per thousand live births but it fell to around 50 by the outbreak of the Second World War in 1939 (it is now 14 per thousand). In the 1900s it was not uncommon for women to speak in the same breath of the number of children they had raised and the number they had buried. The average woman marrying in her teens or early twenties in the 1890s experienced ten pregnancies and spent fifteen years either pregnant or nursing, compared with an average of four years so spent by her counterpart in the years following the Second World War. It is hard to estimate the amount of emotional and physical pain concealed by these statistics.

It is also possible for an observer to point to great material improvements in women's domestic lives during the period covered by this book. Real wages rose substantially after the First World War, allowing those in work to think about moving to a house with a bath or buying a gas stove. For middle-class women it is possible that the modern suburban house of the inter-war years, better equipped with labour-saving devices, with either a resident servant or a daily help and a smaller number of children, provided women with more leisure than either the large household staffs of the

Victorian period or the usually servantless home of the years following the Second World War.

It is however, possible to over-emphasize, first, the extent of the changes and, second, the degree to which they were of real benefit to women. Many working-class women continued to struggle to bring up their families in the 1920s and 1930s with access to only a shared cold water tap. Nor is there much evidence to suggest any real improvement in working-class women's health by the Second World War. Margery Spring Rice found 31.2 per cent of her sample of 1,250 working-class wives to be in 'very grave' health and 15.2 per cent to be in 'bad' health.[7] Moreover, as the survival of children became more certain and housework less onerous, so standards of childcare and housekeeping were inflated. Many middle-class mothers followed complicated feeding schedules devised by (male) infant-care experts during the inter-war years and both working-class and middle-class women strove to maintain elaborate household routines. Nella Last, the respectable wife of a joiner, spoke of pictures and furniture being polished once a week;[8] a prize winner in *Our Homes and Gardens* spoke of dusting pictures and skirtings daily.[9] It is difficult to come to a realistic assessment of the balance between continuity and change experienced by women in their domestic lives during the period under consideration, but one point is clear: married women continued to believe firmly that their primary commitment was to home and family.

The essays in this book seek to further our understanding of women's worlds. They concentrate on the home and family, just as the parallel volume in this series, *Unequal Opportunities*, edited by Angela V. John, concentrates on the workplace.[10] Thus they explore relationships within the family, between parents and children, and husbands and wives, but they also seek to examine the links between women's experience of family and of work, the nature of the relationship with female friends and kin, and the connections between women's experience of family and the exercise of male power, both within the family unit and through the wider social and political system. Of course, our understanding of the sex/gender system can never hope to be complete until we have a deliberate attempt to understand the total fabric of men's worlds and the construction of masculinity.

I

Most accounts of women's domestic lives have been drawn primarily from the prescriptive literature, which conveys a powerful ideology of domesticity.[11] Marriage and motherhood were Victorian woman's 'natural' destiny and it was considered a tragedy if they were not achieved, or if one was achieved without the other. Indeed, the position of the unmarried mother worsened considerably with the passing of the 1834 Poor Law, which sought to place full responsibility for the child on the mother, and again in the 1870s, when the regulations concerning the administration of poor relief outside the workhouse were considerably tightened for both unmarried mothers and deserted wives. The discovery from the 1851 Census that women outnumbered men provoked lengthy discussion under the heading of the 'surplus woman problem', because commentators found it difficult to see what women who could not find husbands would do. The 'angel in the house', sexually passive and refined, whose responsibility it was to oversee the provision of a sanctuary of well-ordered comfort and peace became the literary ideal for middle-class women. In all classes of society, hearth and home acquired the significance of religious symbolism.

The identification of married middle-class women with home and family persisted throughout the early twentieth century. Very few worked outside the home and indeed marriage bars were imposed in the professions during the 1920s and 1930s. However, models for the ideal wife changed substantially. William Beveridge, for example, characterized mariage as a 'partnership',[12] implying that wives were to be regarded more as companions than 'perfect ladies' or 'angels'. But the partnership was not necessarily an equal one, women were still expected to concern themselves with the provision of a domestic sanctuary and, by the 1940s, this included more attention to the emotional support of husbands. For reasons that have not yet been fully explored, but which must be connected to the increasing isolation of the conjugal family, it was no longer expected that wives should be kept in ignorance of their husband's affairs, but rather that there should be a new emotional (and indeed sexual) intimacy between husband and wife leading to a more active, sympathic support role for the wife.

Rather more anxiety accompanied the prescriptions for the 'good' working-class wife. Ideally, working-class families were expected to adhere to the bourgeois family model of breadwinning husband and a wife who employed her time usefully at home, managing the household budget, cooking nutritious, cheap meals, and cleaning and sewing for her family. It was widely recognized that the mother was the 'pivot' of the household, on whom the comfort and integrity of the family depended and, from the late-nineteenth century, social investigators such as Helen Bosanquet, parish visitors, voluntary organizations of all kinds, medical officers of health and health visitors all directed a stream of advice towards the working-class mother.[13] Prior to the First World War, working-class mothers were generally better regarded than their husbands, who were constantly suspected of idleness and drunkeness. The mothers were thought to be well-meaning but all too often ignorant and in need of education as to appropriate methods of infant care and household management. In the years of mass employment following the war, working-class husbands were no longer actively blamed for their personal failure to provide, but the education of mothers was still believed to be crucial, and by the late 1940s, attention had shifted entirely to the mother's responsibility for the emotional as well as the physical well-being of her children. Literature of the Second World War addressed to the forces assumed that fathers would be responsible parents and cooperate voluntarily with the state,[14] but the link made by influential psychologists between affectionlessness, or 'maternal deprivation' and delinquency was a source of increasing pressure on women to be full-time mothers. Maternal 'adequacy' was seen by psychologists and social workers as the key to 'normal' child development.[15]

It is dangerous, however, to infer experience from prescription. It is not clear either how far Victorian middle-class women were the passive decorative creatures idealized by the Coventry Patmore or John Ruskin, or whether working-class mothers were in need of education and advice. Nor is it clear how far women of any social class paid attention to the domestic ideal. It is possible that models for the good wife and mother were unconsciously internalized or that they underwent subtle 'adjustment' to fit more easily with the reality of women's lives, or that they were consciously resisted. Finally, it is not clear how women made sense of the lives they actually lived and how they felt about them.

There are, therefore, many dimensions to be explored in the reconstruction of women's actual experience. In the first place, prescription must be tested against material realities. Were most middle-class women likely to be able to live the rather vacuous life of the 'perfect lady'? Upper-middle-class women were often responsible for the household accounts of establishments where the sums involved amounted to as much as £2000–3000 a year, and where the supervision of small armies of servants could be arduous, as Violet Markham found out when she took over the running of her family home on the death of her mother in 1912.[16] Smaller establishments presented their own difficulties. In Bank's classic work on the middle class and family size, he reckoned that maintenance of the 'paraphernalia of gentility' in the late-nineteenth century required a sum of about £700 a year,[17] and as Patricia Branca pointed out, large numbers of middle-class wives were responsible for making ends meet on incomes of £200–300.[18] Jeanne Peterson's work on medical doctors during the mid-Victorian years shows that the income of a provincial doctor quite often fell with this range.[19] In the case of this occupational group, keeping up appearances, with the minimum of a carriage and a maid to answer the door, was crucial to building a successful practice. We may thus surmise that careful household management was also required of wives, who would have to play an active part in running the home, probably to the extent of helping the general servant with housekeeping chores. Editorial correspondents during the inter-war years continued to complain of the work required of the middle-class wife, particularly in respect to sewing and mending, to make ends meet.[20]

The realities of life for working-class women were much harsher. Magdalen Stuart Pember Reeves summed up the situation well when she commented of Lambeth wives in the early part of the century that 'to manage a husband and six children in three rooms on round about a pound a week needs first and foremost wisdom and loving kindness, and after that as much cleanliness and order as can be squeezed in.'[21] Visitors from the Charity Organisation Society might recommend that wives cook cheap and nutritious porridge and herring, but when the family owned but one saucepan and cooked on the open fire, sticky porridge was not a practical dish, nor was it pleasant to live in a cramped space that reeked of herrings. Water often had to be carried from a communal tap well into the inter-war period and washing involved pounding clothes in a dolly tub and then mangling by hand. Ruth Schwartz Cowan's recent work on domestic technology has shown that improvement in domestic equipment did not necessarily lighten women's labour, for example, the ranges that replaced open fires required constant black-leading.[22] The vivid records we have of women's own experiences, recorded by the Women's Cooperative Guild and published in 1915 as letters on maternity, tell us of women engaging in hard household labour up to the point of childbirth, of frequent pregnancies and poor health (bronchitis in winter, varicose veins, anaemia and prolapses were the most common), and little or no leisure.[23] These women struggled to find time for Guild meetings, but the vast majority of working-class women took no part in political life or community activities.

As to whether working-class women were ignorant of good household management and child care: groups such as the Guild certainly expressed a desire for more information about female physiology and the health of their children. But this is not to say that they necessarily welcomed the intrusion of the health visitor, or advice from middle-class female visitors and Schools for Mothers on nutritious meals that were impossible to prepare in their often overcrowded and insanitary dwellings, where the battle with dirt was invariably lost. Like the more sympathetic investigators of the early part of the century, several historians have concluded that, given their surroundings, working-class mothers did the best they could.[24] On the new council estates of the inter-war period, conditions were better; many women particularly relished having a bath. (Not that all homes of the period provided a bathroom; this novel piece of equipment was secreted under the stairs or the kitchen table in some council houses of the period.) Rents, however were higher on the new estates, which meant that women faced additional problems in solving the eternal food/rent equation. Women and children usually ended up 'going short', the choicest food going to the breadwinner.

This brief assessment of the material realities experienced by women is fleshed out substantially in the essays that follow; they are introduced here merely in order to indicate the possibility of tensions arising from the gap between prescribed and actual behaviour. Carol Smith Rosenberg has suggested that the tension produced by the effort required to achieve a style of life congruent with ideas of gentility, while at the same time running a household and undergoing frequent childbirth, may explain the large numbers of nineteenth-century middle-class women diagnosed as hysterics.[25] By taking refuge in the sick role, women were able to escape their domestic responsibilities, and because doctors considered their condition to be the natural result of female physiological weakness, their behaviour was socially acceptable. This assumes, however, that the domestic ideal was in large part accepted and internalized by middle-class women. Branca also makes this assumption in her work, even though in her interpretation women struggling to achieve a genteel lifestyle on a small income demonstrated resourcefulness and ingenuity.[26] Yet Jeanne Peterson and Carl Degler have questioned the extent to which middle-class women's lives bore any relation to the domestic ideal. Many of the women discussed in Peterson's detailed investigation of the Paget family followed pursuits of their own choosing and also participated in decision-making about their husbands' careers and family businesses, at a time when women were supposed to be ignorant of such matters.[27] And from his study of a rare contemporary survey of American college women during the 1890s, Degler has suggested that Victorian women actively enjoyed sex.[28] Certainly, it was not impossible for women to make use of the fact that they had large numbers of servants to engage in some meaningful work or artistic pursuit, as long as it was not pursued for money. But of course this proviso immediately jeopardized the seriousness of the endeavour.

It is possible, then, that the fabric of middle-class women's lives bore little relation to that prescribed for the angel of the home and even that divergence from the ideal did not necessarily produce tensions. Yet it may be argued that both prescription and material reality imposed real constraints on women's behaviour and expression. Middle-class women, married or single, had few opportunities outside the home. Most did not know where exactly their husbands' workplace was or what it looked like inside, or had any idea of what went on there. Many creative women fully recognized that marriage would in all probability end what little opportunity they had for the useful pursuits permitted them, chiefly reading or philanthropic work. This was the cause of Beatric Webb's agony over her affair with the politician, Joseph Chamberlain. If she married him she would have had to reconcile herself to the life of a society hostess, which she found attractive at one level – it was a socially acceptable and high status 'occupation' – but with little social purpose.[29] Within the constraints of a world in which middle-class women necessarily sought the protection of a man, she was arguably fortunate to marry Sidney Webb, with whom she could share an intellectual life, as well as gain emotional support, and escape the lonely and monotonous routines of the elderly spinster living in the parental home.

Middle-class women's need for economic support, together with the ideology of domesticity that dictated a particular role for women within the home, did serve to place limits on the range of women's choices and on their expectations. The possibilities for resistance were slim. Deborah Gorham and Leonore Davidoff have shown how middle-class women were expected to engage in the arduous social duties of 'calling', no matter whether they liked the practice or not.[30] Indeed, Davidoff has shown how such practices were crucial to the vital social process of distinguishing new wealth from old. Moroeever, women tended to be judged and to judge one another on the terms set by the ideology of domesticity. The concept of the 'good wife' was widely understood and accepted. Exceptional women, who were determined to pursue public activities and lives rarely openly rejected the domestic ideal; rather, they turned its message to their advantage. Thus Josephine Butler fought her campaign against the Contagious Diseases Acts and the double moral standard in the name of the sanctity of home life, and Millicent Fawcett struggled for the vote not to permit women to forsake hearth and home, but rather to allow the voice of mothers be represented at the national level.[31] Thus domestic ideology might be mediated and concern for family used to justify going outside the home to engage in a public campaign or, much more often, to venture into the homes of working-class women to instruct them on household management; large numbers of Victorian middle-class women spent quantities of time 'visiting' the poor.[32]

Working-class women were similarly circumscribed in the choices they were able to make respecting the pattern of their lives. The average wages of adult working-class women hovered around subsistence levels for much of the period covered by this book. The minimum wages set by the wages councils (established in 1909 and then called trade boards) were below the subsistence standard established by Rowntree in 1937. Their regulations applied to one-sixth of all women workers. Thus working-class women who did not marry were hard pressed to support themselves adequately. Once married, however, low and irregular male wages, especially in the period before the First World War, forced women to take up casual work, often charring, or sewing at home or in workshops, in order to make ends meet. The vast majority of working-class women accepted responsibility for the welfare of their families, which entailed considerable personal sacrifice in both material and psychological terms; women went without new clothes, good food and the leisure to pursue activities related to the development of self rather than the welfare of family.

Working-class women also experienced tensions between what was expected of them as 'good wives' and what it was possible to achieve given their material circumstances. Most working-class wives accepted the idea that women should take responsibility for home and family and that men should be the breadwinners; in the context of hard domestic labour and frequent pregnancy it was a model that made sense.[33] However, poverty also dictated that women engage in paid employment as and when necessary to help their families. State legislation, which assumed the existence of the bourgeois family model, thus tended to thwart the working-class wife's effort to sustain her family. For example, school attendance officers, who insisted that girls should attend school regularly and not be kept at home to mind the baby while mother worked, encountered bitter resistance in the late-nineteenth century.

Many working-class wives also fought to reconcile the demands of being a good wife with notions of respectability.[34] For example, carding buttons at home was preferable to making matchboxes because it was a more respectable occupation. In large measure, notions of respectability accorded with the bourgeois family model. Most respectable of all was the wife who did not have to take paid employment. Visible manifestations of respectability included whitened doorsteps and a clean rent book. In the context of primitive domestic technology and often unpredictable income such things were, however, hard to achieve. Moreover pursuit of them was likely to produce a certain conflict between necessary reliance on the help of female neighbours in hard times and the imperative of social distance inherent in the concept of respectability. Broadly speaking, respectability was a concept endorsed by social superiors because it connoted social order and responsibility. However, the working-class wife's criteria of respectability did not match those of social investigators and government inspectors. Infant welfare experts, for example, deplored the amount of time cleaning rituals took to the detriment of attention to babies and toddlers. Women necessarily mediated ideas of the 'good wife' and of respectability in accordance with their material circumstances and different social priorities and belief systems.

Given that the major task of so many working-class wives was concerned with securing the well-being of their families by whatever means possible, their room for manoeuvre was necessarily confined. Labour movement activists, like Ada Nield Chew and Hannah Mitchell struggled to do the week's baking and cleaning sufficiently in advance to allow them to go to meetings.[35] Both were fortunate in having small families before it became the norm for working-class women to do so. Women expected to look after their families and hoped above all for a 'good' husband, that is a good provider. In old established working-class communities before the First World War there was no greater expectation of shared intimacies and companionship between husband and wife than among Victorian middle-class families. The increasing isolation of the conjugal family unit during the inter-war years may have changed this somewhat; certainly Diana Gittins has suggested that those husbands and wives with close joint relationships were most successful in limiting their family size during this period.[36] There is evidence to suggest that many working-class women took pride in the control they exerted in managing the family economy and that they resented the intrusions of state officials or indeed of husbands, in what they regarded as their domain. With smaller families and either the more regular wages or dole money of the inter-war years, less ingenuity was required to make ends meet and less pride accrued from so doing.

Exploration of the way women mediated or resisted the role expected of them, or of the tensions they experienced still does not tell us what meanings they attached to family, home, marriage or children. Such a project is difficult in large part because there are few readily identifiable sources to work with. Many of the authors in this volume have made extensive use of oral history (although only Jamieson and Roberts make it their main primary source material), but even interviews do not always reveal the intimacies of marriage and personal life. Something can be gained from an exploration of more unusual sources, as Barbara Brookes' use of criminal depositions relating to abortion trials shows or, of course, from tracking down the autobiographies, personal letters and diaries more common among middle-class women, as Carol Dyhouse has done. But it is also possible to piece together the ideas of articulate women about the various dimensions of personal life. For example while much has been written on feminist arguments for the vote, very little attention has been paid to women's views of marriage and the family, as Lucy Bland's piece shows. And it is essential that the new insights and understanding produced by fifteen years of analysis of women's position in the family be brought to bear on familiar qualitative and quantitative source materials. Phyllis Rose has recently provided us with a splendid example of this in her work on five well-known Victorian marriages. Previous authors have read in George Eliot, for example, evidence of a chronic need for affection, but Rose sees rather a passionate woman struggling aggressively (with limited opportunity) to love and find someone to love her.[37] This more realistic interpretation is based on a wider investigation and appreciation of the constraints and conflicts experienced by middle-class Victorian women. In this volume, Diana Gittins combines the use of oral interviews, census material and parish records to reconstruct the households of a small Devonshire town and to provide a sensitive commentary on the lives of the women within them. It is, of course, hard to generalize about the female experience. These essays deliberately draw on evidence from a number of different geographical regions, but it remains for further work to confirm or deny their findings for other areas of the country.

II

Parts I and II examine the experience of children and mothers. We have recently been subjected to a rash of mother-blaming literature, from men and women, anti-feminists, non-feminists and feminists. Writing about his mother, Rebecca West, Anthony West has been determined to show that 'she was minded to do me what hurt she could, and that she remained set in that determination as long as there was breath in her body to sustain her malice.'[38] Nancy Friday has argued in her book, *My Mother Myself* that daughters' unhappiness can be blamed on their mothers, who intentionally and often viciously constrain their behaviour.[39] And, writing as a feminist, Dorothy Dinnerstein has sought to demonstrate the disastrous impact of 'mother-dominated infancy' on men, women and society.[40] Historians of the family have also argued strongly that, prior to the nineteenth century, women did not love their children and that 'affective relations' are a feature of the recent past.[41] Absence of maternal affection has been inferred both from demographic statistics, particularly the high infant-mortality rates, and from customs, such as the fact that parents in seventeenth and eighteenth-century Anjou did not attend their children's funerals. Yet as Stephen Wilson has recently observed, other interpretations of this behaviour – for example, that the parents were too grief stricken to attend – are just as possible.[42] Edward Shorter has, nevertheless, gone so far as to suggest that as late as the nineteenth century the high infant-mortality rate among urban working-class infants provides evidence of maternal neglect and, like nineteenth-century observers, he has singled out working mothers for particular blame.[43]

There are two fundamental assumptions at work in this literature: first, that mothers have enormous control over childraising practices; and, second, that there is a workable definition of what it means to be a 'good mother'. But as the essays in this section show, mothers' control over their children is subject to considerable material and ideological constraint. Moreover, the idea of what constituted a 'good mother' varied between classes, between social prescriptions and mothers' behaviour, and between mothers and daughters.

On the whole, the evidence seems to suggest that middle-class mothers did their best to follow social prescriptions in bringing up their daughters. As Carol Dyhouse shows, mothers may have hated calling and card-leaving rituals, but nonetheless brought up daughters to do their 'duty' in this respect. She also shows them respecting taboos regarding sexuality and menstruation despite the anguish that resulted for the daughter. Moreover, fathers could be counted on to enforce ladylike behaviour on the part of daughters; Jex Blake for example, who took a strong stand in refusing to countenance his daughter, Sophia, accepting a salary for teaching mathematics at Queen's College.

For working-class women, it seems that there was a greater gap between the behaviour prescribed for a good mother and their own understanding of good mothering, and that the tensions increased during the period before the First World War. Mothers felt that their first duty was to provide for their children, which might necessitate going out to work. This should not therefore be necessarily interpreted as neglect, or as evidence of lack of maternal affection on their part, but rather the reverse. Similarly, as Lynn Jamieson shows, mothers might have no option but to insist on daughters contributing to the arduous work of the household. Ellen Ross points out that love in working-class homes must be seen as taking the form of service, and the reciprocal obligations of mother and children in respect to labour should not be assumed to be without emotional content. Both Ross and Lewis observe the way in which these shared understandings of the relationship between love and labour were complicated by the additional expectations and interventions on the part of the state during the early twentieth century. The apparatus of health visitors, infant welfare clinics and state elementary schools, with their demands for regular attendance and medical inspection, reduced the labour that children could provide for their families, while increasing the demands on mothers. Indeed, some schools hoped to educate mothers via their daughters.

Historians and contemporaries may have given the impression that there were many more bad mothers than good in the past, but this view is not endorsed by daughters. Both Ross and Jamieson stress what is undoubtedly a much more realistic ambivalence on the part of daughters towards their mothers. As Dyhouse notes, most middle-class women's autobiographies are written by rebels, yet their accounts of relationships with their mothers reveal intimacy as well as rebellion. Jamieson and Ross show that working-class children felt pride as often as resentment about the contributions they were expected to make to the family economy and Jamieson argues that girls resented only the deferential service to brothers that was sometimes expected, but not the giving of help in and of itself and not the fact that the nature of the help they were expected to give was different from that expected of boys. It would appear that most daughters did not feel that their mothers intentionally constrained them, but rather that they understood and appreciated the constraints experienced by their mothers.

It is even more difficult to reconstruct women's experience of marriage and the nature of their relationships with their partners than it is to reconstruct their role as mothers and their relationship with daughters. What did marriage mean to late-nineteenth- and early twentieth-century women? Cicely Hamilton stressed the importance of marriage as a 'trade' for middle-class women.[44] Working-class women also relied on marriage as a means of financial support. There is, however, another side to this emphasis on dependency. Marriage was also seen (and as Beatrix Campbell's recent observations show, is still seen) as a means of achieving not only a higher social status, but also adulthood, which in and of themselves represent substantial secondary gains.[45]

In her previous work, Ellen Ross has argued that working-class marriage did not enjoin romantic love or verbal and sexual intimacy, but required financial obligations, services and activities that were gender specific.[46] This did not mean, as I point out in my own essay, that affection was necessarily lacking, but expectations of marriage and perhaps women's priorities may have been different from that of today, although it is particularly difficult to assess how realistic young single women were about married life. As Pat Ayers and Jan Lambertz point out, there may well have been painful dysjunctures between the romance of courtship and the reality of married life.

The third set of essays focuses on sexuality and reproduction, the most difficult aspect of personal life to research historically. Given the taboo placed on any subject relating to sexuality and the ignorance of both middle-class and working-class women of their physiology, it is difficult to find out either what women thought about sex or what they actually did. The 1890s survey of American college women's sexual behaviour tapped by Degler,[47] or the explicit diaries used by Peter Gay in his book on bourgeois sexuality,[48] are all too rare and

Fem Movement

are also difficult to balance against evidence that some women did internalize the ideal of sexual passivity, such that 'two separate races [confronted] each other over the marriage bed.'[49] To date, students of women's history have concentrated on exploring the records of organizations such as the Women's Cooperative Guild or the papers of individuals who expressed explicit views on sexuality in the course of campaigns against the Contagious Diseases Acts, or in favour of birth control and abortion.[50] Lucy Bland has uncovered some new sources which reveal the views of a number of articulate middle-class women, most of them feminists, on the problems of sex in and outside marriage. The problems they identify are strikingly similar to those discussed by early nineteenth-century Owenite socialists: for example, the nature of sexual desire in men and women, the form of the marriage contract and the possibilities for its reform or abolition, and the responsibilities for children.[51] What is striking is the way in which even these admittedly exceptional women had difficulty both in articulating their ideas within a male framework of beliefs in natural sexual difference and biological determinism, and in coming to terms with their ambivalent attitudes towards marriage and sexual freedom. The latter can only be understood in the social context of late-nineteenth-century marriage and reproduction. As Barbara Brookes explains, reproduction was being situated ever more firmly within marriage and, given middle-class married women's essential financial dependency, even radical women were bound to feel uneasy about free unions and birth control, both of which threatened to divorce reproduction from marriage. Thus before the First World War, women were more likely to argue publicly for a higher moral standard for men than for greater sexual freedom for women. But as both Bland and Brookes show, the emphasis placed during the inter-war years by the new sexologists on sexual companionship within marriage changed the terms of the debate, making it more difficult for women to formulate their own critique.

The dynamics of marital relationships, especially in respect of decision-making, are of crucial importance to our understanding of sexual and emotional behaviour. It is difficult to assess both the extent to which decisions reflected the greater financial or indeed physical power of the husband and the extent to which they were reached by discussion, harmonious or otherwise. As Stacey and Price have argued, power should be understood not only as the circumstances in which the will of one person triumphs over that of another, but the circumstances in which the views, interests or wishes of one category or group (men) are normally given precedence, in which case there is no struggle or conflict, but rather superiority is taken for granted.[52] Rose sees power as the key to understanding the marriage relationship, suggesting that love is 'the momentary or prolonged refusal to think of another person in terms of power' and that a marriage turns sour when the weaker member feels exploited, or the stronger is rewarded for his/her strength.[53] From a consideration of power it follows that we might expect a range of decision-making practices between husband and wife. The model suggested by J. A. Banks in respect to fertility control, which stresses the power of the husband, is likely to be partial.[54] In the majority of cases such a decision was probably negotiated between husband and wife. Brookes' essay shows that the behaviour on the part of lovers and husbands towards women having abortions ranged from support to the crude exercise of domination; in some cases men forced women to abort.

In the last two sets of essays Ayers and Lambertz, Copelman, and Roberts all explore aspects of the everyday pattern of marriage relations, especially with regard to questions of gender roles and money management. Writing of domestic behaviour in the present, Pauline Hunt has wrestled with the problem of describing the status of husband and wife in the traditional male-breadwinner/dependent-wife relationship and concluded that, while the concept of authority reminds us that the male breadwinner's status is legitimated by the dominant ideology, the concept of power points to the coercive undercurrents in the domestic relationship.[55] Ayers and Lambertz's essay supports this view. They stress not the complementarity of male and female roles and tasks perceived by Ross, Roberts and myself, but rather the deceit and tensions, and the potential or actual violence arising primarily from the problems of household budgeting in working-class Liverpool families. Their evidence seems to bear out the findings of Nancy Tomes' study of crimes of violence between working-class husbands and wives in London between 1840 and 1875.[56] Her evidence showed that wife beating occured when the woman failed to carry out a duty assigned to her or when she brought disrepute upon the family, for example by resorting to the pawn shop, or when she interfered with her husband's actions by nagging him to change his ways. Tensions in working-class marriage seem to have centred around questions of male privilege and the allocation of resources.

I argue in this volume, as do Roberts and Ross elsewhere,[57] that the sexual division of labour between male breadwinner and female household manager was a shared ideal, largely because it made sense when the burden of women's household labour and frequent pregnancies was so large. This is not to deny that the male-breadwinner family model discriminated against women as workers and priviledged men within the home.[58] Ayers and Lambertz's contrasting view is valuable, not least because it reminds us of the difficulty in assigning a single interpretation to 'private' behaviour in the past. Oral testimony in and of itself is no more sure a guide than other forms of evidence in this respect because, just as meanings were negotiated between husband and wife, so individuals renegotiate the meaning of events in their lives as time passes.

Looking at the lower-middle-class marriages of teachers, Dina Copelman finds not conflict but mutual support and, more surprising still, not for the traditional sexual division of labour, but rather for women continuing to work after marriage. Women teachers continued to shoulder the primary responsibility for home and family, often with considerable difficulty, but many were able to call on husbands to render both material help and moral support. Interestingly, the position of the married woman teacher was eroded during the inter-war years not by the opposition of husbands, but rather by the male teachers union, the National Association of Schoolmasters, anxious to secure the position of its members, and by local authorities who adopted marriage bars as a publicly acceptable (if in the long term ineffectual) way of creating jobs for unemployed college leavers and as a means of reducing expenses in the wake of public expenditure cuts.[59] Copelman's women teachers appear to have found immense satisfaction in their work. Working-class women were unlikely to do so in the casual charring and sewing jobs they were most likely to pick up. Indeed, as Elizabeth Roberts comments, women who had to undertake full-time paid work in addition to their arduous household chores were pitied by their neighbours. Robert's account of working-class women's strategies to combat poverty illustrates the range and ingenuity of their efforts to secure the welfare of their families.

Women without male support were even more dependent on their ability to earn. Diana Gittins examines the position of widows, unmarried mothers and single women in a small Devonshire textile town. Household census data for 1851 and 1871 finds many of these women sharing a household with married kin. Indeed, there seems to be a parallel here with Edward Higgs' findings for Rochdale from the same censuses. In a study of domestic service, he found that no fewer than 40 per cent of servants were related to their employers.[60]

Suffrage

As Gittins skillfully argues, the obligations of work, kinship and marriage were overlapping ones. Help from kin and neighbours was crucial to married and single women and mutual aid was extended from borrowing and bartering to moral and material support at times of illness and crisis. Brookes' evidence on abortion shows that women often sought the help of other women. It is also true that women's obligations to kin sometimes dominated their whole lives. The fate of the unmarried middle-class daughter caring for elderly parents was often, as Beatrice Webb remarked, a singularly unhappy and isolated one.[61] Gittins shows early twentieth-century parents discouraging younger daughters from marriage and paid employment in order to keep them at home and, apparently, the daughters reported no resentment.[62]

It is also important to assess the role of female kin, neighbour and friendship networks *vis à vis* women's allegiance to home and husbands. It could be argued that these should be seen as expressions of solidarity and empowerment. But as Janet Bujra has pointed out, without control over production or politics, the latter is unlikely (although the rent strikes organized by women, especially during the First World War, are remarkable examples of consumer power). Moreover, female solidarity rarely manages to override class divisions or conjugal solidarity.[63] In fact, female support networks could sometimes act as a brake on more radical thoughts and behaviour. Rosemary Crook has shown that Rhondda women's support for other women during the inter-war years was dependent on their adoption of the conservative moral values of the community.[64]

A striking theme that emerges from many of these essays is the extent to which women's worlds were oriented around the family. Paid employment was usually taken up at different points in the life cycle in response to crises, as and when the family economy demanded it. Women's political activities, whether in the suffrage or labour movements, also tended to be premised on the importance of their roles as wives and mothers. The Women's Cooperative Guild, for example made the welfare of mothers and children the main focus of their early twentieth-century campaigns. Olwen Hufton's comment on the importance of family for eighteenth-century women remained true of women in the late-nineteenth- and early twentieth-centuries: 'One's family of origin shaped one's potential for living and working; one's whole working life, whether one married or not, was colored by notions of family.'[65]

Many of the essays in this volume comment on girls' and

women's ambivalent feelings about family relationships: in respect of paid work and its relationship to domestic labour; between autonomy and dependency in respect of their economic position; and pleasure and danger in respect of their sexuality. While feminist analysis has shown how women's position in the family is central to an understanding of sexual inequality, it is surely the case, as Beatrix Campbell has pointed out in her recent account of the lives of working-class women today, that women 'both accept and resent men's domination' and feel both 'complaint and commitment about domestic life with men'.[66] In all probability, women felt a similar ambivalence in the past, although their expression of acceptance and resentment, complaint and commitment may have taken very different forms. Many of the essays offer evidence regarding relationships at the individual level, which help us to understand the patterns of women's lives and how they made sense of them. Personal relationships could erode or reinforce the role expected of women and mitigate or exacerbate the material realities of their lives. Husbands and children might be a source of support or a constant source of conflict and resentment, and even violence. Female kin and neighbours could be a source of mutual aid and moral support or of instrumental assistance and, at worst, rivalry. The essays that follow also show that the extent to which the boundaries of family extended beyond immediate conjugal relationships to kin and neighbours, and beyond the domestic sphere to the public.

Notes

Place of publication in these and all other notes is London unless otherwise stated.

1 Michelle Zimbalist Rosaldo, 'Women, Culture and Society: a theoretical overview', in M. Z. Rosaldo and L. Lamphere (eds.), *Women Culture and Society* (Stanford University Press, Stanford, 1974). This introduction is not the place to take up in detail the debate over the concept of public and domestic but it should be noted that, while such a separation of spheres appears to fit the recent historical experience of Western women well, anthropologists have found, first, that the dichotomy conflates too easily with public/private and reproduction/production to be a useful conceptual tool and, second, that it has more descriptive than analytical power. Some of the critiques are discussed by Rayna Rapp, 'Anthropology', *Signs* 4 (1979), 497–513.

2 Women over thirty were granted the vote in 1918, but as Linda E. Walker shows, women's work for national political parties was important from the closing decades of the nineteenth century: 'The Women's

Movement in England in the late Nineteenth and Early Twentieth Centuries', unpublished PhD. thesis, University of Manchester, 1984.

3 Lisa Peattie and Martin Rein, *Women's Claims. A Study in Political Economy* (Oxford University Press, New York, 1983), pp. 71–2.

4 Rosaldo, 'Women, Culture and Society'.

5 On Victorian Social Darwinism, see Carol Dyhouse, 'Social Darwinistic Ideas and the Development of Women's Education in England, 1880–1920', *History of Education* 5 (1976); Janet Sayers, *Biological Politics: Feminist and Anti-Feminist Perspectives* (Tavistock, 1982); and Sara Delamont and Lorna Duffin (ed), *The Nineteenth Century Woman: Her Cultural and Physical World* (Croom Helm, 1975).

6 For further comment see Irene Bruegel, 'Women's Employment, Legislation and the Labour Market', in Jane Lewis (ed.) *Women's Welfare/Women's Rights* (Croom Helm, 1983).

7 Margery Spring Rice, *Working Class Wives* (Virago, 1981, first published 1939).

8 Richard Broad and Suzie Fleming (eds), *Nella Last's War* (Sphere, 1983) p. 255.

9 Nicola Beaumann, *A Very Great Profession. The Woman's Novel* (Virago, 1983), p. 110.

10 Angela V. John (ed.) *Unequal Opportunities: Women's Employment in England 1800–1918* (Basil Blackwell, Oxford, 1985).

11 On the ideology of domesticity, see J. A. Banks, *Prosperity and Parenthood* (Routledge & Kegan Paul, 1954); Delamont and Duffin, *Nineteenth Century Woman* (Croom Helm, 1978); Joan N. Burstyn, *Victorian Education and the Ideal of Womanhood* (Croom Helm, 1980); and Deborah Gorham, *The Victorian Girl and the Feminine Ideal* (Croom Helm, 1982).

12 William Beveridge's 'Report on Social Insurance and Allied Services', Cmnd. 6404 (HMSO, 1942).

13 Helen Bosanquet, *The Family* (Macmillan, 1906). On advice to working-class mothers more generally, see Jane Lewis, *The Politics of Motherhood* (Croom Helm, 1980); and Anna Davin, 'Imperialism and Motherhood', *History Workshop Journal* 5 (1978), 9–65. Peter Stearns accepts that working-class women were poor housekeepers: 'Working Class Women in Britain, 1890–1914', in Martha Vicinus (ed.), *Suffer and be Still* (Bloomington, Indiana University Press, 1973), pp. 100–20.

14 Patricia Allatt, 'The Family Seen Through the Beveridge Report, Forces Education and Popular Magazines: A Social Study of the Social Reproduction of Family Ideology in World War II', unpublished PhD. thesis, University of Keele, 1981.

15 On psychological theories, see Denise Riley *War in the Nursery: Theories of the Child and the Mother* (Virago, 1983).

16 Violet R. Markham, *Return Passage* (Oxford University Press, Oxford, 1953).

17 Banks, *Prosperity and Parenthood*.

18 Patricia Branca, *Silent Sisterhood: Middle Class Women in the Victorian Home* (Croom Helm, 1975).

Suffrage (handwritten)

19 M. Jeanne Peterson, *The Medical Profession in Mid–Victorian London* (University of California Press, Berkley, 1978).

20 R. Lewis and A. Maude, *The English Middle Class* (Phoenix House, 1949), p. 78

21 Stuart Magdalen Pember Reeves, *Round About a Pound a Week* (Bell, 1913), p. 19.

22 Ruth Schwartz Cowan, *More Work for Mother. The Ironies of Household Technology from the Open Hearth to the Microwave* (Basic, New York, 1983).

23 Margaret Llewellyn Davies, *Maternity letters from Working Women* (Bell, 1915).

24 Elizabeth Roberts, *A Women's Place. An Oral History of Working Class Women, 1890–1940* (Basil Blackwell, Oxford, 1984); Derek Oddy, 'Working Class Diets in Late Nineteenth Century Britain', *Economic History Review XXIII* (1970).

25 Carol Smith Rosenberg, 'The Hysterical Woman: Sex Roles and Conflict in Nineteenth Century America', *Social Research* 39 (1972).

26 Branca, *Silent Sisterhood*.

27 M. Jeanne Peterson, 'No Angels in the House: the Victorian myth and the Paget women', *American Historical Review* 89 (1984).

28 Carl Degler, 'What Ought to be and What Was: women's sexuality in the nineteenth century', *American Historical Review* 79 (1974).

29 Barbara Caine, 'Beatrice Webb and the Woman Question', *History Workshop Journal* 16 (1983).

30 Gorham, *The Victorian Girl*; and Leonore Davidoff, *The Best Circles* (Croom Helm, 1973).

31 Jane Lewis, *Women in England, 1870–1950* (Wheatsheaf, Brighton, 1984), pp. 104–5.

32 On 'visiting' see especially, Anne Summers, 'A Home from Home: women's philanthropic work in the nineteenth century, in Sandra Burman (ed.), *Fit Work for Women* (Croom Helm, 1979); and Frank K. Prochaska, *Women and Philanthropy in Nineteenth Century England* (Clarendon, Oxford, 1980).

33 On the debate over the family wage see, particularly, Hilary Land, 'The Family Wage', *Feminist Review* 6 (1980); and Jane Humphries, 'Class Struggle and the Persistence of the Working Class Family, *Cambridge Journal of Economics* 1 (1877).

34 On respectability, see for example, Robert Q. Gray, *The Labour Aristocracy in Victorian Edinburgh* (Clarendon, Oxford, 1976); and Patrick Joyce, *Work, Society and Politics* (Harvester, Brighton, 1982). The literature on the labour aristocracy and, more recently, on the labour process also uses the concepts of mediation and negotiation.

35 Doris Nield Chew, *Ada Nield Chew: The Life and Writings of a Working Woman* (Virago, 1982); Hannah Mitchell, *The Hard Way Up* (Virago, 1977).

36 Diana Gittins, *Fair Sex: Family Size and Structure, 1900–1939* (Hutchinson, 1982).

37 Phyllis Rose, *Parallel Lives. Five Victorian Marriages* (Knopf, New

York, 1984), p.211.

38 Anthony West, 'Mother to Son', *New York Review of Books* 31, 1 March 1984, pp.9–11.

39 Nancy Friday, *My Mother/Myself* (Delacort, New York, 1977).

40 Dorothy Dinnerstein, *The Mermaid and the Minotaur* (Harper and Row, New York, 1976), p.83 For a fuller discussion of this literature, see Nancy Chodorow and Susan Contratto, 'The Fantasy of the Perfect Mother', in Barrie Thorne with Marilyn Yolom (eds), *Rethinking the Family* (Longman, 1982).

41 The two best known examples are: Lawrence Stone, *The Family Sex and Marriage in England, 1500–1800* (Weidenfeld and Nicholson, 1977); and Edward Shorter, *The Making of the Modern Family* (Fontana, 1977).

42 Stephen Wilson, 'The Myth of Motherhood Myth: the historical view of European child-rearing', *Social History* 9 (1984).

43 Shorter, *Making of the Modern Family*, chapter 5.

44 Cicely Hamilton, *Marriage as a Trade* (Chapman Hall, 1909).

45 Beatrix Campbell, *Wigan Pier Revisited. Poverty and Politics in the 1980s* (Virago, 1984).

46 Ellen Ross, ' "Fierce Questions and Taunts": married life in working class London, 1870–1914', *Feminist Studies* 8 (1982); and 'Women's Neighbourhood Sharing in London before World War II', *History Workshop Journal* 15 (1983).

47 Degler, 'What Ought to be and What Was'.

48 Peter Gay, *The Bourgeois Experience, Victoria to Freud*, (Oxford University Press, New York, 1984) vol. I, *Education of the Senses*.

49 Jeffrey Weeks, *Sex, Politics and Society* (Longmans, 1981), p.39.

50 See for example, Iris Minor, 'Working Class Women and Matrimonial Law Reform, 1890–1914', in David E. Martin and David Rubinstein (eds), *Ideology and the Labour Movement* (Croom Helm, 1979); Nancy Boyd, *Josephine Butler, Octavia Hill and Florence Nightingale* (Macmillan, 1982); and Sheila Rowbotham, *A New World for Women. Stella Browne: socialist feminist* (Pluto, 1977).

51 Barbara Taylor, *Eve and the New Jerusalem* (Virago, 1983), especially pp.208–14.

52 Margaret Stacey and Marion Price, *Women, Power and Politics* (Tavistock, 1981, p.102).

53 Rose, *Parallell Lives*, pp.8 and 265.

54 J. A. Banks, *Victorian Values: secularism and the size of families* (Routledge & Kegan Paul, 1981).

55 Pauline Hunt, 'Cash Transactions and Household Tasks: domestic behaviour in relation to industrial employment', *Sociological Review* 26 (1978).

56 Nancy Tomes, '"A Torrent of Abuse": crimes of violence between working class men and women in London, 1849–1875', *Journal of Social History* 11 (1978).

57 Roberts, *A Woman's Place;* Ross, 'Fierce Taunts' and 'Women's Neighbourhood Sharing'.

58 In contrast, Jane Humphries has argued without reservation that the

male-breadwinner family model maximized the welfare of all family members, in her 'Class Struggle and the Persistence of the Working Class Family'.

59 Lewis, *Women in England*, p. 199.

60 Edward Higgs, 'Domestic Service and Household Production', in John (ed.), *Unequal Opportunities*.

61 Beatrice Webb's Diary, 1 January 1886, British Library of Political and Economic Science.

62 See also Anthea Duquenin, 'Who Doesn't Marry and Why', *Oral History* 12 (1984).

63 Janet M. Bujra, 'Introduction: Female Solidarity and the Sexual Division of Labour', in P. Caplan and J. M. Bujra (eds.), *Women United, Women Divided* (Tavistock, 1978), p. 30.

64 Rosemary Crook, ' "Tidy Women": women in the Rhondda between the wars', *Oral History* 10 (1982).

65 Olwen Hufton, 'Women without Men: widows and spinsters in Britain and France in the eighteenth century', *Journal of Family History* 9 (1984), 356.

66 Campbell, *Wigan Pier Revisited*, pp. 222 and 73.

Part I
Childhood

Mrs Arthur Savoury and her daughters 1903

1

Mothers and Daughters in the Middle-Class Home, c. 1870–1914

Carol Dyhouse

The social position of a middle-class family in the period 1870–1920 was determined very largely by the status of the Victorian or Edwardian *paterfamilias;* a status which was a product of his rank, occupation and regular income. A secondary, but significant determinant of the family's social standing was its lifestyle, and here the middle-class *wife* of Victorian or Edwardian times, *her* social values, knowledge, taste and organizing skills, were of crucial import. Whatever the income level or degree of 'middle classness', it fell to the wife of the household to be responsible at some level for style of living and domestic routine. If she did not herself adopt the role of housekeeper and cook, she would direct those whose services her husband's means afforded; it was her duty, be she a lower-middle-class housewife or the mistress of a more substantial 'establishment', to monitor levels of expenditure and consumption, and to organize domestic life in such a way as to demonstrate the family's standards and values of respectability to the neighbours and to the world at large.

Amongst the more prosperous sections of the middle class there evolved remarkably consistent sets of rules about the right ordering of domestic life. These rules both reflected and reinforced bourgeois ideology about the right ordering of society generally; the proper distance and relationships to be maintained between men and women, working and middle classes, the old and the young. To aspire to full gentility required a substantial income,[1] but even at the *petit bourgeois* level notions of respectability and correctness were derived from the more affluent, demonstrating the cohesiveness of middle-class ideology. Patterns of middle-class social life had become highly ritualized, particularly in provincial communities, by the turn of the last century. An upper-middle-class home might require the attention of two or three living-in servants but this kind of establishment could only be kept up by the minority of families with an income of around £300 per year or more. Around three-quarters of the Victorian middle class had incomes well below this level, and could afford to employ no more than one domestic servant, a general skivvy, perhaps, or maid-of-all-work.[2]

Distance between social aspirations and what one's income could actually support created constant tensions for middle-class families. As Deborah Gorham has observed, these tensions probably affected women more than men because it was they who were seen as responsible for creating a civilized domestic milieu.[3] It was a hallmark of middle-class respectability that wives did not involve themselves in paid work. The economic dependence of wives and daughters advertised the independence and the status of the male breadwinner. The insulation of women in the private sphere of the home protected their femininity from the contamination of the public sphere at the same time as it secured the domestic comforts of the male. A large proportion of middle-class wives faced the contradictions of trying to live up to the ideal of the leisured lady whilst having to confront the realities of heavy household duties and care of what was often (by modern standards) a large family, with the help of a young general servant.

Ideals sometimes matched and sometimes clashed with realities in Victorian and Edwardian domestic life. We can learn much about ideals from reading the domestic manuals and etiquette prescriptions in women's magazines of the time. For the realities we are dependent very largely upon autobiographical evidence. Women's autobiographies often provide evidence about the patterns of domestic life that characterized the relationships between a daughter and her mother. In one sense they record and summarize the lessons of a home education, although their use by historians raises methodological problems which will be discussed later.

An ideal middle-class residence had to be large enough to give physical and spatial expression to distances between social groups based upon sex, class and age, and to social hierarchy. A large upper-middle-class home would accommodate its servants 'below stairs' in the basement during the working day; at night time they would sleep in the attic. Class distances might be preserved by the existence of a separate 'back staircase' and servants' entries, which also afforded the family protection from the unaesthetic sights of slopping pails and other such evidence of real domestic work. Smaller houses would not have been able to conceal domestic activity in this way, but their owners may still have striven to maintain barriers between themselves and their employees. Mrs C. S. Peel, addressing herself to those 'on a modest income' in *The New Home* (published in 1903) permitted herself to express a hope that even in a smallish house the kitchen would not have to serve as the servants' sitting room, although clearly it often did.[4]

The ideal establishment also made it possible to define separate spaces for the men and women of the household. This kind of sexual segregation was taken furthest in the large Victorian country houses of the period. Mark Girouard has discussed the development of a 'male domain' in the architecture of these houses, the increasingly fashionable provision of billiard rooms, smoking rooms, libraries and gun rooms – all territory sacrosanct to male use.[5] Women had their own territory in the form of boudoirs, dressing rooms and so forth, and the drawing room was generally regarded as a feminine habitat. In a prosperous household where many servants were employed, the organization of the servants' quarters themselves might mirror the patterns of segregation and hierarchy based upon gender and seniority that characterized the family 'upstairs'. The butler, invested with a kind of reflected patriarchal authority, would be privileged with the territory of his own pantry; the cook, a kind of matronly figure in 'her' kitchen, might preside over the servants' sitting room and table, exercising authority over the kitchen maids in the scullery and the housemaids who worked 'upstairs'. Again, smaller establishments could not hope to sustain such elaborate arrangements, but some segregation often remained.[6]

The interior arrangement of a well-appointed gentleman's home also allowed for the separation of children from adults, ideally through the provision of day- and night-nurseries and a schoolroom, conventionally on the top floor. It has frequently been observed that, in families who could afford to employ nannies, nursemaids and governesses, the social distance between parents and children might be considerable, their relationships highly formal. Certainly this was true in aristocratic circles.[7] But even those brought up in more lowly (but still 'solidly comfortable') middle-class homes often spoke of having inhabited, when young, an entirely separate world from their parents. Lilian Faithfull (the daughter of a Secretary at the War Office) growing up in Hertfordshire in the 1870s, recalled that although formalities which had marked the relations between our grandparents and their children did not exist for us . . . we should not have dreamed of invading the rooms of our parents at other than appointed times. We appeared in the dining room for a short time after breakfast, but only at six o'clock did our parents really belong to us for an hour and devote themselves to the 'little ones'. The ceremony of getting ready to go downstairs was no trivial matter of getting rid of sticky fingers or tangled hair. Its value lay in the fact that it instilled a certain awe and reverence into children, and best manners were put on with best frocks both on Sundays and in the evenings.[8]

Similarly Enid Starkie, who grew up in a bourgeois household in Ireland some thirty years later remembered that

We saw our parents very little when we were children and they seemed to belong to another world, a world separated from ours by a great, insurmountable China wall.[9]

Before the age at which boys would be sent off to preparatory school, girls and boys inhabited the same space, and shared similar routines in the nursery world of the comfortable middle-class home. They learned through observing the roles played by their parents and by the servants in the household. Through participating in the rituals of domestic life they absorbed a sense of what their parents regarded as fitting, as proper, as 'natural' in social arrangements. Much of what they learned would have been unspoken, values transmitted as assumptions; knowledge of the 'taken-for-granted' kind. Such knowledge had sharply differing implications to children as individuals, according to their sex.

One of the first and most important lessons learned by the young girl in the middle-class home was that the organization of the household revolved around the needs of the male breadwinner. Some middle-class males – clergymen for example – worked at home. Where this was the case children were usually well schooled by their mothers to keep a respectful distance from the door of father's study, and abjured not to disturb him. The study, a kind of paternal *inner sanctum*, was often out-of-bounds to other members of the household. Enid Starkie remembered that she once illicitly penetrated her father's study and, fascinated by the rows of pens and pencils on his writing tray, dared to try out one of the fine-pointed pencils. The point broke and she fled from the room in panic, never daring to admit her guilt.[10] However, as is well known, the nineteenth century witnessed an increasing separation of home from workplace, and a majority of middle-class men became daily commuters from their suburban residences or villas into the central commercial districts of provincial towns or the City.

This pattern of commuting gave physical expression to the social distance between the public, male world of business and the professions and the private, feminine world of the household. Katharine Chorley's autobiography vividly describes life in Alderley Edge, outside Manchester, from a young girl's viewpoint.

> Every morning in my childhood the business men caught the 8.25 or the 8.50 or the 9.18 trains into Manchester. The times are graven in my memory.

The men always travelled first class; but

> any wife or daughter who had to go into Manchester by one of those trains always travelled third; to share a compartment with the 'gentlemen' (we were taught never to call them just plainly 'men') would have been unthinkable. Indeed, the ladies always avoided the business trains if they possibly could. It was highly embarrassing, a sort of indelicacy, to stand on the platform surrounded by a crowd of males who had to be polite but were obviously not in the mood for feminine society.[11]

Once the 9.18 train had left the station, she remembered

> the Edge became exclusively female. You never saw a man on the hill roads unless it were the doctor or the plumber, and you never saw a man in anyone's home except the gardener or the coachman.[12]

What their fathers actually did in the City remained a closed book to most of their daughters. Small sons would have grown up in the knowledge that one day they would in all likelihood be initiated into this world, but not so their sisters. At some point Katharine Chorley learned that the 'socially elect' amongst Manchester businessmen met for lunch at the Union Club, quintessentially a masculine sanctuary: 'The community quarters of a monastery are not more jealously withdrawn from outsiders than was the Union Club from feminine penetration. No one among our ladies would have dared enquire for her spouse at its portals. That would have been spectacular immodesty'.[13] For women to trespass was not simply to breach convention, it was to commit an indecency, a shaming, polluting form of behaviour. Nor was there any doubt about the relative importance of male and female spheres. When Chorley tried to sketch the faces of her neighbours on the station platform, she thought exclusively of the heads of families and their sons:

I could not sketch the ladies on the same plane as their
husbands and fathers and sons because it would not come
natural to put them on an equality. For the men were the
money-lords; and since for almost every family the community
values were fundamentally economic, it followed that their
women were dependents. They existed for their husbands and
fathers' sakes and their lives were shaped to please masculine
vanity.[14]

It has already been emphasized that the middle-class wife was
responsible for domestic harmony; if she had servants to relieve her
of the worst drudgery she might still feel accountable to her husband
for supervising and coordinating their activities. Young girls would
observe their mother's deference to their father's needs. Enid Starkie
recollected that

My father seemed to me a very important person and this
glamour and prestige were largely due to the general attitude of
the womenfolk of the house towards him. In my mother's
opinion everything he did was right, everything he said had the
weight of divine revelation and it would not have occurred to
her that any one could doubt that every word he uttered was
inspired by perfect wisdom. She considered it right that the life
of a wife, that the life of all women in a household, should
revolve around its male head. Nurse, the maids and even Lizzie
the cook, accepted this attitude without question, and
everything went smoothly.[15]

Ideally, a prosperous upper-middle-class household would function
like a well-oiled machine, with the minimum interference from its
mistress. Esther Stokes remembered that their household in
Streatham had included seven female living-in servants, assisted by a
daily 'outdoor man', 'who did the sort of coals'.[16] Contact
between the family and the domestics was highly formal:
'Mother would go down and see her cook in the morning, to
give orders and that kind of thing. And thereafter, if she wanted to
speak to her for any reason or other bells were rung and the cook
would come up. No mistress would ever go downstairs.'[17] The image
of the gracious lady discussing the day's menus with the cook was an
ideal which must have appealed strongly to the rather more
harassed wives of the lower middle class. Mrs C.S. Peel certainly
knew the power of such a vision: giving advice on the furnishing of
basement rooms in a small town house she suggested that 'The
presence of a small Doulton-ware sink will add to the convenience of
the mistress, who will here arrange her flowers, write her menus,
and give out the stores.'[18]

The lower one descended through degrees of 'middle classness', the more one might be sure its women knew about the dimensions of the endlessly-discussed late-nineteenth- and early twentieth-century 'servant problem'. Servants could be wasteful and careless. The pages of the manuals of domestic advice brim with suggestions for monitoring servants' consumption of heat, light, cleansing materials and foodstuffs. Mrs. Peel suggested that to economize on electricity it might 'be useful to have the switches of the servants' quarters in the mistress' bedroom, so that if she suspects the domestics of reading in bed their lights can be put out.'[19] It is unlikely that servants would have welcomed surveillance of this kind and class resentments between employers and domestic workers in more penny-pinching middle-class households must often have been particularly acute. It would have been the women of the household who would have largely had to cope with such resentments and their manifestation in such forms as studied insolence, cheek and inefficiency.

Daughters learned from observing their mothers in their interaction with servants, or in their own activities, about the social expectation that a wife should be solicitous for her husband's needs. The elaborate ritual surrounding mealtimes in middle-class homes of the period conveyed similar messages, often unspoken, about gender, age, and class in their relation to role and social precedence. Even in the lower-middle-class home meals would tend to be taken at times which fitted around the routine of the man's work. In all probability children would be admonished to sit quietly whilst their father breakfasted behind the newspaper; at other mealtimes he would be served with the largest and the choicest portions; the clearing away would be the work of the women. However, in more affluent households mealtimes – most notably the evening meal when the man of the house was at home – were a highly complex affair, especially when guests were present. Many middle-class families preserved the habit of 'dressing for dinner' with varying degrees of formality, up until the First World War. Katharine Chorley recalled that, although at lunch time one was allowed simply to break off from some or other activity and having washed and tidied one's person to a reasonable extent, to come straight to the table and eat, 'at dinner we had to approach our food formally, assembling first in the drawing-room, silk-frocked and dinner-jacketed according to sex. No slipping into your chair when the rest of the company was seated.'[20]

Many autobiographies contain recollections of children watching the beginning of the adult festivities at dinner parties through the baluster of the staircase. Young children rarely ate with the family in the evening and it was an important occasion when their parents did see fit to let them join their elders at 'late dinner'. Lilian Faithfull describes how her mother took great pains to train her children, especially the girls, in the art of hostessing and dinner-table conversation.[21]

At what age would those middle-class daughters who had brothers have been aware of distinct differences in the way in which they were treated by parents? It is obviously difficult to generalize. Girls were, of course, dressed differently from boys – more fussily as a rule. They were given (as they are today) different toys to play with. In homes where there were not plenty of servants girls might, from an early age, be expected to help their mothers with domestic tasks. Mrs Peel insisted that it was 'most important that a girl should be brought up both in nursery and schoolroom to be tidy and methodical, and to take a pride in keeping her surroundings neat'. Their brothers, however, should simply be encouraged 'to conduct themselves generally as decent members of society and not as savages'.[22] Other manuals gave similar advice.[23] Even in fairly affluent middle-class homes there were often so many children generating so much mending and the like that daughters would be recruited into helping. Helena Swanwick (née Sickert) remembered that when she returned to her home in London after a period at a school in France she was required to spend hours mending the household linen and 'the "men's" underclothes'.[24]

Where mothers were particularly hard-pressed, it was not uncommon for older daughters in a family to be given the responsibility of looking after younger brothers and sisters. Even in a household employing two servants, Lily Whichelo became a second mother to four younger siblings; bathing them, escorting them on outings and helping with the housework at the same time.[25] Jean Curtis Brown, the daughter of a Presbyterian Minister in the Merseyside district in the 1900s, tells us that because her mother was so occupied with church work and with looking after her husband (whose health was precarious) she was, as a young girl, looked after almost entirely by her teenage sister, Elizabeth.[26]

The degree to which girls accepted the differences in treatment from that meted out to their brothers varied. Lilian Faithfull considered that the majority thought it quite natural to be looked down on by their brothers: 'In family life, sisters are not as a rule treated with . . . consideration until long after school-days. If there is a fishing expedition their lot is to put on the worms for the eldest brothers, or to stay at home, and they meekly chose to serve.'[27] Molly Hughes, the youngest child and only daughter of a family growing up in London in the 1870s found herself alternately petted and patronized by her four older brothers, whom she hero–worshipped. Her mother expected her to wait on her brothers but Molly insists that she harboured no resentment about this.[28]

Other girls found themselves far less happy with the restrictions and prohibitions which increasingly hedged them around as they attained puberty. At this time their treatment contrasted very strongly indeed with that of their brothers, who were likely to be enjoying an enhanced sense of self-esteem that accompanied being sent away to school; that sense of having acquired the first instalment of worldly experience on their route to adult manhood. I shall return to the theme of resentment and rebellion later.

Girls were schooled from an early age in the conventions of modesty and reticence. Victorian unease about bodily functions might manifest itself in prohibitions and obsessional avoidance of 'indelicacy'. It was not uncommon for many middle-class women to be embarrassed to have to mention the lavatory by name. Ursula Bloom remembered that in the 1900s her family and friends suffered agonies of shame when they were unable to cloak their visits to the lavatory in total secrecy. At children's parties, she confessed, they were always urged not to drink too much in order to avoid the embarrassment of having to ask where 'it' was.[29] Ursula Bloom, Naomi Mitchison and Katharine Chorley all recall the elaborate system of social segregation and taboos which applied here – servants, men and women of the family all had separate lavatories.[30] Katharine Chorley described how

> Mother was very particular about anything which symbolised decorous behaviour as between males and females. The downstairs lavatory, for instance, was sacrosanct to the men of the family and their guests, the upstairs was reserved with equal exclusiveness to the females. Woe betide me if I was ever found slinking into the downstairs to save time. Conversely, the good breeding and social knowledge of any male guest who was suspected of having used the upstairs while dressing for dinner was immediately called into question.[31]

Given all this embarrassment about bodily functions, it is not surprising that we know so little about girls' sex education generally and about their experiences of the menarche and of menstruation. As Deborah Gorham has observed, manuals of advice written for young girls at the time mention the subject – if they mention it at all – only in the most veiled and allusive manner.[32] Beryl Lee Booker, whose Edwardian upper-middle-class upbringing is recounted in her autobiography *Yesterday's Child*, described her own experience as traumatic whilst assuming that she was not unusual in this respect.

> The old-fashioned policy of silence did real harm. Girls suffered terrible mental torture and shock. I know I did when for two days I was in the grip of a pain I'd never before known, with such terrifying results that I rushed to my brother and confided in him that I'd broken something inside and thought I was dying. Arthur telephoned to the family doctor who came rushing round, as we were alone that evening, Mother, Father and the governess being out. He soon reassured me – all was well and normal – and he gave me the kindly, homely advice on such matters I should have received at least two years earlier. But I had a severe mental shock.[33]

Where a mother was herself embarrassed by menstruation this would be communicated to her daughter who would also be likely to feel shamed by her body and unclean. Naomi Mitchison (née Haldane), the daughter of an intellectual upper-middle-class family living in Oxford in the 1900s, has left us with a vivid description of her experience of the menarche:

> I was twelve, still at the Dragon School, unsuspecting. I had little or no pubic hair, my breasts were ungrown and did not in fact develop until my mid-teens. And then there was blood on my blue serge knickers. I was quickly pulled out of school and I never went back. I couldn't quite understand why, only it seemed that it was something about me which was shameful and must above all never be mentioned to a school friend.[34]

Naomi Mitchison reminds us that disposable sanitary towels were not in use until around the time of the First World War. Problems of hygienic management and laundering must have been considerable, especially when one remembers the *secrecy* surrounding the whole business. Mitchison recalled that in her day men knew nothing or next to nothing about menstruation: 'Soon after we were married Dick told me that he had been given to understand that ladies had something in the nature of a headache every month.'[35]

All in all it is difficult to believe that girls would have found it easy to feel positive about their sexuality. Marked off from their brothers through possession of this shameful secret of menstruation, they may well have cursed fate and resented their mothers for the implications of being born female. As a young girl living in Buxton, Vera Brittain penned a significant entry in her diary on 4 March, 1913:

On the way to golf I induced mother to disclose a few points on sexual matters which I thought I ought to know, though the information is always intensely distasteful to me and most depressing – in fact it quite put me off my game! I suppose it is the spiritual – & intellectual – development part of me that feels repugnance at being brought too closely into contact with physical 'open secrets'. Alas! sometimes it feels sad to be a woman! Men seem to have so much choice as to what they are intended for.[36]

Schooling was often seen as of secondary importance to the influence of the home in the education of middle-class girls. They might be educated entirely at home, with or without the help of a governess. The more prosperous families might send their daughters to expensive and select boarding schools for a while; the less wealthy were more likely to patronize small homely 'academies' which aimed to foster those same ideals of feminity that were nurtured in the middle-class home. An examination of the curriculum (both formal and informal) of the majority of girls' boarding schools of the period will show that social values and objectives took precedence over academic goals: girls were educated with their marriage prospects and the ideal of the 'cultivated homemaker' in mind. Even the newer more academically oriented girls' day schools founded in the last quarter of the nineteenth century deferred to contemporary estimations of the importance of home influences. Frances Buss, founder of the famous North London Collegiate School, remained a staunch champion of the virtues of day schools rather than boarding schools for girls because she believed that girls derived a major part of their education from family life. The majority of girls' high schools provided lessons only in the mornings: afternoons, it was felt, were more appropriately spent at home. Most of the Girls' Public Day School foundations did not introduce the principle of afternoon school until well into the present century. The last thing that most middle-class parents wanted was for schooling to foster any inappropriate vocational aspirations in their daughters. Neither 'worldly' ambitions nor too much bookishness made for marriageability in girls, and they *did* want their daughters to make 'good' marriages.[37]

Adolescent girls then, spent long periods at home and even those who received substantial amounts of regular schooling generally returned home when their schooldays were over, to remain there until they married. Working outside the home to 'fill in time' before marriage, though increasingly common in the case of girls from lower-middle-class families, did not become the norm for the class as a whole until after the First World War. Katharine Chorley's father was not at all happy when his daughter announced that she wanted to go to Cambridge: 'he did not approve of women invading his own university.' But he was even more put out by Katharine's announcement that she wanted to go to Cambridge in order to equip herself to do a proper job.[38]

Helena Swanwick describes how after her father died money was in short supply. She herself was very keen to find work and found several opportunities to take on private coaching and part-time lecturing in economics. Her mother was, however, deeply ambivalent about her daughter's taking paid work. When Frederick Swanwick and Helena became engaged, Mrs Sickert tried to explain to her future son-in-law the sources of the conflicts which had increasingly marred her relationship with Helena. 'Don't you see that I *can't* have her living in my house and earning her living like a man?' she exclaimed.[39]

What kind of life did a 'daughter-at-home' lead? At her mother's side she might well be initiated into the social routines of the middle-class married women of the day which often centred in the afternoons around 'calling'. Many autobiographies contain full descriptions of this highly complex and ritualized activity which functioned to establish and confirm social position and to cement the relationships between middle-class families in the neighbourhood. Jean Curtis Brown described how

> Mother spent nearly every afternoon calling, it was one of her many duties. And what an infinitely complicated social rite that was!
>
> She never went out in the afternoon without a thin silver case containing a selection of Father's cards (small) and her own (big). These she 'left' on people in varying numbers according, as I remember, to whether it was a first visit to new people, or a return visit, or a visit made after recovery from an illness. If Father were not with her, and he seldom was, the corner of the card or cards was turned down.[40]

She went on to explain that there were three types of calls. The first was when one did't expect or want to see the hostess, in which case one simply left the card with the maid, who deposited it on the silver tray which was conventionally kept on a table in the hall for this purpose. It was important that the card should be left at four o'clock, that is, at the appropriate time for calling. The second type of call was when one was admitted by the maid because her mistress had confirmed that she was 'at home', that is, prepared to receive callers. Cards were still left on the silver tray just the same. Finally there was the institution of the 'At Home Day'. In the district in which Jean Curtis Brown spent her girlhood, every respectable matron held these once a month:

> These magic dates, First Thursday or Second and Third Tuesdays, were sometimes engraved on the visiting cards. On this day the hostess had to be at home, sitting in her best afternoon dress in the drawing room at four o'clock, having provided a large and good tea. In the natural cycle of calling, the ladies revolving every afternoon round the houses of the neighbourhood as in some complicated dance, I suppose it seldom happened that nobody came on one's At Home Day; though I remember Mother saying, as she surveyed the scene after one of her 'days', 'Only six this afternoon! What *shall* we do with all the cakes?' But sometimes twenty ladies or more would come, the front door bell pinged all afternoon, feather boas and umbrellas littered the hall, the silver salver overflowed, Mother and the maids were exhausted, and we had a cold supper.[41]

When well-to-do daughters 'came out' they had their names printed beneath their mother's (or widowed father's) names on the cards. Although the increasing number of journals addressed to adolescent girls and manuals of etiquette often advised on the formalities of calling, mothers remained the main teachers and their daughters would learn by accompanying them. Many were less than wholehearted about this. Katharine Chorley remarked: 'The day was indeed a black one on which we found that our mothers had had their cards reprinted and that our names figured below theirs on the disgusting little white slips. But we, too, were drilled and disciplined.'[42] The fact remained that the system itself was seen as socially obligatory. Mothers themselves might dislike calling, but they would see it in the light of a necessary social *duty*.[43]

Philanthropy, of course, was regarded as a suitable activity for middle-class women and many a daughter served an apprenticeship alongside her mother in organizing bazaars, charity teas, jumble sales and the like. The ideal of the gracious lady bestowing her favours on cottagers (especially the tenants on husband's or father's estates) was a tenacious one, not always removed from reality. Lady Henry Somerset remembered her mother, Lady Somers, grooming her daughters in this respect. Isabel and Adeline were allotted special baskets which they were to keep for carrying puddings, jellies and grapes to elderly or sick tenants on the family's estate at

Eastmor.[44] Lower down the social scale, mothers were more likely to be involved in sales of work for local missionary societies or the Girls' Friendly Society. Vera Brittain remembered that as a 'daughter at home' in pre-war Buxton she had been pushed into visiting her mother's 'district' in the village of Burbage near Axe-Edge, there to distribute copies of *Mothers in Council*.[45] Jean Curtis Brown's mother was deeply involved in church work and philanthropic ventures of all kinds. When the time arrived for the Annual Sale of Work in the Church Hall her daughter remembers their house having to accommodate, somehow, enormous piles of hideous tea-cosies, babies' jackets and hand-painted calendars.[46] Daughters, like their mothers, would often be recruited into the manufacture of 'fancy goods' for such stalls. Jean added: 'Naturally I was roped in. I plaited hair-tidies and painted revolting Christmas cards – angels, smudged or Aberdeen terriers looking like wart-hogs – and I handed round tea, walking so slowly to avoid spilling that the tea was always cold before it reached its destination.'[47]

It was commonly regarded as the responsibility of the middle-class mother to facilitate her daughter's initiation into the social circles in which a future husband might be found. In upper- and upper-middle-class families, 'coming out' involved a highly elaborate series of undertakings, sometimes culminating in the girl's presentation at Court. In 'the best circles', as Leonore Davidoff has described, large sums of money would be invested in expensively coutured gowns ready for 'the season'.[48] The rules governing presentation at Court were formidably complex: articles in girls' magazines of the period frequently featured articles on this theme, along with photographs of high society debutantes. But even in the less exalted circles of the provincial debutante there was a substantial code of etiquette to be learned – how to fill in dance-cards, how to conduct oneself in the company of young men of a higher, lower or similar social status to oneself on the dance floor, on the tennis court or at the dinner table. Mothers were responsible for initiating their daughters into these mysteries, and for ensuring that all the social activities in which their daughters participated were appropriately chaperoned. Both Vera Brittain and Katharine Chorley have left us with full descriptions of the very rigid codes of behaviour which were adhered to in this process of their being fed into what the latter described as 'the complex mechanism designed to enable young men and maidens to meet and mate in circumstances which could be controlled by their elders'.[49]

The life of a 'daughter at home' was not one calculated to appeal to a budding feminist. Helena Swanwick described her own experience of returning home after school in Neuville in the third chapter (entitled 'Girls in Waiting') of her autobiography *I have Been Young*. The synopsis of the chapter's contents begins with a terse disinclination to compromise: 'I become a girl in waiting and don't like it.' Both Vera Brittain's and Katharine Chorley's accounts of their experiences as 'daughters at home' bristle with impatience at what they considered to have been a pitiful waste of time. Vera Brittain's account is particularly uncompromising; blistering in its contempt for what she had come to see as the shallow snobberies of the provincial middle class.[50]

However, these accounts raise important questions about our use of autobiographical evidence in the writing of history. There are at least two related questions which we need to ask ourselves. Firstly, what kind of people – in this case women – were likely to *write* autobiographies? Secondly *why* did they choose to write them? I will take these questions in turn.

Most of the autobiographies which have been drawn upon as 'evidence' in this chapter were written by highly intelligent and unusually articulate women. It could be argued that such women would be likely to have been particularly critical about their girlhood in the family; usually hostile to the constraints of a domestic environment. That they would not *necessarily* have been so is demonstrated by the case of M. V. Hughes, who never became a feminist and offers us what might be considered to be a rather idealized account of her childhood and family life.[51] Most of the writers I have drawn upon were, however, feminists or, rather, they *became* feminists in adult life. I have used their accounts to illustrate patterns of domestic life, but to infer that their rebellion against social prescriptions was in any way representative would be more hazardous. Even so, it would be rash to suppose that all those who were *not* usually ambitious, or feminists, were wholly happy with their lot. In 1912 Josephine Pitcairn Knowles wrote a book entitled *The Upholstered Cage* in which she lengthily and critically dissected the social impotence and frustrations of the suburban 'daughter-at-home', the 'mollusc Mary' unable to work, marry or mix in any interesting society.[52] The author tells us that her book grew out of two public lectures which she had earlier given on the subject, which had generated a huge and sympathetic response. Like George Gissing's novel, *The Odd Women*, (1893), the book emphasized the vulnerability of a girl without marriage prospects, whose parents have assumed that she will never have to earn her own living.

These and other sources suggest that the frustrations and

uncertainty that might be experienced as a 'daughter at home' were by no means confined to a tiny feminist minority. But the problem of representativeness is not the only difficulty facing the social historian who draws upon autobiography as evidence. Related to the question of *who* might choose to write about the past there is the question of *why* and *when* they come to do so. Autobiographies are very different from diaries in that they are written with hindsight and usually from the vantage point of maturity if not old age. One implication of this is that in selecting what to write about and how to write about it many authors are guided by the intention of charting a straight line of development from what they were as children to where they are as adults. Most of the autobiographies used in this chapter were written, as it has been observed already, by feminists and by women who achieved some degree of eminence in life: they were 'achievers'. It is not at all unlikely that this would have made them less tolerant, in retrospect, of the more trivial experiences of their youth than they were at the time. Looking back, they emphasized 'formative' experiences as those which counted. In the case of women whose adolescence was lived on the eve of the First World War, one must expect to find a particularly determined sifting through of experiences, together with a ruthless dismisal of 'frivolity'. The cruel impact of the war with its devastating losses had a deeply astringent effect on the psychological outlook of many young people: Vera Brittain's *Testament of Youth* is, of course, primarily about this.

Both Vera Brittain and Katharine Chorley looked back upon their girlhoods as from the far side of a deep ravine. It was difficult for them to write about the past without imbuing their accounts with a sense of uneasiness, a sense of marking time. It is particularly instructive to compare Vera Brittain's diary of 1913-17 with *Testament of Youth* in this context. The early entries of the former convey an image of a thoughtful but very exuberant young girl, much involved in dancing, parties and pretty clothes. She records her delight in receiving compliments about her clothing and her satisfaction at being in demand on the dance floor. The first entry (for 1 January, 1913) fairly bubbles with gaiety:

> We danced the New Year in at the Garretts yesterday evening; I don't know why I enjoyed it so much, except that I suppose it is gratifying, when there are too many girls at a dance, never to have to dance with girls or sit out.[53]

Compare this with the following rather dour passage in *Testament of Youth*:

> At my first dance, the High Peak Hunt Ball, I appeared
> modestly attired in the conventional white satin and pearls; this
> ingenuous uniform entitled me to spend the greater part of the
> next few weeks gyrating to the strains of 'Dreaming' and 'The
> vision of Salome' in the arms of physically boisterous and
> conversationally inept young men.[54]

The difference between the two passages is striking. In 1939 Vera
Brittain herself observed that 'Today I feel only a remote family
relationship with the girl who lived in Buxton and went to Oxford.'[55]

It is scarcely surprising to find the young Vera far less distanced
from her mother in the diaries than she depicts herself in *Testament
of Youth*; although her comment on the censoriousness of the
conventional Buxton matrons in the latter is clearly based upon
observations recorded in the former. In relation to the horrified
response that her desire to go to Oxford aroused in her mother's
friends Vera remarked that

> It has just struck me today . . . that it is scarcely ever men who
> raise objections to a woman's being given what her talents
> deserve, but always other women. At first it seems
> extraordinary that women should be the retrogressive members
> just when the era of their true glory and justice is beginning to
> dawn. But I suppose it is that women are sharply divided into
> two classes, the old-fashioned, who can see nothing, and the
> new-fashioned, who see all.[56]

Katharine Chorley similarly insisted that it was the *ladies* of Alderley
Edge who were the staunchest defenders of conservatism. If any
woman tried 'to stake a claim for herself' she observed 'all the other
women bunched together on the side of the challenged male'.[57]

Many of the writers whose autobiographies have been drawn upon
in this chapter describe troubled relationships with their mothers.
Enid Starkie depicts herself as never having seen eye to eye with her
mother after the day when the latter made her hand round cakes
decorated with anti-suffrage colours at a garden party which she
organized in honour of the Anti-Suffrage League.[58] Naomi
Mitchison, Helena Swanwick and Jean Curtis Brown all appear to
have been through periods of serious conflict with their mothers.
Molly Hughes, on the other hand, writes of an extremely intimate
relationship with her mother, Mrs Thomas; from her autobiography
comes the impression that they never exchanged a cross word. Lilian
Faithfull dedicated her autobiography *In the House of My Pilgrimage*
to her mother; in her preface to *I Have Been Young*, Helena
Swanwick indicted hers. Advice columns in girls' magazines of the

period, and chapters in manuals and encyclopaedias of useful knowledge written for adolescent girls frequently discussed the difficulties of mother-daughter relationships, conveying the impression that tensions were indeed very common.

But we should resist the temptation to present conflict and tension as wholly characteristic of mother-daughter relationships when the latter were at the adolescent stage, nor should we stray into representing mothers too simply as the main agents of their daughters' oppression. Certainly mothers tended to provide their daughters with the latter's earliest models of 'femininity'. But one cannot assume that mothers themselves possessed simple, unambiguous personalities wholly at ease with their social roles, nor that daughters learned from their mothers passively, like blotting paper simply absorbing impressions. Almost everything written by feminists interested in psychoanalysis over the last ten years indicates a very different process. Work by Nancy Chodorow and Adrienne Rich has emphasized the conflicts and deep ambivalences involved in mothering in patriarchal society.[59] If one was compelled to generalize about the nature of mother–daughter ties then perhaps 'ambivalence' would emerge as a key theme.

Certainly an appreciation of the ambivalent nature of mother–daughter relationships helps one to understand (for instance) Vera Brittain's relationship with her mother. If *Testament of Youth* was all we had we would be left with a clear picture of rejection, of a young girl determinedly and consistently rejecting her mother's values and lifestyle. Yet reading the diaries yields a very different picture: as an adolescent, Vera clearly had periods of real intimacy with her mother, and they often seem to have united in defence of a more liberal stance in discussion on matters of religion, marriage and 'the feminine predicament' against Vera's father. The evidence is by no means consistent, but then personalities and relationships are by no means always consistent either.

There are novels written by women in the late-nineteenth and early twentieth centuries which 'speak volumes' about the nature of the mother–daughter relationship. May Sinclair's *Mary Olivier* (1919) is outstanding in this respect, and is based very much on the author's own experience.[60] Although 'fiction' rather than 'fact' (if we are to use such deceptively simple categories), the novel has the advantage over many autobiographies of the period in allowing complexity. The author is not trying to present a simple account of her past, of her development from one point to another. Through the skilful use of symbolism, and through the exploration of fragmentary states of consciousness she is sensitive to ambiguity, and to contradictions – she does not try to 'iron them out'. Similarly Virginia Woolf's novel *To the Lighthouse* (1927), although it does not deal directly with the mother–daughter relationship, tells us an enormous amount about the author's own ambivalence towards 'femininity' through her exploration of the life of Mrs Ramsay, the central mother figure in the novel, based on Virginia Woolf's memories of her own mother.[61]

Bibliographical Notes

Many of the themes which have been raised in this chapter are dealt with more fully in my book *Girls Growing up in Late Victorian and Edwardian England* (Routledge & Kegan Paul, 1981). This also explores girls' schooling in some detail and considers the experiences of working- as well as middle-class girls. Deborah Gorham's *The Victorian Girl and the Feminine Ideal* (Croom Helm, 1982) also deals centrally with girlhood in the middle-class family. Patricia Branca's *Silent Sisterhood, Middle Class Women in the Victorian Home* (Croom Helm, 1975) remains important reading. Branca's interpretation, particularly her use of 'modernization' theory remains controversial but her work serves as a useful corrective to any exaggerated notions of the 'passivity' of the Victorian matron. Leonore Davidoff's *The Best Circles: Society, Etiquette and the Season* (Croom Helm, 1973) provides a wealth of insight into the functions and rituals of upper-middle- and upper-class society. On the *origins* of domestic ideology and the influence of evangelical religion upon concepts of women's sphere, Catherine Hall's essay 'The Early Formation of Victorian Domestic Ideology', in Sandra Burman (ed.), *Fit Work for Women* (Croom Helm in association with the Oxford Women's Studies Committee, 1979) is seminal. Jenni Calder's lavishly illustrated *The Victorian Home* (B. Y. Batsford, 1977) is enjoyable and entertaining reading.

There is not space to list autobiographies here, although there are so many that illuminate our understanding of family and domestic life during the period. However, I believe Katharine Chorley's *Manchester Made Them* (Faber & Faber, 1950) is quite exceptionally useful, as the many references made to the text in this chapter will indicate.

Notes

1 See J. A. Banks' classic discussion of 'the paraphernalia of gentility' in *Prosperity and Parenthood: A Study of Family Planning Among the Victorian Middle Class* (Routledge & Kegan Paul, 1954).

2 P. Branca, *Silent Sisterhood: Middle Class Women in the Victorian Home* (Croom Helm, 1975), pp. 38–48, and T. McBride, 'As the Twig is Bent:

The Victorian Nanny' in A. S. Wohl, (ed), *The Victorian Family* (Croom Helm, 1978), pp. 44–5.

3   D. Gorham, *The Victorian Girl and the Feminine Ideal* (Croom Helm, 1982), pp. 11–12.

4   Mrs C. S. Peel, *The New Home; Treating of the Arrangement, Decoration and Furnishing of a House of Medium Size to be Maintained by a Moderate Income* (Constable & Co., 1903), p.74.

5   M. Girouard, *The Victorian Country House* (Clarendon, Oxford, 1971), pp. 24–6.

6   Peel, *The New Home*, pp. 208–9, 140.

7   See, for instance, the Duchess of Westminster, *Grace and Favour: Memories of Loelia, Duchess of Westminster* (Weidenfeld and Nicolson, 1961), p.54.

8   L. M. Faithfull, *In the House of My Pilgrimage* (Chatto & Windus, 1925), pp. 17–18.

9   E. Starkie, *A Lady's Child* (Faber & Faber, 1941), p. 36.

10   Ibid., p.37

11   K. Chorley, *Manchester Made Them* (Faber & Faber, 1950), pp. 114–15.

12   Ibid., p. 149.

13   Ibid., p. 136.

14   Ibid., pp. 149–50.

15   Starkie, *A Lady's Child*, p. 36.

16   T. Thompson, *Edwardian Childhoods* (Routledge & Kegan Paul, 1981), p. 179.

17   Ibid.

18   Peel, *The New Home*, p.81.

19   Ibid., p.66.

20   Chorley, *Manchester Made Them*, p. 102. See also Gwen Raverat's description of Cambridge dinner parties in the 1900s, in *Period Piece, A Cambridge Childhood* (Faber & Faber, 1952), p.78.

21   Faithfull, *In the House of My Pilgrimage*, p. 18.

22   Peel, *The New Home*, p.239.

23   See (for instance) Eliza Warren's *How I Managed My Children from Infancy to Marriage* (Houston and Wright, 1865), cited in Gorham, *The Victorian Girl*, p. 167.

26   Jean Curtis Brown, *To Tell My Daughter* (Rodney Phillips & Green, 1948), p. 18.

27   Faithfull, *In the House of My Pilgrimage*, p.45.

28   M.V. Hughes *A London Child of the 1870s* (Oxford University Press, 1977), p.7.

29   U. Bloom, *Sixty Years of Home* (Hurst & Blackett, 1960), pp. 97–8.

30   Chorley, *Manchester Made Them*, pp. 101–2; N. Mitchison, *All Change Here* (Bodley Head, 1975), p. 16.

31   Chorley, *Manchester Made Them*, pp. 101–2.

32   Gorham, *The Victorian Girl*, p.85.

33   B. Lee Booker, *Yesterday's Child 1890–1909* (John Long, 1937), p. 104.

34   Mitchison, *All Change Here*, pp. 11–12.

35   Ibid., p. 12.

36 A. Bishop (ed.) *Chronicle of Youth, Vera Brittain's War Diary 1913–17* (Victor Gollancz, 1981), pp. 30–1.

37 C. Dyhouse, *Girls Growing Up in Late Victorian and Edwardian England* (Routledge & Kegan Paul, 1981), especially chapter two.

38 Chorley, *Manchester Made Them*, p. 250.

39 Swanwick, *I Have Been Young*, p. 144.

40 Brown, *To Tell My Daughter*, p. 89.

41 Ibid., p. 91.

42 Chorley, *Manchester Made Them*, p. 153.

43 Ibid., p. 152.

44 K. Fitzpatrick, *Lady Henry Somerset*, (Jonathan Cape, 1923), p. 69.

45 V. Brittain, *Testament of Youth, An Autobiographical Study of the Years 1900–1925* (Victor Gollancz, 1933), pp. 51–2.

46 Brown, *To Tell My Daughter*, p. 91.

47 Ibid.

48 L. Davidoff, *The Best Circles: Society, Etiquette and the Season* (Croom Helm, 1973), pp. 51–2.

49 Chorley, *Manchester Made Them*, p. 262.

50 Brittain, *Testament of Youth*, p. 59.

51 M. V. Hughes, *A London Child of the 1870s* (Oxford University Press, 1977), and *A London Girl of the 1880s* (Oxford University Press, 1978).

52 J. Pitcairn Knowles, *The Upholstered Cage* (Hodder & Stoughton, 1913).

53 Bishop, *Chronicle of Youth*, p. 25.

54 Brittain, *Testament of Youth*, pp. 50–1.

55 Bishop, *Chronicle of Youth*, p. 25.

56 Ibid, p. 40. Compare with the account in Brittain, *Testament of Youth*, p. 73.

57 Chorley, *Manchester Made Them*, p. 150.

58 Starkie, *A Lady's Child*, pp. 93–4.

59 N. Chodorow, *The Reproduction of Mothering: Psychoanalysis and the Sociology of Gender* (University of California Press, Berkeley, 1978), A. Rich, *Of Woman Born: Motherhood as Experience and Institution* (W. W. Norton, New York, 1976).

60 M. Sinclair, *Mary Olivier* (Cassell & Co., 1919).

61 V. Woolf, *To the Lighthouse* (L. & V. Woolf, 1927).

Glasgow Green c.1900. Women and girls laying out washing to dry

2

Limited Resources and Limiting Conventions: Working-Class Mothers and Daughters in Urban Scotland c.1890–1925

Lynn Jamieson

The interaction between mothers and daughters is more than just emotional. Financial and material factors also play an important part. Indeed, among working-class families in Scotland during the late-nineteenth and early twentieth centures, the practical dimensions of mother–child relationships played a major role in determining the emotional content of those relationships. Mothers were conventionally charged with managing the working-class family budget, and their relationships with sons and daughters were shaped by the constraints they experienced, in particular by very limited financial resources and a household division of labour that reflected a pervasive gender hierarchy.

It was possible for children as well as adults to contribute to the working-class household economy. As earners, children could make important financial contributions to family income; as domestic workers, they could significantly ease the burden of household toil. However, the role of working-class girls was somewhat different from that of boys. They had different opportunities, developed different skills and, most importantly, had different demands made of them within the family, particularly by their mothers. This paper looks at mothers' influence on the contributions boys and girls made to the household, and at children's (particularly daughters') reactions to differential treatment. Essentially, the ways in which mothers treated sons and daughters helped to structure gender hierarchy. However, this was not necessarily recognized by either mothers or the children themselves: gender differences were always apparent but hierarchy was not. In describing the different ways in which boys and girls contributed to the household, I show the extent to which mothers' demands of their boy and girl children were shaped by their material circumstances.

My data are oral histories: semi-structured interviews with 38 working-class women and 26 working-class men born around 1900. All the respondents were brought up in the cities or industrial towns of Scotland. In these interviews I asked respondents many questions about details of family life, focusing specifically on their changing relationship with their parents as they grew up. Responses were tape-recorded for subsequent transcription, summary and analysis.[1]

The material conditions of working-class life differed substantially from those of the present. Indicators of 'the quality of life' derived from official statistics and reports (mortality rates, average height of children, housing standards, etc.) all compared unfavourably with the present. Families were larger and materially poorer than we would expect today. Working-class people worked longer hours, either in paid employment, or in domestic work at home, in order to make ends meet. In these respects growing up as a working-class boy or girl in urban Scotland was not radically different from growing up in the same category in any other industrialized community at the turn of the century. Indeed, in what follows, Scotland is treated as a case study rather than a unique case.

Although all members of working-class households tended to contribute to the domestic economy, there was a conventional division of labour, particularly between mother-housekeeper and father-earner. The families of my working-class respondents did not necessarily have a mother 'at home' and a father 'at work'. Almost a third did not live with their mother and father throughout childhood, death being the major cause of disruption. Moreover, in a third of respondents' households, mothers were engaged in paid employment. Among fatherless households, not surprisingly, the majority of mothers worked for wages. But even among the intact families a quarter of mothers were working. Nevertheless, the conventional gender division into 'housewife' and 'provider' was recognized as the norm or ideal; it was universally taken for granted that domestic work was primarily a mother's responsibility and that paid employment for married women was exceptional or extraordinary. Among my respondents, attitudes to married women working ranged from perceiving it as a tragedy or disgrace, to, in one case only, evidence of exceptional energy and independence.[2]

Unless a household was motherless, domestic work was performed by the wife and mother in the first instance. This included management of the household budget, providing appropriate food and clothing, nursing, cleaning and generally caring for all members of the household. As a number of authors have emphasized,[3] material circumstances ranging from the state of domestic technology to family size made domestic labour extremely arduous. Together, the material circumstances of the work and the pervasive assumptions about women's responsibility for that work constrained the physical and emotional space mothers had for their children, and resulted in mothers making particular demands of their daughters. In households in which 'everybody did their bit' of domestic labour, mother was still the orchestrator. She delegated tasks. Material circumstances might have made it virtually impossible for a mother to maintain standards of housework without assistance, but then convention dictated that when it came to passing on arduous domestic work it was daughters who were first in line.

It is important to remember that parents of the period were in no way embarrassed by appeals to traditional authority; parents were to be obeyed simply because they were parents. They expected deference and obedient service from their children, and felt they had a right to ask children to contribute to the household in ways that would lighten their own burden. Notions of traditional authority also permeated the relationships between husband and wife, men and women. Such views meant that daughters – both as children and as young women – were liable for a double dose of service. The lives of daughters in Jimmy's family were an extreme example. His father was almost a caricature of the traditional patriarch. After their mother's death his sisters had to serve his father directly: 'He never spoke to us in the house. Never heard his voice. And if he wanted a cup of tea, he rattled his spoon in his saucer for my sister to pour out his second cup of tea. Oh, it wasn't a very easy life!'

In making greater demands on their daughters, mothers were thus not only drawing on their traditional parental authority, but also respecting conventional notions about gender divisions. The allocation of domestic work to women was and is part of a broader and pervasive set of assumptions concerning appropriate behaviour for women and men. These assumptions were not made in the family and imported to other areas of society but were, like similar assumptions today, grounded in actions and possibilities simultaneously enforced 'at home', 'at work', in toil and in pleasure. Most importantly, the labour market was and is structured in a way that underpins a view of women as domestic workers first and paid workers/earners, second.[4] Gender differences sustained in different arenas are mutually reinforcing. For example, the difference in earnings of boys and girls, women and men was and perhaps still is a material circumstance that influences family relationships, including the way that mothers treat boys and girls.

Respondents' experiences of contributing to the household indicate that there were considerable differences in the number and weight of demands mothers made of them. I discuss first respondents' experiences of doing housework and then their experiences of earning. In both sections the experiences of boys and girls are compared.

Doing Housework

My respondents spoke of a range of domestic tasks that were delegated to them as school children: 'going the messages' (shopping), cleaning cutlery, polishing brass, cleaning shoes. In some households these tasks were done only by girls, but in most cases they were children's rather than girls' jobs. However, the heavier, more difficult household tasks of cooking, washing, floor scrubbing were rarely delegated to boys. George described a typical division of labour when talking of his house during the Friday night cleaning, an event common to most households:

> Friday night was always a night that was a cleaning night. And after you came home from school, if you weren't going out with the milk [delivering milk: the most common part-time work of school children] you went the messages for the Saturday. And that was the night you cleaned the house. Everyone of us had their part to play in those days. There was no linoleum like what it is now, just the bare boards, and these boards had to be scrubbed with what they called silver sand. Dry-scrubbed, and then you went over it with water. These boards would be smooth. You'd think they'd varnished it. And after the floors were washed – my sisters they did the washing of the floors – the newspapers were put down and woe betide you if you dirtied the floor.

Some tasks – digging the garden, fetching the coal and, in some households, washing the windows – were more likely to be done by boys. But this did not balance the division of household tasks. Far more schoolgirls spent long hours in housework than boys. Moreover, girls usually continued to do some housework after they had entered full-time employment. Even if they were living and working away from home they were often expected to make a contribution in their time off. Mary, for example, was a shop assistant living with a woman who kept a small 'Jenny a' Things' (a shop stocking a wide variety of everyday items – 'all things'). She worked long hours but had a half day: 'Sometimes I wished I hadnae. I had to go home to my mother's and do washing.' Housework was not demanded of boys once they were in full-time employment.

Through the experience of doing housework for their mother was learned more than just how to do certain tasks. Daughters also developed a set of ideas about what ought to be done in the role of housekeeper and a set of standards by which to measure their own and others' performance in that role. Mothers often supervised children's efforts and imposed standards on them:

> I can mind the first time I done the stair. I was sorry I ever offered. It was a wooden stair, you see. Here I hadnae done it to my mother's liking and she came oot and looked at it. She says, 'No Ina! That's no right. No. You'll get a knife wi'ye and you get into the corners.' I says, 'Well I didnae know I had to dae that.' 'Well', she says, 'You do a thing, you do it right.'

Standards were not determined by each individual mother-housewife for herself, however. The practice of cleaning the house on Friday night, for example, was a widespread tradition. Women were judged by their family and neighbours, at least in part according to their housewifery. In trying to explain to me why their mother was a 'good mother', respondents often talked in terms of her skill and energy as a housekeeper: the cleanliness and order of the house, the ability to make good food from very little, her potted meat, her thrift. It was in the interests of mothers, then, to make their efforts visible. Mary's mother for example, when she said, 'Eat up all your rice 'cause there's an egg in it to make it rich for you,' was declaring her good housewifery to her children as well as encouraging good food habits.

In addition to the role of family and neighbours in shaping standards of domestic labour, the state, in the shape of the teacher, newly created school nurse and health visitor could also bring influence to bear. A number of respondents talk of having paraffin rubbed in their hair to keep them clear of vermin. Crissie linked this explicitly to 'the school inspection' (the medical inspection of school children was introduced in 1907). This was one instance of an increased number of routes through the child from school to home, created or consolidated by late-nineteenth- and early twentieth-century legislation.[5]

Just as standards of housework and childcare existed independently of the discretion of the individual mother-housewife, so it was with notions concerning appropriate behaviour of sons and daughters. The pervasiveness of something close to the idea that domestic work is women's work was illustrated by many respondents, particularly men. Men often described their childhood involvement in housework with the explanatory addendum that they had no sisters. Similarly other men explained their lack of participation with reference to their sisters. For these respondents the rules were quite clear, men did domestic work only if there were no women to do it. Indeed, there was one job which a man never took on: that of full-time domestic worker. If the mother died a woman would be expected to step into her role. Several respondents were taken away from school early when one of their parents died, and while there are instances of both daughters and sons entering full-time paid employment early because of a father's death, only daughters left school early to become full-time housekeepers.

Thus, in accordance with conventional gender divisions, mothers made girls do more housework than boys; young women were expected to continue helping with housework, young men were not. This gave daughters some experience of 'women's role', and some opportunity to identify this role as an aspect of the subordinate position of women in the gender hierarchy. My evidence suggests, however, that mothers rarely set about deliberately and consciously socializing their daughters into the role of future housewives.

The clearest test of mothers' intentions is to examine the extent to which they 'taught' their daughters to be housekeepers. Although they 'taught' standards of housework through supervising delegated tasks, there was very rarely a sense of a progressive programme of learning; what was taught depended on the needs of the household rather than the state of the daughter's knowledge. When circumstances resulted in a girl of thirteen or fourteen taking on the role of housekeeper she usually had to learn on the job. For example, Agnes made 'mainly mince and tatties' after her mother died because it was easy. She remembered having a terrible disaster on her first wash day:

> I remember the first washing I did. I used to have to stand on a stool. [It was] a great big wooden tub. One day I was washing sheets. [I was] twelve years old. And I thought to myself, 'Well I'll get some chloride of lime.' That was the stuff we used to use long ago. And I sprinkled it on the top of the sheets in the pot. Put the pot in the fire to boil them to wash them. When I took the sheets out they're a' in ribbons. I'd put too much in.

Those daughters who carried the heaviest domestic burden were those whose mothers were absent or particularly overburdened or debilitated. On the other hand, some mothers limited their demands to the traditional children's tasks, being able and preferring to do the bulk of the housework themselves. Very few, like Jane's mother, made special efforts to involve their daughters in what they were doing in an educational way: 'If mother was baking she would give us a little bit of dough and a bottle for a rolling pin, and showed us how to roll out scones. As we got on [older] we had to make the dough ourselves and do it.' Only Hatty's mother made a sustained effort to teach her daughters a range of skills explicitly flagged as being characteristics of a good wife. This included advice about managing money:

> Mother used to say, 'Well, it will no be my fault if you dinae turn out to be a good wife.' We tain our teaching off my mother, that you had to do right. If you were going to get married you had to do the right thing. And my mother when we were getting married used to say to us, 'Now remember never take on but what your husband knows. Never. If you feel you need anything, save up for it and wait till you've got the money to buy it. But if you feel you need it and you've no got the money, tell your husband. Get his opinion before you do anything.' And she used to say to us, 'There's one thing you've got to remember when you get married. See that you pay your rent and that you pay your way, your societies [various insurance-like savings schemes]. Never let that go out. See that you pay your rent, even if you have to live on bread and margarine.'

For most daughters, any knowledge of the management of money, as with housework, came from doing or observing rather than from advice about a future role of wife. Hatty's mother was exceptional in many respects. While doing much more to explicitly train her daughters as good wives, she also presented an example of an extremely independent woman:

> My mother was a very independent person. She wouldn't draw on his [father's] salary. That's what you could do long ago. She

wouldnae do that, she'd rather go out to work and when my
father [a seaman] came to an English port he would get his
salary and send money up to mother and perhaps go away to
Russia again. My mother was a very thrifty woman.

Hatty apart, in so far as mothers encouraged daughters to be more
domestically minded than boys, they did not make any explicit links
to wider views of either the girl's 'future' or 'women's place' more
generally. The daily contributions mothers made to fostering gender
differentiation were only indirectly responsible for making 'good
wives' of their daughters. The demands made of daughters seemed
to come from mothers' perceptions of household needs rather than
from a sense of responsibility for the future housewifery skills of
their daughters.

So far I have presented a picture of mothers demanding help from
their daughters out of necessity. There is nothing simple about this
necessity however. It is not reducible to a set of material
circumstances (including income, housing, furnishing and facilities,
family size and composition, domestic technology, health and
energy) that created a large burden of housework. Rather, it was
shaped by authority structures and rules of conduct that dictated
that certain tasks could not be asked of men or boys, at least as long
as there are girls there to do them. The burden of work was also
shaped by standards of housework. Base-line standards were far
wider than any individual family, that is they were socially not
individually produced. The work asked of daughters was dictated by
the mother's desire to attain the degree of domestic order she
believed to be acceptable, as well as by ideas about female
responsibility for housework.

Earning, Pocket-Money and Freedom to Come and Go

As well as contributing to the household through housework,
shopping and childcare, working-class children often also brought
home contributions of money and goods. Children under fourteen
(the school-leaving age) often foraged for fuel, did casual and holiday
work, and had part-time jobs. They were not working for
pocket-money. It was generally understood that any money earned,
even small sums, would be handed over 'to the house'. Pocket-
money was given out by mother. This system of handing over all
earnings and getting pocket-money back persisted when children
entered the workforce, but with variation by gender. Both girls and

boys took it for granted that they would be leaving school and entering some form of full-time employment at fourteen. With the exception of a few girls who were full-time houseworkers and five respondents who stayed on at school beyond fourteen, all were earning a wage by then. The experience of earning differed in a number of respects for boys and girls, young men and women: first because, young women living 'at home' were almost always also houseworkers as well as earners; second, they rarely earned as much as their brothers; and third, their disposable income was often less than that of their brothers.

About half of my respondents, but proportionately more boys than girls, did part-time work while still at school, the majority delivering milk. More boys than girls worked for shops, delivering and doing back-shop work, which tended to mean long hours. There was one type of work that only girls did: scrubbing stairs and cleaning other people's houses for money. For some girls, then, there was an overlap between doing housework and earning. Belle, for example, did housework at home and was paid for a routine housework job, as well as 'going with the milk':

> I washed stairs, [for] a man who worked beside my father, and his wife died. I got sixpence and that was a lot of money for washing the stair. So he said 'Will you scrub the bunker?' It was a great big white bunker. It was a Friday I had to go and scrub the bunker and scrub the floor – brown linoleum on the floor. And I got a shilling if I done the kitchen bunker and my mother got the shilling.

Carrying a heavy burden of housework at home could preclude having a part-time job. I asked Maggie if she did any kind of paid work when she was at school: 'No I never had a chance 'cause my mother was oot working. I had to be in the hoose with the bairns, washing and everything at twelve or thirteen years old'.

Although to be burdened to this extent was unusual, all girls did housework and it was typically experienced as something they had to do throughout their young lives, whether or not they were earners. In either case it was normally mother who said what had to be done. George and Mary, quoted above, have already indicated the compulsory character of children's involvement in housework. Ina made this very clear: 'On a Friday night everything had to be cleaned and put back again. Oh I'd [to do] all that, and if I was late in coming in my mother was there meeting me at the school. I'd be playing and she'd give me a row for being late'. Some boys also had to do housework but for them it was confined to a specific life-cycle stage and almost never overlapped with full-time earning.

Unlike housework, early earning, that is earning prior to leaving school, was not experienced as something that had to be done because of a parental demand or expectation. Johnnie illustrates the sense of choice when I asked if he had to work: 'Didnae have to do anything. Did it because I was always energetic. I could see the way my mother was struggling'. Involvement in part-time employment was not typically the result of pressure from mother or father. This is despite the fact that parents, particularly mothers, stood to gain from the part-time work of school children, since it was taken for granted that earnings would be handed over 'to the house'. Earning money beyond the household was not part of the traditional, deferential and obedient service parents expected of children. The fact that early earning was voluntary, and early housework was not, further exaggerated the lower potential housework offered for building self-confidence and a sense of self-worth.

When it came to entering full-time employment, gender differences were negligible in a number of important respects. First and foremost, this was an inevitable event for both girls and boys, and respondents' accounts suggest it was generally an event of similar significance for both. The satisfaction Johnnie expressed at being able to help mother was remembered by a number of respondents, both women and men, as a part of the pride they felt when they earned their first full-time wage. This is described in rather dramatic terms by Eric: 'And the joy of getting your pay on Friday and handing it over to mum. That was good. Her face would light up and a tear in her eye.' I asked respondents when they thought they felt 'grown up'. Many said it was when they started work. Jenny replied, laughing: 'When I left the school I thought I was keeping the hoose.' Several respondents remember liking the idea that they kept the house, even if their earnings were insufficient in reality. Thus both women and men talked in terms of a new sense of contribution and responsibility to the household.

The experience of earning was nevertheless different for women in a number of respects. Most importantly, women's average earnings were considerably less than those of men. Typically the wages of young people were low, but by the age of twenty-one the vast majority of male respondents were earning more than 25 shillings a week.[6] Several were earning a few pounds. Some women, however, never escaped low-paid work and continued to earn less than a pound a week well into their twenties. The difference in their earnings was reflected in the amount of spending money young women and men had, although pocket-money did not mirror wages in any exact way. Young women usually had less to spend than young men. Since it was mothers who, on the whole, controlled the family budget, including pocket-money, it could be argued that they contributed to these gender differences. But it is more in keeping with the evidence of women workers' low wages to suggest that mothers failed to redress the inequalities of earnings generated in the labour market.

Initially, all respondents received a small amount of pocket money but at some stage a substantial proportion started to 'keep themselves'. There were two systems, either a set sum, 'digs money', was paid over and the rest of the wage retained, or pocket money increased. In both cases the understanding was that clothes and anything else required in addition to board were the young earner's responsibility, although this was not necessarily strictly adhered to, inasmuch as mothers would often continue to buy things for their children. The transition to 'keeping themselves' and particularly to 'paying digs' meant an increase in the disposable income of the young person. Among my respondents, few women ever paid 'digs money' and a larger proportion of women than men never 'kept themselves'.

From a small sample it is difficult to establish confidently the going rate for 'digs money', particularly given the difficulty in allowing for inflation during the war period.[7] My evidence suggests that the going rate was higher than the earnings of low-paid workers, but for someone earning good wages the system of paying digs was the most advantageous, as Andrew observed: 'In those days it was 25/−. I gave her [mother] more after [in later years] but that was the usual thing. If you got board you thought you were the Lord of the Isles. You always had a pound in your pocket and a pound was your best friend'. Jenny was one of the few women to earn good wages. She was a time-served french polisher:[8] 'Oh I was keeping myself. My mother gave us a winter rig-out and a summer rig-out. 'Now', she says, 'your apprenticeship is finished, you'll keep yourself, and you'll know the value of money'. That was alright. We were making good pays, right enough . . . I remember one week I got about seven pounds extra'.

Jenny was unique among the women respondents in having such a sum at her disposal. Far more common was the experience of having very little. Some women, like Betty, received very little pocket money well into their twenties and yet were expected to be able to satisfy their needs from that small amount: 'You may have got 3d or

6d and we were in the penny bank in the church, and we went up religiously with the bank-books and maybe just putting in 3d or 6d. Then, maybe you were needing something or there was something you wanted for yourself, then you would get it'. The 'needs' of many women respondents never expanded with their income, but rather remained small with their pocket money.

Differences in earning were not the sole cause of gender differences in spending money. There were additional pressures that encouraged mothers to depress the pocket-money of girls or inflate that of boys, pressures which resulted in boys having more freedom than girls. Boys and young men could be seen as 'needing' more pocket-money because they 'got out' more and because the conventions of courtship required young men to pay for expenses incurred when a young couple 'went out'. Some daughters talked of how they did not need as much money. Rosie talked of the 6d a week spending money she had when she was 'going out with' her future husband:

> Well, I didnae really need anything to spend, actually. There wasnae so many – well we didnae get so much to the pictures then and even at that it was the only place you could go . . . I was only allowed out three times a week anyway. Half-past nine Sunday and ten o'clock through the week, sometimes half-past nine. And if I didnae do what I was told I was kept in and deprived of my nights out.

Young people did not have complete freedom to come and go. The overwhelming majority continued to be governed by their parents in a number of ways, despite the fact that they were earners, but sons were generally given more leeway than daughters. Even if they were still told when they had to be home at night, parents did not check up as closely on sons as they did on daughters. Mothers and fathers were routinely watchful of when their daughters came home and intervened if she lingered with a young man outside the house. This reflected fears both of sexual misconduct and for their daughters' reputations.

For those young men, particularly apprentices, who experienced a marked increase in earnings during their late teens/early twenties, greater freedom was bound up with their status as earners. For some respondents there was a link between paying 'digs' and having more freedom. Eck gave an elaborate account of this when trying to explain why his brother Joe had more freedom than him:[9]

> Aye Joe! He came and went as he liked. [I asked: How come he managed to come and go as he liked?] Well, he paid his way ye

ken. I wasnae paying for my digs like. I was handing over my
wages. He was paying his digs. I had the five shillings a day at
the pony driving. Well, I didnae pay my digs off of that. I just
handed my mother the pay and got my pocket-money back.

The link between greater freedom and the status of the earner was
less sharp for young women for a variety of reasons. Fewer
experienced a similar marked increase in earnings and disposable
income. Also, as women, their freedom was always more restricted.
Free time was reduced by housework; the range of ways in which
they spent their free time was more limited; and the rules of sexual
conduct required them and their parents to be more cautious of
where, when and with whom they 'went out'. Both sons and
daughters took earning to be a natural part of growing up and both
were proud to be earners, but there were more opportunities for
young men to feel that their status was enhanced by earning.

Acceptance or Resentment of the Daughter's Position

My data suggest that the willingness with which daughters accepted
responsibility for housework varied according to their assessment of
their mother's needs and intentions. Some respondents were less
willing helpers because they felt they were treated unfairly. In some
cases differences in pocket money and in freedom between
themselves and their brothers were factors contributing to this
feeling of unfairness. A few felt their mother wittingly and
unnecessarily made invidious distinctions between boys and girls.
For others, differential privileges and demands did not influence
their response to mothers' requests for help; they saw mother as
having no choice but to ask.

Respondents recognized that demands made on a daughter were
typically influenced by the overall burden borne by her mother,
which in turn depended on many factors – the mother's health and
energy, the size of the family, and the amount of other assistance she
received. A number considered themselves unlucky to have been of
an appropriate age to help when their siblings were too young or
otherwise unavailable. Betty makes this clear:

I sympathise with a person that's the oldest girl because she
does get it put on her. She [younger sister] would get out.
When she come out of the school my mother would say, 'Get
the wee one ready'. Well she would take her [the wee one] oot
. . . and she would leave her at the side of the road and play at

jumping ropes . . . I had to go in and scrub the floor or wash. I was standing at the green – hanging up clothes [standing] on a tin box or something because I couldnae reach the line.

Some daughters came to do housework willingly: they felt close to their mothers, sympathized with how much they had to do and regarded them as having no choice but to demand help when they did. A number of daughters explained the amount of housework they took on in terms of their affection for their mothers. Tilly was an example. In the quotation below she moves from talking about compulsion to voluntary participation:

We had to help, you see and then . . . of course, mind you I was different from the rest of the family. I always wanted to help my mother. Her and me were very close to each other, whether it was with me being the youngest I don't know . . . I've had more to do with her than any of them. In fact her and my father both died in my house.

When talking about her school days, Betty complained about the lot of an eldest daughter, but later she described how she voluntarily carried on helping her mother even after she was married, in spite of a considerable burden of other work and opposition from her husband:

I wasnae very far away from her [mother]. At seven o'clock I had to leave them [her own two children] sleeping . . . and slip across to the washhouse for an hour and get the washing done and come back for to get them away for school. I used to take all the washing and this is the truth . . . Now I was washing for all they lads [brothers and father] that was working on the coal lorry. You know the kind of towels and sheets I had. I used to go twice a week for her. [Her husband found out and demanded to know] 'Whose going to bring they kids up if anything happens to you. You've another two sisters and you know they're making a damn fool of you. I don't mind you helping if one of them would go wi' ye.' The other two was never inside a washhouse. But I couldnae see. It was my mother. I couldnae see that.

Betty was no longer doing what she was told but was 'choosing' to help because of sympathy for her mother. At the same time it was as if she felt that she had no choice – she could not tolerate seeing her mother without help. Daughters who 'stayed at home' to look after their mothers similarly talked in terms of 'choice':

Anyway I got this when my father died [Jean was aged 14]: I was the eldest and I would have to see my mother through. And

> I did, because my brothers were both married. They married
> within a year of each other. Mother and I were left. Then we
> just carried on taking in boarders . . . Mother had the boarders
> and I had to go home [from work in the hoisery factory] and
> work at night. There was nothing else for it. [Jean's mother
> died when she was forty-one] . . . and I didn't marry till after
> that. I've never grudged it.

For many daughters with brothers close to their own age, the
recognition that their mothers had no choice but to ask their help
was prompted in part by the assumption that certain things could
not legitimately be expected of their brothers. These daughters took
for granted that they and their mother were bound by the rule that
domestic work was largely women's work. Discontent at having to
do housework did not necessarily amount to a rejection of the
categorization of domestic work as 'women's work'. Young women
could feel uneasy with the fact that they had to do housework; they
could doubt that it was legitimately *their* work, but yet recognize that
there was nobody else to do it, meaning no other suitable woman. In
this situation, daughters remained uneasily reconciled to doing
housework in the knowledge that their mother had nowhere else to
go for help and could not be left to do it alone. Belle speaks for
daughters in this category. She is only atypical in that she did have a
target on which to pin her unease – her sister Dot who was at home
to help her mother. In Belle's view this sister should have done all
the housework not done by her mother and thus have freed earners
(like her and her sister Peg), from housework:

> But Peg was the best worker of the lot to my mother. Even
> though we were working from six to eight at night in Alder
> McKae's [munitions factory, Edinburgh] she'd say, 'Come on
> we're the first served, we'll wash up to save my mother.
> Mother's leg is awfie sore. Come on!' [I said] 'Peg, it's unfair.
> We're in the factory all day.' And we'd a single sister Dot. She
> was supposed to be keeping the house. She'd be sitting reading.

Belle did not take for granted that all daughters should do
housework because they were daughters. She wished to make a
distinction between daughter-earners and daughter-houseworkers
and it is this division she appeals to when complaining about having
to do housework. And yet, because it was universally taken for
granted that a full-time houseworker could only be a woman, her
brothers could invoke the same earner/houseworker division when
concluding that housework was women's work.

Not all daughters felt in sympathy with their mothers. A few respondents felt that their mother clearly favoured their brothers in a number of ways which could not be accounted for in terms of having no choice in the matter. In other words, they reported favouritism and discrimination that rankled. Mary, for example, wryly remarked: 'They were the apple of my mother's eye. Nothing could go wrong with the boys' (she had just described how she and her sisters had to wash the white gloves and polish the patent leather shoes which their brothers wore 'to the dancing'). In this case girls were manifestly being forced to serve their brothers. Annie made similar complaints with reference to her brother:

> My mother was more lenient with the boys than she was with the girls. She preferred boys of course. My mother used to think boys shouldn't have to do anything in the house, that was a girl's place you know . . . I was the last one out of the house [last child to leave home except her unmarried brother Sandy who never left] . . . It was a case of do this for Sandy and do that for Sandy. He was treated like a baby honestly. . . . She wouldnae see the wind blowing on him, sort of style.

What caused Annie and Mary resentment was not that their mothers were demanding help with housework but that they were expected to give deferential service to their brothers. This experience forced them to see not just gender difference but hierarchy. Much that implies hierarchy to a sociologist can be treated as unexamined difference in everyday life. The objective facts of gender-based divisions of labour at home and in the labour force, the greater restrictions placed on the movements of daughters by parents and, indeed, the more limited freedom of movement accepted by women of all ages, did not typically excite resentment. Having to serve brothers, particularly when both brother and sister were earners, was unavoidably experienced as subordination in a relationship between self and brother. However, children could always interpret the hierarchy they experienced as resulting from deviant behaviour on the part of their particular parents, rather than as evidence of wider male domination.

There were a handful of respondents who complained of such discrimination but then there were also a few mothers who actively discouraged their daughters from working for their brothers or 'the family'. Ina's mother for example: 'I can mind of saying to my mother, "Mum, what's going to happen to the boys if anything happens to you?" [Mother replied] "They'll no do for you what you do for them." That always stuck [in my mind]. So she says, "Put them in a home."' As with those experiencing active discrimination against them, Ina perceived this as idiosyncratic favouritism, rather than acknowledgement of an understood sex/gender system in which men came out on top.

Conclusion

Throughout the paper I suggest that mothers' contributions to gender inequalities must not be overstated. Although mothers had authority in the domestic sphere, they did not have complete freedom in which to treat sons and daughters equally. Social pressures and material factors play an important part in structuring family relations: for example, in determining that women rather than men become housewives.

In support of this my data suggest, first, that the overwhelming majority of mothers were not preoccupied with bringing up their daughters to be good housewives and their sons to be good earners. For example, mothers did not put pressure on their school-aged sons to go out and earn in the way they demanded housework from daughters. Such pressure would not have been as consistent with their immediate needs for assistance, or with the limits of their parental authority, even though such demands would have mirrored the conventional division of labour between adult men and women. The evidence suggests that mothers were preoccupied with their housekeeping responsibilities rather than the moulding of their children into future roles.

Second, while respondents' experiences of doing housework and earning indicated differences between boys and girls that supported the dominance of men, the demands mothers made – in respect of housework, for example – reflected their structural and material position. Mothers were the organizers of limited physical and financial resources while further constrained by conventions – prevailing high standards of housework, and the pervasive assumption that domestic work was women's work. Limited resources and limiting conventions resulted in heavy demands being made of daughters. Thirdly, limited resources and limiting conventions supported gender differentiatioin and hierarchy, even when mothers did not respond by demanding more housework and depressing the privileges of earning in the case of their daughters. Mothers' decisions about whom to ask to do what were thus heavily constrained, even if they did not intend to make any invidious distinctions between sons and daughters.

The extent to which different degrees of experience of domestic work in childhood have profound and lasting effects on boys and girls is unclear. Literature on the contemporary family indicates a variety of possibilities:[10] psychological (willingness to serve); practical (sensitivity to 'what needs doing' and appropriate skills to do it); and ideological (women's greater housewifery skills reaffirm the wisdom of the gender-based division of labour). Generalization is, however, difficult given that the range and variation in burdens of domestic work carried by school-age children in the early twentieth century were considerable. There were, for example, a few boys doing more housework than some girls.

In any case, whatever their actual experience, my evidence suggests that all family members took it for granted that a whole range of household tasks were women's work. Certainly, both boys and girls accepted that many such tasks were mothers' responsibility and that only certain categories of women were appropriate substitute mothers. This is what men were saying when they explained having to do housework by the absence of sisters, and this was why a thirteen-year-old girl could be taken out of school to stand in for a deceased mother while her older brother was never considered.

It is not until they themselves were earners that young women faced the contradictions in the division of labour they accepted between earner and housewife-mother, and by implication between men's work and women's work. Although boys and girls entered full-time employment at the same age and with equal pride, the status of earner did not carry the same privileges for women. The continued availability of teenage daughters as mothers' helpers was an important attenuating factor. If young women understood the division of labour between their parents as complementary separate spheres, they now learned that earning and domestic work were not mutually exclusive in their own case. They discovered that domestic work was still to be their responsibility; they were again reminded that this work was women's work and were simultaneously initiated into the contradiction in categories that constituted their own status as 'women workers'. Mothers' systems of redistributing household income further supported invidious gender distinctions between earners in their late-teens and early twenties. High earners paying 'digs' (predominantly men) kept a larger proportion of their salary than low earners, who received pocket-money (predominantly women). Finally, the greater watchfulness parents kept over daughters further reduced the possibility of girls experiencing earning as liberating. Taken together, these factors helped depress the significance of the status of 'earner' for young women. Among my respondents, women did not boast of the privileges of having money in their pockets and freedom to come and go. Although women worked, the status of worker, whether anticipated or not, generally remained elusive.

But again, even when the distinctions mothers made between boys and girls were minimal, gender hierarchy was implicit in other status divisions within the family that were universally supported: children must respect adults, 'non-workers' must respect 'workers'. The fact that fathers were presumed to be the ultimate authority in the household underpinned the daily demands mother made for obedient service from her children. The rule that only women were to be full-time houseworkers reflected the fact that full-time house-workers routinely served full-time paid workers. Some women partially recognized the links between these status divisions and gender divisions. Like Belle, they felt that the respect they should have been afforded as full-time adult workers eluded them as they crossed status boundaries to help their mother.

For many respondents the existence of a gender hierarchy was occluded by their affection for mother. They could see their mother toiling, they knew how they were supposed to help. Help involved action; it did not require analysis of the gender-based division of labour. For daughters, this meant willingly taking on domestic work. Even those who believed that 'workers' ought not to do housework did so; helping mother was a natural, from-the-heart exception to that general rule. The sense of choosing to help masked the constraining and discriminatory sex/gender system. Not surprisingly, gender hierarchy was most readily visible to respondents who were out of sympathy with their mothers, particularly those who saw their mothers as blatantly favouring boys.

Bibliographical Note

All the names quoted in this paper are fictitious (I promised anonymity to my respondents) but this work was possible thanks to all those who were interviewed and those who assisted in finding respondents. I am here drawing on a wider body of material collected for my PhD. thesis, 'The development of "the modern family": the case of urban Scotland in the early twentieth century', Edinburgh University, 1983. I was inspired to use retrospective interview by the work of P. Thompson, particularly, *The Edwardians: The remaking of British Society* (Paladin, 1977). A recent and relevant publication using similar techniques is that of E. Roberts, *A Woman's Place: An oral history of working-class women 1890–1940* (Basil Blackwell, Oxford, 1984).

There are many pieces of femininist and feminist-informed literature (both historical and contemporary) that deal with internal family dynamics and gender socialization while refusing to see the family as markedly separated off from wider social processes. An early example L. Davidoff, 'Mastered for life: servant wife and mother in Victorian and Edwardian Britain', *Journal of Social History* 7 (1974), 406–28. More recent work includes relevant sections from the more general M. Barret, and M. McIntosh, *The Anti-Social Family* (Verso, 1982) and C. Harris, *The Family and Industrial Society* (George Allen & Unwin, 1983) or, with a greater emphasis on psychological factors, M. Poster, *Critical Theory of the Family* (Pluto, 1978) and N. Chodorow, *The Reproduction of Mothering: psycho-analysis and the sociology of gender* (University of California Press, Berkeley, 1978).

Notes

1 The fact that this material is from the viewpoint of the child has advantages and drawbacks. It provides insight into the family from a neglected perspective but then any one perspective is inevitably partial. I have occasionally been tempted to infer mothers' attitudes from children's (remembered) experiences of their behaviour. This is obviously dangerous and I have, therefore, tried to be cautious when so doing. Background information on all respondents can be found in my 'The Development of "the Modern Family": the case of urban Scotland in the early twentieth century', unpublished PhD. thesis, Edinburgh University 1983. For discussion and evaluation of the use of oral history see P. Thompson *The Voice of the Past: Oral History* (Oxford University Press, Oxford, 1981).

2 For further relevant discussion of the view that married women should not 'have to' go out to work and indeed should only do so if 'forced to', see E. Roberts, 'Working class women in the North West' *Oral History* 5 (1977) 14–28 and *A Woman's Place: an oral history of working class women 1890–1940* (Basil Blackwell, Oxford, 1984).

3 R. Schwartz Cowan, *More Work for Mother: the ironies of household technology from the open hearth to the microwave* (Basic, New York, 1983) has detailed the persistent and extensive burden of domestic work for the North American housewife throughout the twentieth century. Descriptions of the nature of domestic labour in Britain are scattered throughout numerous studies. A classic article arguing that the burden of housework is not the result of material resources and technology alone is that of L. Davidoff, 'The rationalisation of housework' in D. Barker and S. Allen (eds), *Dependence and Exploitation in Work and Marriage* (Longman, 1976). One British author who, like Schwartz Cowan, treats

the extent of the domestic burden as having fostered a gender-based division of labour is J. Humphries, 'Class struggle and the persistence of the working-class family, *Cambridge Journal of Economics* 1 (1977), 241–58.

4 Many feminist authors have documented aspects of how the labour market operates in this way. Two key theoretical articles are those of R. D. Barron, and G. M. Norris, 'Sexual Divisions and the Dual Labour Market', in Barker and Allen, *Dependence and Exploitation*; and A. Phillips, and B. Taylor, 'Sex and Skill: notes towards a feminist economics' *Feminist Review* 6 (1980), 79–88. For useful summaries of relevant discussion see J. Wajeman, 'Work and the Family: who gets "the best of both worlds"?' and J. Siltanen 'A Commentary on Theories of Female Wage Labour', both in *Women in Society*, The Cambridge Women's Studies Group (ed.), (Virago, 1981). For interesting but little-known British empirical work specific to the period discussed here, see J. Bornat, 'Home and Work: a new context for trade union history', and S. Taylor 'The Effect of Marriage on Job Possibilities for Women and the Ideology of the Home: Nottingham 1890–30', both in *Oral History* 5 (1977), 101–23 and 46–61.

5 J. Donzelot, talks of the 'Policing of families' in *The Policing of Families: Welfare Versus the State* (Hutchinson, 1979), although my evidence suggests that he overstates his case.

6 Before decimalization, there were twenty shillings (20/−) in the British pound and twelve pence (12d) to each shilling.

7 Since my oldest respondent was born in 1888 and the youngest in 1908, their early earning years actually span the First World War.

8 'Time-served' describes a person who has completed a full apprenticeship.

9 Eck is a diminutive form of Alec which is, in turn, a diminutive of Alexander.

10 In fact a variety of groups of literatures are relevant here. Much has, of course, been written on gender socialization; a British example is S. Sharpe, *'Just like a girl': how girls learn to be women* (Penguin, Harmondsworth, 1976). There is also literature specifically on housework; see, for example, A. Oakley, *The Sociology of Housework* (Martin Robertson, 1974). In addition, more general 'family sociology' often makes relevant comments, for example on the consequences of different previous housework experience for the divisions of labour on marriage.

Part II
Mothering

Picture from a scrapbook relating to St. Pancras School for Mothers c.1910

3

Labour and Love: Rediscovering London's Working-Class Mothers, 1870–1918

Ellen Ross

In the early 1900s controversy over 'the deterioration of the English race', working-class mothers generally figure as ignorant and neglectful. The autobiographical accounts created by their children, on the other hand, portray confident, portly, managing women, constantly working and planning for their households. The voice of the women themselves is seldom found in the voluminous literature on working-class family life a century ago. In this essay, which centres on working-class motherhood in London for the two generations ending 1918, I want neither to celebrate nor to judge mothers, but to make them historical subjects: to examine the work which having children demanded of them, the expectations it created, the emotions it may have generated, and the ways in which women experienced the pressures transforming it.

The dissemination of psychoanalytic models of child development since the early 1940s and, since the 1960s, theories of early childhood cognitive development, have weighted mothers today with unprecedented responsibility for their children's formation. While the physical work of mothering has been dramatically eased over the past century by such varied advances as antibiotics and modern plumbing, the emotional job has been expanded; every resource, and every failing, of the mother are constantly at play in modern notions of childraising. As Sheila Kitzinger formulates the contrast, the 'relational and sentimental features' of mothering have come to dominate the 'service aspects'.[1] Kitzinger's is a fair characterization of the change in ideologies about motherhood, but it wrongly implies that in today's pattern there is more emotion invested in mothering than in the past. I propose, instead, that we examine the meanings that 'service' carried for contemporaries. In London poverty, mothers' domestic work – sewing, cleaning, nursing and especially supplying and preparing food – provided their families' only sources of comfort, and was often essential to sheer physical survival. In consequence, these caring services carried even more emotional resonance both with mothers and their families than they do today. (As household providers of care and food, mothers have continued, of course, to exercise such power in their households, in addition to sacrificing their own comfort and nutrition for their husbands and children.)[2] Perhaps the deep appreciation of food in a hungry people helps explain the extra-ordinary detail with which Victorian and Edwardian Londoners have remembered into old age such domestic activities as shopping and cooking, and may indeed have lent mothers the larger-than-life stature they are given in so many working-class autobiographies.

In the two pre-war generations my study describes, the cluster of practices and ideas which we think of as belonging to 'mother' were falling into recognizable places, just as the word 'mum' was becoming a standard part of the English language.[3] The introduction of compulsory education by the School Board for London in the early 1870s had thrown household economies and patterns of mother–child reciprocity into disarray, postponing for several years the point at which children could go out to full-time jobs.[4] What developed in the course of the following decades was an uneasy truce between working-class mothers and the School Board. Women kept 'sick' children at home, or lied impressively to the Board's representatives when summoned to explain their children's truancy. The cultural and juridical assumption that children belonged with and to their mothers rather than to their fathers is mostly a product of this era, as is the view that mothers have an inescapable role as intermediaries between children, on the one hand, and the appropriate professions and state agencies, on the other. It was, too, in the decades just before the First World War that the medical and social-work professions staked out their claims, as experts, to determining working-class standards of childcare. London mothers may have benefitted from the state and charitable programme (school meals, old-age pensions, improved medical facilities, the maternity benefit, etc.) introduced in the early twentieth century. Yet a subtle transformation in the mother–child relationship was gradually taking place, by which women were given more responsibilities toward their children, while children remained their dependants for a longer period. Settlement worker Anna Martin, writing just before the war, was certain that compulsory education, in the context of other social and legal changes, had constituted a 'speed-up' for England's working-class mothers. From their tiny household budgets, wives had to supply children's boots, white pinafores for girls, changes of underlinen, cleaning materials, 'scraps of cheap finery for the school parties', death insurance and hot Sunday dinners. 'The schools are veritable harrying machines,' she concluded.[5]

As a subject of thought and scholarship, motherhood is only now being 'discovered' by feminist scholars, with most emphasis on childbirth and the first months of the baby's life.[6] Historians of women have not yet launched a parallel effort to reconstruct motherhood as a part of social history in the West; this has been left to historians of the family, such as Ariès, Shorter, and Stone, for whom the experiences of husbands and children are most central. Feminist historians have, however, explored the mountains of advice literature written for the consumption of middle-class mothers,[7] and motherhood often figures between the lines in many attempts to uncover the political or work experiences of adult women. A small body of recent work addresses itself to specific questions in the recent history of motherhood in Britain; my own work is a contribution to this project.[8]

In this sketch of a social history of motherhood in England I draw on a range of methods and assumptions: from social and family history, works on the social functions of the state, ethnographic studies of childraising, and recent feminist efforts at placing women's consciousness at the centre of studies of both paid work and reproduction.[9] For reasons of space, and because my own research on London mothers is far from complete, I take up some issues and not others – contraception, abortion, and childbirth itself being the greatest gaps.

Having Babies

Even if viewed narrowly as a biological event, motherhood was all encompassing. Childbearing among the poor began soon after marriage and continued into middle age. Figures for England as a whole show that in the cohort of women who married in about 1860, 63 per cent had five children or more; only 12.3 per cent of the women who married in 1925 had this many children. The 1911 Fertility Census found that almost 20 per cent of women who had completed their childbearing by that year had *eight* or more children![10]

Continuous childbearing, however, had become the fate only of poor women, as the middle classes had begun in the 1850s or so to have smaller families.[11] Fertility differences between the rich and the poor had existed in the eighteenth and early nineteenth centuries in England (and in many other countries), but the contrast in England was far greater in 1901 than fifty years earlier.[12] The 1901 census revealed great differences in London birthrates by district, and thus by class. They ranged from an annual 283 births per thousand wives ages 15–45 in Bethnal Green, to 295 in Stepney, 283 in Shoreditch, 233 in Hackney, 183 in well-off Hampstead, and only 163 in the City of London.[13] While fertility began to decline in all the classes from the 1880s, table 3:1 suggests the rather small size of the fertility decline in poor districts before the First World War,

TABLE 3:1   FERTILITY RATES FOR SOME LONDON BOROUGHS, 1880–1934 (Births per thousand married women of reproductive age)*

Borough	1880–1	1890–1	1900–1	1909–11	1922–4	1934
Bermondsey	306	290	273	223	175	105
Bethnal Green	313	298	283	226	166	101
Hackney	291	257	233	169	130	91.0
Hampstead	261	222	183	121	100	71.7
Kensington	255	226	201	149	121	87.4
Lambeth	284	266	243	164	125	87.6
Paddington	255	227	203	151	114	83.6
Poplar	302	286	282	219	173	108
St Marylebone	288	280	276	148	105	64.9
Shoreditch	297	277	272	225	183	115
Southwark	279	261	252	201	155	100
Westminster	238	210	174	124	87.9	66.6

Note: *Legitimate and illegitimate births combined (the legitimate rates are about 1 per cent lower than the combined ones). For the years 1880 to 1901, 'reproductive age' is 15–45; for the following years, it is 15–49.

Source: Based on T. A. Welton, 'A Study of Some Portions of the Census of London for 1901,' *Journal of the Royal Statistical Society* 65 (1902), p. 493, table VIII; and John W. Innes, *Class Fertility Trends in England and Wales 1876–1934* (Princeton University Press, Princeton, N.J., 1934), Appendix II, p. 134.

compared with the much faster drop in the better-off areas. Between 1880 and 1901, for example, the fertility rate in a solid working-class district like Poplar declined 6 per cent; the rate of deeline in Hampstead was nearly 30 per cent in the same period and in Kensington 21.2 per cent. The dramatic drops in family size in working-class neighbourhoods were not to come until the inter-war years. Thus, in the period under discussion, women of London's working poor lived their adult lives surrounded by babies and children, and undergoing frequent pregnancies.

Fertility rates only hint, of course, at the ways women experienced their reproductive lives. The *Maternity* letters, collected just before the First World War by the Women's Cooperative Guild, are thus invaluable supplements to the abstractions of fertility statistics. The letters describe women's exhausting round of housework or factory jobs in late pregnancy, 'bad legs', the grief and worry of a pregnancy during a period of illness or unemployment in the family, the anguish of a dead child.[14] Childbearing histories gathered by midwives and hospitals provide other glimpses into the experience of maternity. The elaborate case histories of the General Lying-In Hospital on York Road in South London from the early 1880s (when the hospital became a model antiseptic maternity centre) show dramatically that actually giving birth represents only a small point in the experience of reproduction. For example, Mrs Pratt, a 32-year-old Vauxhall woman, came to the hospital to have her seventh child only one day after her husband of twelve years had died of consumption. She was not well, complaining of swelling of the face and hands. She had had her first child eleven years before, followed by two others, all of whom were living. Mrs Pratt had then had a miscarriage and, subsequently, twins, who had both died. After the twins there was another child, now three years old. This time (winter, 1884) the patient had a large healthy girl, and she did fairly well in the hospital, despite her grief and more oedema in the legs and feet. When, ten weeks later, the doctor visited her at home (which was very unusual), he found her supporting herself by mangling, her face still bloated, and the new baby very ill with thrush.[15] Of 39-year-old Mrs Rittman's five children, only two were alive when she checked in at the hospital early in 1884 to have her sixth, a five-pound girl who was born immediately. One of Mrs Rittman's children had died of 'convulsions', another of whooping cough (at sixteen months), and another of 'inflammation of the brain' at two-and-a-half years. She had also had one miscarriage. This patient worked as a charwoman to support her remaining children and her husband, a compositor, who was laid up with lung disease. They lived 'in poor circumstances' in a tiny turning off Walworth Road. She reported a reasonably healthy pregnancy, though she complained of a sore stomach, 'perhaps from leaning against washtub,' the physician noted. Several days before the birth, Mrs Rittman's membranes had ruptured, and she 'has been standing at the wash tub every day since and had one continuous dribble,' wrote the admitting physician with some sympathy.[16]

Motherhood was interwoven with sacrifice and self-denial in patterns that changed with a woman's life cycle. Over and over again, we hear of pregnancy as a period of special hardship. It involved more work and often less food than usual and could be accompanied by great anxiety, as women prepared for the confinement and tried to equip themselves for the new baby. 'Often weak and low spirited,' 'depressed throughout,' 'much mental depression', the General Lying-In doctors wrote of their patients' pregnancies. 'Patient has not had good food during her pregnancy,' reads the case notes of a 33-year-old woman having her sixth child. 'She cried on this question being put to her.' 'Has been unable to get much meat,' appears in the case record of a young St Pancras woman having her first child at the Hospital. Some of the 'saddest cases' Evelyn Bunting met at the Saint Pancras School for Mothers in the 1900s were women in the last months of pregnancy, weak with hunger: 'the extra expense of the coming confinement hangs over her like a black cloud.'[17] The School provided not only a baby clinic, but cheap meals for pregnant and nursing mothers, and earnest lectures on their need, and right, to eat.

A new baby indeed represented a substantial expense. A professional nurse-mother, interviewed by a London County Council (LCC) inspector, reported that a ten-month-old, for example, consumed 2/4d in milk each week, and also required additional food, soap, starch, fuel, and sometimes rent; the child thus cost her more than she could collect from the natural mother, which was, in the 1890s, 5/– per week.[18] A 1915 estimate (made before the ravages of wartime inflation) of the costs of a cot, flannel clothing, and a perambulator, was £2 9/–, assuming that the babyclothes were the second-hand variety available in bundles at pawnshops.[19] Other expenses included the midwife, whose fee averaged 10/– in about 1910; possibly a nurse to help at home for a few days, and the mother's lost wages or housekeeping skills, worth a good deal in cash. These were all viewed as 'woman's expenses' which would have to be met out of the housekeeping money, the rather inelastic 'wage' she received each Friday or Saturday from her husband. Thus all the major women's groups were scandalized when, having succeeded in getting the maternity benefit attached to the 1911 government insurance package, they found that its 30/— was to be paid to the husband (it was amended in 1912 to go directly to the woman). In all, it is not surprising that a woman's response to an impending birth was likely to be, not joyful anticipation, but worry, work, and sacrifice.

Mothers expected that infant care would be a major responsibility, in contrast to the care of older children. For while women viewed it as normal to sacrifice and to 'give' to their infants, they expected children older than six or so to substantially look after themselves. Baby care among the poor involved relentless physical labour: heating water for bathing and laundry, carrying heavy buckets, emptying coppers; all at a time when breast-feeding seriously undermined a woman's stamina.[20] 'Mrs A', one of the Somers Town women taking cookery lessons from Florence Petty, 'the Pudding Lady' associated with the St Pancras School for Mothers, had four children under school age to look after. Water for household use had to be carried into their ground-floor rooms from a tap in the yard; laundry was done in a washhouse in the same yard. (Many of the 'Pudding Lady's' other mothers lived on higher floors and had to carry water up forty or fifty steps from outdoor taps.) For cooking, Mrs A had only a small open fire, two saucepans, and a frying pan. It is not surprising that she 'seemed helpless' at times amongst the babies, or that they were not very clean until the visitor offered to help bathe them.[21] The voluminous nappies used by all classes, which were folded over several times, must have been the scourge of washdays. Higher levels of birth defects than today's, more premature and 'weakly' infants, and a far greater incidence of infectious diseases not only made babies' lives precarious, but exacted extra work and vigilance from mothers. *Baby: The Mother's Magazine*, founded in the late-nineteenth century by the entrepreneurial Ada S. Ballin for a middle-class readership, is filled with detailed articles on the nursing of children's diseases, and gives a vivid picture of the work and knowledge all mothers needed to combat childhood diseases: 'The Care of Epileptic Children', 'How to Take and Chart Temperatures. An Art which Every Mother Should Understand,' 'The Nursing of Enteric Fever', 'Whooping Cough', etc.

Infant-care practices among the poor were worlds apart from those of either conventional or progressive middle-class opinion, which prescribed rigid schedules for all vital functions (eating, sleeping, and elimination), chilly rooms, a bland milky diet, and a good deal of physical separation from adults in cot, playpen, and nursery.[22] Among the working class, babies got a great deal of carrying and attention from parents, siblings, and passing friends and neighbours. They were held constantly, nursed on demand if possible, included in family and street activities (and taken into pubs by their mothers before this became illegal in 1908), and fed in all but the earliest months tastes of sweets and family dinners. Babies commonly shared the parental bed, a practice which experts never tired of denouncing (see the discussion of 'overlaying' below). Fabian Women's Group researchers doing a study of child nutrition were nonetheless impressed with the results of ordinary baby care they encountered in pre-war Lambeth. The cheerful babies were crawling vigorously, standing, and saying many words before the end of their first year. 'Poor things,' said a Bow woman in 1915 as she looked at her own shabby, emotionally needy older children; 'When they're little's the only joy they get.'[23]

Maternity involved an awareness that a new baby's hold on life was fragile. In Grace Foakes's Wapping, when a new baby was presented to neighbours, people asked 'Has it come to stay?' Foakes's own mother, at the birth of a weak little boy, clearly prepared herself and her family for the baby's likely death, telling her other children: 'He hasn't come to stay; he's only lent to us for a little while.' A letter by another Bow woman reveals the tentative quality of her attachment to a new baby; 'You ask me to name the baby [she wrote to settlement worker Clara Grant] and if God spares it I will name it Vilet [that is Violet]!.'[24] If we assume that babies become increasingly 'human' with each week of life, establishing stronger and stronger ties with those around them, then deaths of babies in the later months of the first year or, indeed, later in childhood must have been far more painful for parents than neonatal deaths. Arthur Jasper's *Hoxton Childhood* is filled with dead babies: a niece, a nephew, a friend's child, and their weeping parents and grandparents.[25] A Lambeth pub cleaner (herself born in 1901) wrenchingly described her one-year-old daughter's death (in the 1920s):

> I had three Caesarians . . . And we had a little girl . . . she only
> lived to twelve months. She had gastric enteritis. They're more
> advanced now with it. She was alright, then my landlady said
> 'Polly, I don't like the look of her. Run her up the hospital.' So
> we put her in a whatsname, got a cab. Cheap in those days –

about three bob. Took her to Waterloo. I never used to drink then, couldn't afford it. I was sitting on the window ledge outside the street door and a policeman came by . . . He said 'there's a little girl in Waterloo Hospital. You'd better go at once.' When I gets there, she's taking her last breath. I couldn't see her die. I couldn't . . . Chokes me. It's a bit of life they've had.[26]

At turn-of-the-century London, about 15 per cent of babies died in their first year. Figures varied tragically, though, between districts. In well-off Hampstead, as table 3:2 shows, the rate was closer to 9 per cent in 1901–3. In Hackney, which included a good many better-off workers, the figure was 131 per thousand live births (that is, about 13 per cent); in Southwark, 160; and in Shoreditch, 186 per thousand, a figure twice as high as Hampstead's.[27] Older babies' lives were also threatened, though they were susceptible to different illnesses than infants. Epidemic diseases – measles, scarlet fever, and whooping cough especially – were more likely to kill them than

TABLE 3:2 AVERAGE ANNUAL INFANT MORTALITY IN LONDON, 1901–3

London district	Infant deaths per thousand live births
Bermondsey	147
Camberwell	136
Chelsea	143
Finsbury	166
Hackney	131
Hammersmith	136
Hampstead	92
Holborn	115
Poplar	157
Shoreditch	186
Southwark	160
Stepney	156
St Marylebone	145
St Pancras	145
Westminster	123
Woolwich	120

Source: E. W. Hope, *Report on the Physical Welfare of Mothers and Children*, (Carnegie UK Trust, 1917), vol. I, p. 212.

infants' illnesses like diarrhoea, 'convulsions', bronchitis, pneumonia, and 'atrophy and debility' (categories used by health officials). Thus, while in Hackney 24.5 per cent of all deaths between 1871 and 1875 were those of infants under a year old, those aged one to five still comprised a large group – 15.5 per cent of all deaths. In 1880, children under 5 accounted for almost half of the total number of deaths in Hackney (477 per thousand).[28]

While these are huge losses (the rates are over ten times as high as those of many European countries and the USA today), they are moderate in comparison with earlier London death figures, which were staggering. In England as a whole, infant death rates had improved until the 1850s; there was no further progress until the twentieth century, though general death rates, for all ages, continued to decline substantially in the same period. [29]

Infant deaths were concentrated in the very first few months of life, and have, over the past century, become still more so. To cite the figures compiled in 1904 by the energetic St Pancras Medical Officer of Health: in 1876, 68.1 per cent of infant deaths took place in the first three months, while in 1901, 76.5 per cent occurred then. The first month was the most dangerous for babies, as it has continued to be. Such figures suggest that rather than the quality of childcare, pre-natal nutrition and complications of childbirth were important factors in the loss of babies. 'The deaths of infants under one month old are to a large extent not preventable,' declared the Paddington Medical Officer in his 1905 Annual Report.[30]

Middle-class observers widely assumed that the poor valued infant life cheaply, and accusations of neglect, ignorance, and even deliberate infanticide run as a *leitmotiv* through official discussions of working-class infant health. Commentators closely scrutinized, for example, the nearly universal working-class practice of buying burial insurance for infants for signs that parents neglected or even killed their babies and pocketed the insurance.[31] 'Overlaying' or accidental smothering, usually in bed (actually the cause of a very small proportion of infant deaths in the years we are examining) was another active target of infant health experts. The enlightened St Pancras School for Mothers shared these worries. The clinic sold a cheap cradle made from a banana box and entreated its clients to put babies into these rather than keeping them in the parents' bed at night. Figures on such smothering deaths are clustered on weekends, particularly Saturday night and Sunday morning; they suggest that overlaying was an accident that was more likely when parent went to sleep with alcohol in their systems and thus lost, I would speculate, their usual semi-conscious vigilance, which normally protected the infants at night.[32]

Neighbourhood public opinion was intensely hostile to those suspected of cruelty to children. Crowds of women mobbed and hooted women accused of starving 'farmed-out' infants when they appeared in court, and extra police guards were sometimes required. In general, matrons rather closely watched neighbourhood children. When, after 1874, the LCC established an inspection system for homes taking in nurse-children, neighbours were one source of information for the inspectors. The National Society for the Prevention of Cruelty to Children (NSPCC) inspectors also relied heavily on neighbours' testimony.[33] Some professional nurse mothers actually sought formal LCC inspection for their homes to escape insinuations that they might be 'baby-farming.'[34]

Child health was indeed an urgent maternal concern. Edward Berdoe, an East End doctor with a large practice among the very poor, wrote, in the early 1890s, of the extremes to which women pushed themselves when a family member was sick: 'After a long illness of a member of a poor household it is a common thing for the mother to break down from scanty feeding and anxious watching.' Poor people spent proportionally more of their income on doctors and chemists than their richer neighbours. Even women getting medical relief (that is, payment by local authorities for doctors' bills) were 'every exacting', Berdoe wrote. They demanded frequent visits by the physician, reported regularly for their medicines, and kept close watch on children's symptoms, describing them carefully. Berdoe's only criticism of his East London mothers' health practices was that 'they too often view troubles of the skin in a tolerant light'.[35] a view with which school authorities would have concurred. Doctors who saw fee-paying patients complained, however, that they were not called until too late when children were sick, as mothers tried until the last minute to avoid having to pay the 2/– fee for a home visit. Medical journals also decried the wide use of patent medicines like Godfrey's Cordial, which contained such high doses of opiates. A West Ham junior school inspector was also typical in complaining of the 'queer remedies' local people favoured, such as tea leaves applied to children's inflamed eyelids while others noted the ineffectual but common practice of warding off whooping cough by subjecting a child to the fumes of the gasworks.[36] It may well have appeared that, with regard to illness, 'people [were] taught that Providence sent the complaint and Providence intended it to remain.'[37] In fact, with their restricted financial and social access to formal medical knowledge, women quite aggressively followed a mixed regime of folk remedies, patent medicines, and actual 'medical' cures.

As in most cultures where women have many children spaced closely together, the real mother–child 'dyad' existed only for a short time: during the period in which the mother was nursing the infant and before the next child. Tension inevitably arose when the much coddled and beloved infant was replaced. Those concerned with infant health viewed this 'ex-baby' as a special candidate for illnesses. Ex-babies were said to be thinner and more poorly nourished than their younger siblings. It was in the second year of life, rather than the first, that poor children generally began to grow 'delicate' and fall behind in growth, wrote one knowledgeable nutritionist.[38] An additional handicap for ex-babies was that their curiosity and mobility were totally incompatible with their families' small quarters, with their exposed grates, basins of hot water, or supplies for home industries, such as matchbox making. During much of the day, toddlers were often confined to high chairs, or strapped into ordinary seats, waiting in frustration for an older sibling to return from school and take them out.[39] The break with the mother that comes with weaning, or the birth of another child, is a notoriously agonizing one in the life cycle of children in a great many cultures. In London working-class culture it was perhaps more painful for children because of the greater intimacy between mother and baby, and the relatively limited availability of siblings (who had to attend school) as full-time replacements. A.S. Jasper became an ex-baby very late, at the age of five. He experienced the sharpest anguish when his place in bed with his mother was usurped by his baby sister, and compensated for his loss both through his relationship with a nurturing 'caretaker' sister, and through learning to share his mother's work caring for the new sister.[40]

'Poor Old Mum': Mothers and Children

Hard work was not only the fate of the poor at the workplace, but also a highly emotionally charged 'currency' in intimate relationships. 'Work' defined the obligation of husbands to wives: a man who 'worked for' a woman and her children, regularly supplying her with most of his wages, was functioning as her husband. One who did not do so risked losing that status, as we can glimpse from the bigamy cases brought before the Central Criminal

Court of London. Wives owed husbands work too, and their failure to cook or clean was the man's most frequent justification for wifebeating.[41] Mothers' love, as I noted above, was expressed in work – that was most engulfing when children were infants and toddlers. Most women expected that their children would reciprocate as soon as they were old enough. Joy Parr has labelled the years between six and twelve (or fourteen, depending on the school-leaving age legally in force) the 'caretaker' years, when children's contributions to their households consisted mostly of errands, childcare, and other kinds of domestic assistance for their mothers.[42] In this system, mothering was understood quite explicitly to involve labour and effort; as children grew into 'caretakers' they acquired an intimate knowledge of the intricacies of this work, as is vividly illustrated by the recipes for cheap meals, and formulas for a whitewash remembered over a lifetime to be included in autobiographies.[43]

The pattern of heavy domestic contributions by children is the dominant one in non-urban cultures whether agricultural, pastoral, or some combination of the two.[44] Mothers' discipline is closely tied to extracting the work children can do toward insuring household survival; fetching water and gathering firewood tend to be children's jobs in societies where these tasks have to be done daily.[45] Despite their 'modern' urban setting, London households generally required no less labour: fetching water and disposing of it; heating it; helping with the several processes involved in doing laundry; or getting fuel by buying it, gleaning it, or waiting in long queues to receive it from charities. These were overwhelmingly children's jobs and women with no available children often used those of neighbours, either paying them small sums or reciprocating by providing services for their mothers. However, childcare was probably the single greatest children's responsibility, which meant that last children were privileged, as they were freed of this pervasive and often unwelcome task.[46]

Mothers' demands on children were heavy, and they tended to uphold a standard for the maintenance of clothing and shoes that we would consider utterly unrealistic. Discipline was primarily (though not exclusively) a maternal responsibility, though accounts of mothers' anger are rare in working-class autobiographies. Mothers, whose frustration and irritation do sometimes bristle through their children's memoirs were more likely to discipline with slaps and cuffs than with 'formal' spankings. Florence Petty, the St Pancras nutritionist, characterized working-class discipline as rather lenient, but occasionally 'whimsically severe', a style which also suggests that 'discipline' often took the shape of irritable outbursts by harrassed women facing too many simultaneous demands. One Hoxton woman, whose daughter's response to her request was too slow, threw a potato at the offending child, while another insisted on hitting her children routinely, though her husband opposed it, saying, as their daughter remembered it much later: 'Don't hit the children. The world will be 'ard enough to them when they grow up.' But the woman responded (indicating that this arena belonged entirely to her): 'Mind your own business. I'll bring 'em up in my way.'[47]

Money circulated from children to parents as well as the other way, a reciprocity dramatized by the regular and often intricate exchanges of cash between mothers and children in households living at a subsistence level as well as those more comfortably off. A Deptford mother, who had worked extraordinarily hard over a period of years to equip her teenage daughters to go into service at age fourteen or fifteen, confidently expected specific contributions from them in return. She told Ellen Chase, her rent collector: 'I gave all the girls except Hannah just a half fit-out, and they gave me their wages until they were seventeen; after that they kept their money and finished out their sets of clothes. Deb is nearly through this now'.[48] Or look at the much more short-term exchange carried out daily in the Old Nicholl in the late 1880s; at number 12, Half Nicholl Street, according to notes kept by the Rev. Arthur O. Jay on his parishoners, a 16-year-old daughter working for the very low wage of 4/6d per week had a carefully worked-out arrangement with her mother. For each of the five weekdays the mother (who got the girl's whole wage weekly) returned 4d to the girl for her dinners. The daughter also got bread and butter for lunch and tea and, it was specified, got her breakfasts and suppers at home as well. A neighbour's testimony at an Old Bailey trial for 'uttering' counterfeit coins reveals the fluidity of the movement of cash between mothers, their neighbours, and their working children. Mary Ann Bennett, the wife of an engineer's fitter, was a defence witness at the trial of her Battersea neighbour, Emily Budd. Bennett reported that she had gone to the accused woman's house on the afternoon of the 'crime' to borrow a shilling with which to buy the family dinner. A quarter of an hour later, Budd's son arrived home from work with some money, and Bennet got her shilling. A half-hour after that, Budd went back to the Bennet's and lent the Bennet boy 4d with which to pay his fare to Lambeth. Whether the junior Bennet got some money at his Lambeth destination is not known; the court record does state by 8:15 Mrs Budd had been repaid completely.[49]

Children who left school to become wage earners reached a new milestone: they had become their mothers' partners and breadwinners, often a cherished goal. The historical record is clear on the pleasure and relief of mothers when the first child got a full-time job. Women waged chronic war with the School Board over their right to install their children as earners. Furthermore, it was mothers, far more often than fathers, who found their children – even sons – their first position. Studies of household budgets documenting the family cycle of poverty and well-being all over Britain show that women with teenagers who had begun to earn experienced their first leisure and comfort (such as a glass of beer at a pub) since the earliest years of marriage.[50]

Children's contributions are by no means all the product of the grim sense of duty that motivated Kathleen Woodward or George Acorn, both upwardly mobile London teenagers from desperately poor households, whose break with working-class life generated autobiography. Pride in assuming a mark of adulthood, the expectation of more spending money and privileges within the household, and a deep desire to 'help mother' motivated young people to contribute most of their first earnings without open complaint. But boys' wages were usually higher than girls', and the girls had usually been doing more helping throughout their school years; so male autobiographies far more than female describe the anticipated (or achieved) pleasure of giving mothers money. We might well speculate that other issues enter the picture for boys, especially the satisfaction of supplementing the father as breadwinner. Henry John Begg's formulation of his boyhood dream 'to help' might stand for many others: 'That was my one prayer, if I could only find some money or get hold of some money to help my mother. Yes. I used to feel so very very sorry for poor old mum you know. Perhaps I'd see her sitting there crying, you know, well, don't know what her trouble was you know.'[51] Will Crooks, describing his childhood in the 1850s and 1860s in Poplar, recounts a vivid memory of waking up at night to see his mother crying 'through wondering where the next meal is coming from', as she explained. The boy whispered to himself: 'Wait till I'm a man! Won't I work for my mother when I'm a man!' Indeed when, at age thirteen, he earned his first half sovereign, he came running home with it: 'Mother, mother, I've earned half a sovereign, and all of it myself, and it's yours, all yours, every bit yours!'[52] The words of a Pentonville girl, born in 1896, are very similar, yet she was the sixth child, clearly not the first to take a paid job. After working for 3/6d as a 'learner' in a garment factory for six months, she finally graduated to better earnings. 'Oh – the first – the first time I earned ten bob. Oh I had a little thin – ten shilling piece – wasn't I half pleased when I brought it home to my mum. She gave me sixpence out of it.'[53]

'School Stories'

Working-class mothers had the power, generally speaking, to command much of their children's time and labour into their teens, and sometimes longer. Girls had much heavier obligations than boys, yet the First World War separation allowance controversies revealed many thousands of young service men supporting their parents in whole or part.[54] Mothers unselfconsciously expected teenagers to subordinate their own pleasures and ambitions to the household's requirements. The conflict inevitable in such relationships was uncovered, but also heightened, when children did well in school, and were being encouraged by teachers to remain past the legal school leaving age, or to switch to secondary schools. The educators viewed their pupils as individuals rather than as family members, and encouraged the children (or at least those whom they singled out as gifted) to 'make something of themselves'; extra years of education and their centrifugal effects on families have been major themes for generations of British working-class writers. The 'school stories' of successful pupils who had to leave, whether presented as spare narrative, novel or film, carry a variety of meanings in peoples' accounts of their lives: that one was clever and promising; that a chance in life was lost; and, finally, that the comfortable and reassuring power of mothers has a harsh edge.

The household rows created by an older daughter's secondary schooling convinced a Hoxton mother that her other children, all clever pupils, should leave school as quickly as possible. The older girl, the only scholarship student at Bishopsgate School in Spitalfields, could find no place at home to do her lessons, and was in a state of constant worry over it. 'She used to end up in tears nine times out of ten,' said a younger sister interviewed as an old woman in 1975. So the mother refused to let the next daughter even try for the scholarship and she harrassed the eldest until she too left at fourteen. Another brother on a trade school scholarship left at thirteen to get a job. 'Mother wanted us to leave school as soon as we could really,' the sister mildly told the interviewer.[55]

The 'school story' of another East London woman, born in 1905 near London fields, is harsher. The household lived in the direst poverty on the wages of the father, an ailing casual dock labourer, and whatever work the mother could get. Evictions and semi-starvation defined Mrs Benjamin's childhood. Here is her bitter account of her thwarted attempt to continue at school:

> In 1916 [when she would have been eleven] I went in for a scholarship and I won a scholarship to the Bluecoat School, and my parents never told me. One day the teacher told me I'd won. She said 'only rich children can go to the school where you've got a place you're very lucky; but you're very unlucky to have the mother that you've got, because she won't say yes or sign her name.' An aunt of mine had promised to buy my first lot of books, and there was going to be a grant. I said 'Where is the school?' and she said, 'It's in Sussex, near Brighton,' and I said 'What will I be when I grow up' and she said 'Most probably a school teacher.' That was the last I heard of that. When I went home I said to my mother, 'The teacher's asked me to appeal to you, to let me go to this school.' She said 'You take your chances like the others.' There was nothing else that I could do.[56]

For Elizabeth Flint, an Aldgate-born woman who later published two very vivid autobiographical volumes, school occupied a treasured retreat from the rough and blowsy world that radiated out from her mother's warm kitchen. Her first volume, *Hot Bread and Chips*, is an extended 'school story'. A lonely young widow, a neighbour, living 'respectably' on a dead husband's pension, befriended Flint as a pre-school child and taught her about a world of polite greetings and well-dusted chair legs. It was Mrs Hacket, the neighbour, or sometimes Flint's gentle father who shared the girl's enthusiasm for her school lessons. 'Long ago I'd learnt not to talk to mum about school. "Lot of rubbish they tell you there," she said. "Look at me. I left school when I was eleven, I did, and glad to. Fair drove me mad the whole thing did," she said.' Only when she was in the most indulgent of moods did the mother listen to the daughter's school chatter while stroking her hair and offering her ginger beer.[57]

As a serious pupil, Elizabeth Flint was always fighting for space and quiet in which to do her school work, but when she made any open demands, her mother would threaten to remove her from school entirely. Often, she took refuge at Mrs Hackett's. Very reluctantly, because the older children were earning and the father doing well, Flint's mother let her daughter compete for a scholarship that would continue her education until age fifteen. The girl begged her mother to join the audience at the new school's first Speech Day, and, sitting at the front, Elizabeth scanned the room eagerly for signs of her. She returned home to find her mother still there, dressed in her Sunday clothes: 'It was them other mothers, Liz, that's what. Why, some of them came in cabs, they did, right up to the door. I couldn't.' As an adult. Flint commented on this childhood incident: 'The school was to be forever between her and me – the school and what I learned there. It was a long, long time before I could put it into words.'[58]

'School stories' are especially compact ways of expressing the complexity of working-class family feeling as experienced, in their turn, by young adults: the pull of love for mother from which followed the need to help and provide for her; the lure, for a lucky few, of other worlds, resources and pleasures – lonely and risky. To say that families 'then' were close-knit in contrast to our own, or that people were willing to 'sacrifice' for each other, sentimentalizes the intense emotional and material bonds connecting mothers and children in the generations before the First World War. Protests against the stark internal commandment to 'help mother' were certainly common, and took the form of everyday rebellious gestures of (for boys in their teens) staying out in the evenings at a music hall, working boys' club or the street corner, or (for girls as well as boys) not 'reporting' extra income like tips or overtime so as to keep more spending money. Beyond this, few were tempted; the ties connecting children with their mothers felt like ties to life itself.

Bibliographical Note

Readers who want to clarify for themselves the 'problem' that motherhood presents in feminist thought are urged to read: Nancy Chodorow, *The Reproduction of Mothering. Psychoanalysis and the Sociology of Gender* (University of California Press, Berkeley, 1978); Adrienne Rich, *Of Woman Born. Motherhood as Experience and Institution* (W. W. Norton, New York, 1976); Jessie Bernard, *The Future of Motherhood* (Dial Press, New York, 1974); and Helena A. Lopata, *Occupation Housewife* (Oxford University Press, New York, 1971). Important new works on pregnancy, childbirth and the early months of motherhood are Hilary Graham, 'Women's Attitudes Toward Conception and Pregnancy', in R. Chester and J. Peel (eds), *Equalities and Inequalities in Family Life* (Academic Press, 1977); Hilary Graham and Lorna McKee, *The First Months of Motherhood* (Health

Education Council, 1980, Monograph No. 13); Mary G. Boulton, *On Being a Mother. A Study of Women with Pre-School Children* (Tavistock, 1983); and, finally, several books by Ann Oakley: *Becoming a Mother* (Martin Robinson, Oxford, 1979); *Women Confined. Towards a Sociology of Childbirth* (Martin Robinson, Oxford, 1980); and *The Captured Womb. A History of the Medical Care of Pregnant Women* (Basil Blackwell, Oxford, 1984).

Elizabeth Badinter's *Mother Love. Myth and Reality* (Engl. tr., Macmillan, New York, 1981) is a problematic book which is primarily a sketch of changing ideologies of maternal duty and childcare in France rather than a true social history. I found the chapters on the seventeenth and eighteenth centuries very useful, however.

On motherhood in England before the First World War, see: Anna Davin, 'Imperialism and Motherhood'. *History Workshop* 5 (1978); 9–66; Carol Dyhouse, 'Working-Class Mothers and Infant Mortality in England, 1895–1914', *Journal of Social History* 12, (2) (1978), 248–67; Diana Gittins, *Fair Sex. Family Size and Structure 1900–1939* (Hutchinson, 1982); and Jane Lewis, *The Politics of Motherhood* (Croom Helm, 1980).

Of obvious use for the study of the history of motherhood are Stephen Humphries, *Hooligans or Rebels? An Oral History of Working-Class Childhood and Youth 1889–1939* (Basil Blackwell, Oxford, 1981); and James Walvin, *A Child's World. A Social History of English Childhood 1800–1914* (Penguin, Harmondsworth, 1982). I also recommend Trevor Lummis's 'The Historical Dimension of Fatherhood: A Case Study 1890–1914', in Margaret O'Brien and Lorna McKee (eds), *The Father Figure* (Tavistock, 1982).

Notes

For the use of oral history transcripts I am indebted to the kindness and the interviewing skills of several people or groups: Mary Chamberlain, Hackney People's Autobiography, Raphael Samuel, and Paul Thompson (for permission to use the 'Family Life and Work Experience' archive at the University of Essex). Ramapo College and the American Council of Learned Societies generously provided funding for this research.

1 Sheila Kitzinger, *Women as Mothers. How They See Themselves in Different Cultures* (Vintage Books, New York, 1980), p. 25.
2 See J. Finch and D. Groves (eds), *A Labour of Love: Women, Work and Caring* (Routledge & Kegan Paul, 1983). On mothers and meals, see Hilary Graham, *Women Health and the Family* (Wheatsheaf, Brighton, 1984), especially pp. 131–5; and Ann Whitehead, '"I'm Hungry, Mum," The Politics of Domestic Budgeting', in Kate Young et al. (eds), *Of Marriage and the Market* (CSE Books, 1981).
3 As one commentator has coolly described motherhood:

> Motherhood integrates not only certain procreational and interactional processes, not only links sex with both love and

children but also is a site of pedagogy and socialisation, exists in a system of transmission of property and status, is a locus of legal rights and obligations, is a unit to which state benefits are disbursed . . . plays a key part in the organisation of consumption and cohabitation, is the point of mediation of medical and hygienic norms to homes and males via children . . . and so forth (Nikolas Rose, 'The Pleasures of Motherhood,' *m/f* 7 (1982), 82–6, 84).

The widespread national use of 'mum' may be dated from the 1880s, according to the *Oxford English Dictionary*.

4 See David Rubinstein, *School Attendance in London, 1870–1904: A Social History* (University of Hull, Hull, 1969), Occasional Papers in Economic and Social History, No. 1, chapter 2 and throughout.

5 Anna Martin, 'The Mother and Social Reform, II', *The Nineteenth Century and After* 73 (June 1913), 1235–55, 1240. Excellent discussions of state intervention as shaping definitions and obligations of mothers are Anna Davin, 'Imperialism and Motherhood', *History Workshop* 5 (1978), 9–66; Jane Lewis, *Politics of Motherhood* (Croom Helm, 1980); Pat Thane, *The Foundations of the Welfare State*, (Longman, 1983) and Elizabeth Wilson, *Women and the Welfare State* (Tavistock, 1977), especially chapter 3.

6 Here I am thinking of the works of Chodorow, Graham, Oakley, Rich, etc. cited in the bibliographical note above.

7 See, for example, Denise Riley, *War in the Nursery. Theories of the Child and Mother* (Virago, 1983); Ann Dally *Inventing Motherhood. The Consequences of an Ideal* (Schocken Books, New York, 1983); Christina Hardyment, *Dream Babies* (Oxford University Press, Oxford, 1984); and Barbara Ehrenreich and Deirdre English, *For Her own Good* (Doubleday, New York, 1978).

8 For late Victorian and Edwardian England (as well as the inter-war years), Davin, Dyhouse, Gittins and Lewis, cited in the bibliographical note above, have made a wonderful start in very difficult terrain. My essay makes extensive use of material, and references from their work.

9 See, especially, Sarah Eisenstein, *Give Us Bread, but Give Us Roses* (Routledge & Kegan Paul, 1983); and Rosalind Petchesky, *Abortion and Woman's Choice* (Longman, New York, 1983).

10 'Report of the Royal Commission on Population', PP (1948–49), vol. XIX, p. 26, table XVII; 'Fertility Census of England and Wales', PP (1911), vol. XIII, Part 2, p. xliii, table XVI.

11 Patricia Branca, *Silent Sisterhood. Middle-Class Women in the Victorian Home* (Croom Helm, 1979), chapter 7.

12 Dennis Wrong, 'Class Fertility Differentials Before 1850', *Social Research* 25 (1958), 70–86;81. See also A. Newsholme and T.H.C. Stevenson, 'The Decline in Human Fertility in the United Kingdom and Other Countries', *Journal of the Royal Statistical Society (JRSS)* 69 (1906), 34–87; 66–7.

13 T. A. Welton. 'A Study of Some Portions of the London Census for 1901', *JRSS* 65(1902), 447–500, 493, table VIII; see also the comparisons in Newsholme and Stevenson, 'Decline in Human Fertility', p.67.

14 Margaret Llewelyn Davies (ed), *Maternity. Letters from Working Women* (1915) (W. W. Norton, New York, 1978).

15 Doctors' Case Records, General Lying-In Hospital, January–March 1884, case no. 12, Greater London Record Office. I am extremely grateful to the GLRO archivists for recognizing the value of these records and calling them to my attention. My references to them are based on a very preliminary reading.

16 Ibid., Case no. 16 (Mrs Rittman, age 39; married 15 years).

17 Ibid., January–September, 1881, case no. 32, a 32-year-old married woman having her sixth child in seven years; January–March, 1884, case no. 19; Dora Bunting, Annie Barnes, and Blanche Gardiner, *The School for Mothers* (Horace Marshall & Son, n.d. [1907]). See the excellent discussion of the work of this clinic in Anna Davin's 'Imperialism and Motherhood,' pp. 36–43.

18 Only later, when children could eat with the rest of the family, did the costs go down ('Report from the select Committee of the House of Lords on the Infant Life Protection Bill' [H.L.] and the Safety of Nurse Children Bill [H.L.] PP (1896), vol. X, Qs. 1086–7). While a child breast-fed by its own mother would have been cheaper to maintain, the nurse-mother quoted in the text was presumably spared the expense of new equipment for the baby.

19 Janet Lane-Claypon, *Report on the Provision of Midwifery Service in the City of London*, Reports to the Local Government Board on Public Health and Medical Subjects (HMSO, 1917), no. 111, p. 48.

20 To judge from the scattered statistics that exist, 75–85 per cent of working-class London women breast-fed their babies. A study done in Paddington in 1904, in which 862 poor homes with new babies were visited during the year, found that 77 per cent were breastfeeding, and 11 per cent using a combination of breast and 'hand' feeding (Borough of Paddington, *Report of the Vital Statistics and Sanitary Work for the Year 1905*, pp. 5–6). In St. Pancras, in 1904, 63 per cent of 3- to 6-month olds were totally breast-fed, and another 13 per cent partially, so. In the first 3 months, 82 per cent of babies were wholly, and ten per cent partially breast-fed (G.F. McCleary, *The Early History of the Infant Welfare Movement* (H.K. Lewis, 1933, p.82).

21 F. Petty et al. *The Pudding Lady. A New Departure in Social Work* (Steads Publishing House, 1910), pp. 36–8.

22 Eric Prichard's lectures to health visitors on infant care might serve to represent middle-class professional opinion; see his *Infant Education* (Henry Kempton, 1907). Others as diverse as Margaret McMillan and Truby King had fairly similar views, at least on the care of infants specifically.

23 Magdalen Stuart Pember Reeves, *Round About a Pound a Week* (Virago, 1979), chapter 8; E. Sylvia Pankhurst, *The Home Front. A Mirror to Life in England during the World War* (Hutchinson & Co., 1932), p. 402.

24 Grace Foakes, *My Part of the River* (Futura, 1976), pp. 78, 24; 'Fern St. Settlement, Bow,' *The School Child I* (12) (February 1911), p. 3.

25 A. S. Jasper, *A Hoxton Childhood* (Centerprise, 1969).

26 Polly N. born in Drury Lane in 1901, brought up in Lambeth. As an adult, she worked as a theatre and pub cleaner. Interviewed by Mary Chamberlain in London, November 1983.

27 Liverpool had an infant death rate of 169 per thousand, while Oldham's rate was higher than that of most London boroughs (E. W. Hope, *Report on the Physical Welfare of Mothers and Children*, Carnegie UK Trust, 1917 vol I, p. 212). Compared with several other countries, Britain's infant mortality rates were quite high. West Australia, Switzerland, Denmark, Scotland, New South Wales, Ireland, Sweden, and New Zealand all had lower rates (Margaret McMillan, *Infant Mortality*, ILP pamphlet, n.d., but 1903 figures, p. 6).

28 Hackney Sanitary District Board of Works, *Report of the Sanitary State of the Hackney District for the Year 1875*, p. 31 table X; *1885 Report* p. 22, table VII.

29 In the period 1730–49, about three–quarters of London children died by age 5. By 1770–89, the figure was 'only' 51.5 per cent; for 1810–29, slightly under a third (M. W. Beaver, 'Population, Infant Mortality and Milk', *Population Studies* 26 (1973), 243–54, 246; G. F. McCleary, *The Early History* (pp. 1–3). There is an excellent discussion of infant mortality in Anthony S. Wohl, *Endangered Lives. Public Health in Victorian Britain.* (Harvard University Press, Cambridge Mass., 1983), chapter 2.

30 In 1876, 35 per cent of infant deaths in one London district took place in the first month of life; in 1901, 44 per cent (McCleary, *Early History*, pp. 32–33). In the USA, to cite 1978 figures, over two-thirds (68.8 per cent) of infant deaths are in the first month (Abraham M. Rudolph (ed.), *Pediatrics*, 17th ed., Appleton-Century Crofts, Norwalk, Conn., 1982, pp. 6–7); *Paddington Vital Statistics for the Year 1905*, p. 46.

31 National Conference on Infant Mortality, *Report of the Proceedings* (P. S. King, 1908), p. 166: 'Report from the Select Committee on the Children's Life Insurance Bill' [H.L.] PP 1890, vol. XIII; and the 1896 hearings on the same subject PP 1896, vol X.

32 'Report of the Inter-Departmental Committee on Physical Deterioration', PP (1904), vol. XXXII, Q.13001. One medical commentator suggested that breastfeeding babies who took in alcohol with their mothers' milk may have become sluggish and less able to squirm to safety in bed (W. H. Willcox) 'Infantile Mortality from "Overlaying"', *British Journal of Medicine*, (24 September, 1904), 753–5; 754. In any case, the vast majority of 'overlayings' were certainly accidental.

33 For example, *East London Observer*, 11 July, 1868 (a woman tried for neglecting an infant in her care), and PP (1896) vol. X, Q. 171.

34 PP (1896), vol. X. Q. 1037.

35 Edward Berdoe, 'Slum-Mothers and Death-Clubs. A Vindication', *The Nineteenth Century* (April 1891), 560–3.

36 Eric Pritchard, 'The Regulation and Control of the Manufacture and Sale of Foods and Drugs for Infants', National Conference on Infantile Mortality (1908); Virginia Berridge and Griffith Edwards. *Opium and the People. Opiate Use in Nineteenth-Century England* (Alan Lane, 1981), chapter 9; 'Inter-Departmental Comm. on Physical Deterioration', Q. 8006. On gas fumes for

whooping cough, see Foakes, *My Part of the River*, p. 77.

37 'Inter-Departmental Comm. on Physical Deterioration', Q. 8072.

38 Bunting et al., *The School for Mothers;* Pember Reeves, *Round About a Pound a Week*; and especially Petty' *The Pudding Lady*, p. 2.

39 Pember Reeves, *Round About a Pound a Week*, chapter 8.

40 Jasper, *Hoxton Childhood*.

41 On the work women and men 'owed' each other, see my '"Fierce Questions and Taunts": Married Life in Working-Class London, 1870–1914', *Feminist Studies* 8 (3) (1982), 575–605; 580–81.

42 Joy Parr, *Labouring Children. British Immigrant Apprentices to Canada, 1869–1924* (Croom Helm, 1980), chapter 1; see also the fascinating discussion in Carolyn Steedman's *The Tidy House. Little Girls Writing* (Virago, 1982) pp. 125–8.

43 Among the most striking published London autobiographies describing the period before the First World War are (besides Jasper's *Hoxton Childhood* and Foakes's *My Part of the River*): Alice Linton, *Not Expecting Miracles* (Centerprise, 1982); Elizabeth Flint, *Hot Bread and Chips* (Museum Press, 1963); Dorothy Scannell, *Mother Knew Best* (Macmillan, 1974); and Raphael Samuel, *East End Underworld. Chapters in the Life of Arthur Harding* (Routledge & Kegan Paul, 1981).

44 Margaret Jarman Hagood, *Mothers of the South: Portraiture of the White Tenant Farm Woman* (University of North Carolina Press, Chapel Hill, 1939); Beatrice B. and John W. M. Whiting, *Children of Six Cultures. A Psycho-Cultural Analysis* (Harvard University Press, Cambridge, Mass., 1975), pp. 83, 105–8; Beatrice B. Whiting (ed.), *Six Cultures. Studies of Child Rearing* (John Wiley & Sons, New York, 1963).

45 B. B. and J. W. M. Whiting, in *Children of Six Cultures*, attempt a rough correlation between the severity of maternal discipline, and mothers' material need for childrens' assistance.

46 Anna Davin, in 'Girlhood in Nineteenth-Century London' (PhD. thesis, University of London forthcoming), fully explores children's labour, including their responsibilties for childcare and other domestic chores.

47 Petty, *Pudding Lady*, p.11; Raphael Samuel, interview in Autumn 1974 with Mrs S. born in Bethnal Green in 1884 (typescript in the interviewer's files), p. 36.

48 Ellen Chase *Tenant Friends in Old Deptford* (Williams & Norgate, 1929), pp. 172–3.

49 Charles Booth Collection, B80, Notebooks of the Rev. Arthur O. Jay, communicated to Booth in February, 1889, *Booth Papers*, London School of Economics; Central Criminal Court of London (Old Bailey), *Sessions Papers* vol. 101 (1884), 223.

50 As examples of a large literature: Sir Arthur L. Bowley and A.R. Burnett-Hurst, *Livelihood and Poverty* (Ratan Tata Foundation, 1915); and B. Seebohm Rowntree, *Poverty: A Study of Town Life* (Macmillan, 1901).

51 Kathleen Woodward's *Jipping Street* (Virago, 1983) is a novelized autobiography; George Acorn, *One of the Multitude: An Autobiography of a Resident of Bethnal Green* (Heinemann, 1911); Begg is a pseudonym for a

man born in 1884, one of ten children of a packing-case maker. He spent most of his childhood in Battersea (Family Life and Work Experience Archive, collected by Paul Thompson and Thea Vigne, housed at the University of Essex, file no. 225).

52 George Haw, *From Workhouse to Westminster. The Life Story of Will Crooks*, M. P. (Cassell and Company, 1911), pp.3, 7.

53 Family Life and Work Experience Archive, no. 284, p.52. This woman, born just off King's Road, came from a family of eight children.

54 Pankhurst, *The Home Front.*

55 Raphael Samuel's interview with a woman born in Hoxton in 1905, February 1974 (typescript), pp. 5–6.

56 Manuscript copy of Mrs Benjamin's autobiography, not paginated, Hackney People's Autobiography, London.

57 Flint, *Hot Bread and Chips*, pp. 68, 98, 108–9.

58 Ibid., pp. 110–11.

Nurses' rounds in Hackney c.1900

4

The Working-Class Wife and Mother and State Intervention, 1870–1918
Jane Lewis

There is little doubt but that most late-nineteenth century investigators were repelled by urban working-class neighbourhoods. The smells, noise and excitement associated with working-class home and street life were deplored by the middle-class philanthropist seeking to bring order out of perceived chaos. As Helen Bosanquet put it: 'The great problem with this class is how to bring them to regard life as anything but a huge chaos. The confusion which reigns in their minds is reflected in their worlds.'[1] For commentators like Helen Bosanquet, ideal family behaviour was based on a middle-class model, which involved paying close attention to the moral training of children and making careful provision for the future, especially regarding the education of children. (J. A. Banks recently suggested that during this period the (male) occupational groups that developed a meritrocratic career pattern and a concomitant future-time perspective also showed the fastest fall in fertility and developed the most rigid separation of spheres between the sexes.)[2] In this middle-class model of family behaviour, men entered the public world as breadwinners and officeholders, and woman's sphere was the home. Her task, according to the likes of Sarah Ellis and Hannah More, was not only to keep the house neat and clean but to so order it

> as to suit the tastes of all, as far as may be without annoyance or offence to any. Not only must a constant system of activity be established, but peace must be preserved or happiness will be destroyed . . . not only must an appearance of outward order and comfort be kept up, but around every domestic scene there must be a strong wall of confidence which no internal suspicion can undermine, no external enemy break through.[3]

Throughout the period under discussion, and beyond, the responsibility of women for creating a 'haven in a heartless world' remained, even though the prescription as to how this was best achieved and the wife's precise role within the home with respect to ther performance of household tasks changed considerably.

Middle-class commentators were in no doubt that the fundamentals of this model of family behaviour were crucial to the well-being of society as a whole. Dr William Ogle explained to the Royal Statistical Society in 1890 that:

> There are men who toil because work is a pleasure to them and there are others who toil because work is a duty; but the great majority of men are only stimulated to labour that in amount or character is distasteful to them by the hope that they may be able, in the first place to maintain themselves, and secondly to marry and maintain a family . . . If therefore, the well-being of a state consists in the mature well-being of people, a country is then most flourishing when the largest proportion of its population is able to satisfy these two natural desires.[4]

A breadwinning husband and dependent wife and children were thus believed to secure male work incentives and hence national stability. Drawing on the work of the French sociologist Frederick le Play, Helen Bosanquet referred to the male-breadwinner family model as the 'stable family' and remarked that it was the 'only known way of ensuring with any approach to success that one generation will exert itself in the interests and for the sake of another'.[5] When they looked at the working-class family, middle-class observers looked first and foremost for an appropriate division of labour between husband and wife that would both secure the family's moral and economic integrity and safeguard the socialization of its children. Working mothers were thus castigated for the additional danger they posed to the health and welfare of children. As Brian Harrison observed a decade ago, the moral and the social are intertwined during the late-nineteenth century.[6]

It is also clear, although the reasons are not, that middle-class observers were paying considerably more attention to the working class family from the 1870s on. We should probably look for the roots of this new-found interest in the 1860s, when voluntary visiting and the mother's meeting took hold, with the publication of Mrs Bayly's famous *Ragged Homes and How to Mend Them* (1860).[7] It may well be that there is a link between this activity and the crisis of the poor law during the 1860s, recently examined by Michael Rose.[8] Certainly, during the late-nineteenth century, the state was increasingly prepared to regulate aspects of life hitherto considered private, including the sexual.[9] In 1870, two measures that had significant effect on the working-class wife and mother were passed: the Elementary Education Act and the first Married Women's Property Act, which was designed primarily to protect the earnings of working-class women and which may be linked to the debate about wife beating and the separation and maintenance legislation of the later 1870s. From then on there is what might be called an invasion of the working-class family, still chiefly through the agency of voluntary visitors, although increasingly by locally employed state officials such as the school attendance officer and, by the early twentieth century, the health visitor. Charles Bosanquet assured his readers in 1874 that 'the London poor are accustomed to the notion of being visited and are more inclined to complain of being neglected than to look on the visitor as an intruder.'[10] This description of the doorstep response of the working-class family (in practice, of course, the working-class mother) is open to question, but there is no doubt about the amount of visiting that was going on.

There has been a strong attachment on the part of middle-class observers to an ideal model of family behaviour (which can be documented through to William Beveridge and indeed to the present)[11], and this has been the basis of an increasing interest in the working-class family from the late-nineteenth century onwards. However, much recent work on the working-class family, and particularly on working-class women and social policy, has emphasized the way in which state policy was formulated either with the express intention of encouraging the male-breadwinner/ dependent-wife family form or, more usually, with the assumption that this form was the 'correct' one and must therefore be presumed to exist amongst the working class.[12] In neither case are these arguments wrong, as the following examples demonstrate. Anna Davin has suggested that none of the (admittedly traditional) explanations offered for the passing of the 1870 Education Act serve to explain why girls were included in the measure: women had no votes and thus there was no need to make provision for them, nor can the demand for a more literate labour force be invoked where girls are concerned. Board-school textbooks, however, reveal a striking emphasis on what was viewed as the proper role of working-class women.[13] The virtues of good domestic management and infant care were stressed throughout the board-school readers and encouraged more directly, as Carol Dyhouse has shown, by lessons in 'housewifery', which became more a part of the curriculum in the early twentieth century.[14] Similarly, I have argued that, before the First World War, infant welfare centres sought to inculcate middle-class methods of child raising and that protective legislation and national insurance regulations were used as an indirect means of both controlling the kind of work open to women ouside the home and limiting the access of married women to employment benefits.[15] The assumption was that adult women would be supported by their husbands, to quote the 1931 Royal Commission on Unemployment Insurance: 'industrial employment cannot be regarded as the normal condition (of married women).'[16]

Thus there is no doubt that policy-makers do have a firm idea about the kind of family they wish to support, and that their assumptions regarding the desirability of the male-breadwinner form is of central importance to our analysis and understanding of the formation of social policies affecting the working-class family. The point has often been made that the evidence collected by Rowntree showed that the wages of a labourer in regular employment were insufficient to keep a family of 2–4 children from primary poverty.[17] Policies that assumed the existence of a male breadwinner and female and child dependents (the outstanding example is national insurance) were, as they are today, therefore bound to ignore the economic realities of the working-class family and, in particular, the contributions and entitlements due to the working-class wife. It is probable that wives and children as a group gained least out of the liberal welfare reforms.

However, this does not say anything about the perceptions of working-class women themselves, which are of course notoriously hard to uncover. But, by thinking again about the characteristics of what was considered to be ideal family behaviour, in conjunction with what we now know about the working-class wife's world during the period, it is possible to come to some admittedly speculative conclusions about the aspects of state intervention in the family that concerned her most. This is an important and neglected exercise which moves away from the study of policy 'from above' and focuses more attention on policy implementation and the kinds of reconstruction we need if we are to understand how policy was received.

In what follows I would like to suggest, first, that the broad fundamentals of the male-breadwinner family model – with its concomitant sexual divisions – were ideals *shared* by working-class men and women as well as by middle-class observers and policy makers. This meant that working-class wives accepted in large measure the primacy of their responsibilities to home and children and the secondary nature of any wage earning they might engage in. Second, with the greater understanding of the meaning of home and family to the working-class wife that recent research has given us, I will suggest that there was the possibility of resistance and resentment on the part of working-class wives whenever state policy threatened either their management of the fragile family economy or their domestic authority. For the most part such a situation arose as a result of the state's increasing preoccupation with the health and welfare of children rather than as a result of measures such as national insurance, or changes in family law with respect to separation and maintenance legislation for example, which, as Iris Minor has shown, were largely irrelevant to working-class women.[18]

The Family Wage: A Shared Ideal

At some point in the nineteenth century – the precise time and place is far from clear – the family wage emerged as an important bargaining point for the trade-union movement and with it came the idea that, ideally, the wife's place was at home, or at least that any wage earning she did was of secondary importance. Henry Broadhurst's 1877 speech at the TUC Annual Conference is one of the best illustrations of this attitude; he saw it as the duty of male unionists 'as men and husbands to use their utmost efforts to bring about a condition of things, where their wives should be in their proper sphere at home, instead of being dragged into competition for livelihood against the great and strong men of the world.'[19] Similarly, Tom Mann gave evidence to the Royal Commission of Labour in 1894 that he was 'very loth to see mothers of families working in factories at all, adding that he considered 'their employment has nearly always a very prejudicial effect on the wages of the male worker.'[20] During the late-nineteenth and early twentieth centuries the family wage had become the major bargaining counter of the general labour unions and sweated workers; skilled workers relied more on value theory in wage bargaining, although they were ready to fall back on the idea of a family wage as soon as the market price began to fall.

By the 1890s, it was uncommon for the wives of skilled men to work and the ability to keep a wife had become a measure of working-class male respectability.[21] (The erosion of this powerful idea after the Second World War would make an interesting and important study.) The 1876 Commission on the Factory Acts and the 1889 Select Committee of the House of Lords on the Sweating System, for instance, heard copious evidence from male chainworkers to the effect that women's place was in the home. (The position in the chainmaking trade was particularly acute because of the large numbers of women who entered it during the late 1870s from nailmaking.) In 1889, the Select Committee heard a plea from a male unionist for the restriction of married women's work on the grounds that 'when the married women turn into the domestic workshops they become competitors against their own husbands and it requires a man and his wife to earn what the man alone would earn if she were not in the shop.'[22] The Commissioners were more anxious about the immorality of men and women working alongside each other and the dangers working mothers posed to the welfare of the human race, although women factory inspectors, for example, admitted that working women usually needed their earnings. Male unionists may well have been prepared to go further than many civil servants and politicians in their desire to prohibit women from any work that involved them in direct competition with male workers.

The family wage system was, for both sides, an ideal not a reality. In practice, middle-class commentators often exhibited ambivalence towards the proper role of the working-class wife because they seriously doubted the willingness of the working-class husband to provide.[23] If the husband failed to support his family it was considered better that the wife go out to work than the family come onto the poor law. This was a major consideration in the debate over the Married Women's Property Act of 1870, which gave legislative protection to women's earnings. In the words of the National Association for the Promotion of Social Science which campaigned for the Act, 'if the industrious factory woman were able to deposit in the savings bank a portion of her earnings in her own name the school pence for her children would be very seldom withheld'.[24] And as Pat Thane has pointed out, this ambivalence regarding the proper role of poor women became much greater in cases of widow or unmarried mother, where male financial support was definitely no longer forthcoming.[25]

Male workers who in practice did not earn a family wage agreed to women working in traditional female tasks. For instance Nancy Osterud's work has shown that male hosiery workers in Leicester opposed married women's work unless it was in the traditional area of seaming stockings.[26] This provided a necessary supplement to the family income, but women doing the same work as men would have threatened not only men's wages, but their masculinity. The male chainworker giving evidence to the Select Committee in 1889 added an interesting aside to his complaint against married women workers: 'during the time she was in the shop her domestic duties are being neglected'.[27] This was probably a genuine concern of the working-class man as well as the middle-class investigator.

These attitudes as to the proper division of tasks between husband and wife were shared in large part by the female leaders of the labour movement. In 1894, Gertrude Tuckwell (Secretary and later President of the Women's Trade Union League) advocated 'the gradual extension of labour protection to the point where mothers will be prohibited from working until their children have reached an age at which they can care for themselves',[28] and the Women's Labour League agreed that mothers with children under five should not be employed.[29] On the whole, women trade unionists felt that the withdrawal of female labour would benefit male wages and have the additional advantage that working-class homes would be better ordered and managed. Thus, while Mary MacArthur, for example, spoke in defence of married women workers' higher sickness claims to the Departmental Committee on National Health Insurance in 1914, she nevertheless also expressed the fear that to make any improvement in their position under the scheme would 'discriminate in favour of the wage-earning woman as against her uninsured sister, whose need is often as great [and] will result in a state premium on the industrial employment of married women'.[30] This is very similar to the argument put up by the Government Actuary against 1918 proposals to provide additional Treasury support to women workers after childbirth. Apart from the financial aspect, he feared the 'inducement' such a benefit would give to married women to go out to work.[31]

Working women in their turn showed little enthusiasm for a job outside the home as well as one within it. As Elizabeth Roberts' oral evidence has shown, women who worked full-time tended to be pitied by their neighbours.[32] In view of the laborious nature of domestic labour during the period this is not surprising. Working-class women seem to have shared the idea that if they did work it should be at a woman's job for a woman's rate. There is copious evidence of women refusing to do 'men's work'. Ramsay MacDonald reported the response of a female printing worker as 'I know my place and I'm not going to take men's work from them.'[33] Similarly, women on the whole were in favour of protective legislation, although there is some evidence that they objected to its inflexible nature. Married women seem to have worked primarily in accordance with the dictates of the family economy. Very few (10 per cent) worked full-time, but very many took up casual employment as and when necessary. As the recorded memories of the Women's Cooperative Guild members show,[34] even the respectable working-class woman might expect to resort to casual work when her husband was sick or unemployed, albeit that she might take in lodgers and homework in the form of sewing or washing before she hawked fruit or went out charring. There is little evidence of working-class wives working for the 'modern' individualistic motives Joan Scott and Louise Tilly see emerging during the early twentieth century.[35] Women defended their *right* to work – but not more – in face of the strenuous efforts of the infant welfare movement and John Burns (President of the Local Government Board), in particular, to prohibit it.

Undoubtedly, it can be argued that the struggle for a family wage was conducted at the expense of the woman worker and that within the family men benefitted disproportionately because they gained the full-time household services of their wives. Moreover, to the extent that the family wage was never realized, women shouldered a double burden of household work and paid employment, and received little assistance from legislation such as national insurance, which assumed female economic dependency to be the norm. But we look in vain for working-class women's objections to either the family wage system or to social provision made through the labour market, which assumed the existence of such a system, although whether Jane Humphries is right to argue that the family wage was a consciously adopted strategy on the part of both the working-class husband and wife, designed to maximize the family's welfare, is also doubtful.[36] It is true in so far as a woman's first concern was her husband's capacity to provide and in so far as she regarded her own paid employment as secondary, but rather than being a matter for calculation and deliberation, the sexual divisions implied by the male-breadwinner family model fitted the realities of the working-class wife's experience.

The Meaning of Working-Class Marriage

Working-class marriage during the period under discussion consisted of a complex system of reciprocal obligations and is perhaps best understood as an economic and emotional support system. Ellen Ross has reminded us that the marriage contract did not enjoin romantic love or verbal or sexual intimacy, but required financial obligations, services and activities that were gender specific.[37] Marriage according to Lady Bell, the wife of the Middlesborough ironmaster, was 'merely an incident in the daily work',[38] and from his study of working-class autobiographies, John Burnett has concluded that marriage partners tended to be described in terms of solid calculation and that compatibility of temperament and affection seemed to be more important than sexual attraction.[39] Wives judged husbands according to the 'amount he allowed them', in the words of Mrs Pember Reeves.[40] The centre of most working-class wives' worlds was their children and wives saw their responsibilities in terms of managing the household economy and keeping the household together. These responsibilities were, for the most part, accepted and research indicates that wives were tolerant of occasional abuse if they felt themselves to be guilty of some dereliction of duty, whereby husbands were judged to have 'just cause' for violent behaviour.[41]

Middle-class observers recognized the importance of these household tasks while overplaying the extent to which such work could ever become women's exclusive concern. Henry Higgs commented in 1893 that good housekeeping was the crucial variable which could 'throw the balance of comfort in favour of one workman whose wages are much below those of another'.[42] Booth, of course, sought to establish the degree to which thriftlessness on the part of the wife contributed to poverty, and included a category called 'drunken or thriftless wife' separate from that of 'drink' in his list of nine causes of poverty.[43] On balance, most observers agreed that mothers (unlike fathers) could be relied upon to exert themselves on behalf of their children and that mismanagement resulted more from ignorance than vice. Much of the direct intervention into the working-class family was thus aimed at educating women in household management and childraising. But of course when money ran short, whether through neglect, illness or unemployment on the part of husbands, wives automatically pursued a series of strategies including resort to neighbours, kin, credit and casual employment. In instances where the husband proved unwilling to provide, the wife was likely to look elsewhere for support. The 1912 Royal Commission on Divorce took copious evidence to this effect, the nature of which is neatly illustrated by the testimony of Miss E. Lidgett, a poor-law guardian. Miss Lidgett described a case where the Guardians had taken a whole family into the workhouse, the father being 'hopelessly out of work'. Eventually, in what then would have been interpreted as a generous gesture on the part of the poor-law authorities, the wife was freed in order to give her a chance to build up a home again. She immediately began to live with another man and had more children by him, complaining to Miss Lidgett that the Guardians would not allow her to visit her children by her first husband who remained in the workhouse. She 'stoutly defended' her new home, saying that the first husband 'was no husband for her and the one that worked for her she respected'.[44]

However, in emphasizing reciprocal obligations and the element of 'solid calculation' in working-class marriages, it would be wrong to assume that affection was lacking. The view of some historians and sociologists that working-class family relationships moved from the brutal and segregated to the affective and joint,[45] is borne out neither by the observations of more acute contemporary social observers such as Margaret Loane,[46] nor by the more recent findings of Elizabeth Roberts for certain northern towns, of Trevor Lummis for East Anglian fishermen's families or of Gareth Stedman Jones for London,[47] all of whom have recorded the development of a firmly based home culture, with Roberts and Lummis's oral testimony providing considerable evidence of domestic affection. There was, of course, also neglect and abuse, some of which was wilful. But, as evidence to the 1912 Royal Commission on Divorce showed, between 50 and 80 per cent of couples obtaining legal separations under the legislation of the 1870s and 1880s were reconciled, usually as a result of an improvement of the husband's financial position.[48]

Thus the picture that is beginning to emerge of the working-class wife's world is, first, that it was severely limited in spatial and cultural terms (all contemporaries commented on the working-class wife's lack of leisure and Hugh Cunningham was able to find little evidence of any female pastimes).[49] Second, it involved an ardous mix of activities that cannot conveniently be classed as belonging either to the realm of consumption or production, but which often entailed heavy labour.[50] Kathleen Woodward's mother's bitterly expressed sentiments; 'wash, wash, wash, it's like washing your guts away,' cannot have been untypical. And yet, as Elizabeth Roberts has remarked, these were lives of purpose and by no means devoid of either affection or mutual support within the family and the neighbourhood.[51] Working-class wives of this period cannot be categorized as either victims or free agents. Their lives were certainly severely restricted, but there is reason to conclude that very many derived a sense of self-worth from their domestic responsibilities and authority.

Working-Class Mothers' Perceptions of State Intervention

Growing state concerns with motherhood as a 'social function' led to a series of interventions,[52] some of which disrupted and challenged the activities and responsibilities viewed by the working-class mother as her prerogative. By the early twentieth century a strong ideology of maternalism, fuelled by eugenic concern about the quantity and quality of the 'race', made the health and welfare of children a national priority. The state could not intervene on behalf of children without affecting the role of parents. Legislation spawned new officials at the local level, who in practice dealt primarily with the working-class wife who, in turn, found that the mandates of these officials often placed either impossible demands on the fragile household economy, or tended to undermine her domestic authority.

It has often been pointed out that compulsory elementary education deprived the working-class family of essential earnings, which gave cause for resentment. In addition, the ability of the wife to supplement the family income was also impaired. One of the chief causes of absence of working-class girls from school was, as Thomas Wright noted, 'the baby difficulty'.[53] A woman who kept an older child at home from school to mind the baby while she worked invoked the wrath of the school attendance officer – 'men of little education and known authoritarianism',[54] according to Robert Roberts – and risked a summons to attend the 'B' meeting of the School Board Divisional Committee, where 'a stream of tired looking mothers with an occasional father' were required to give details of the family's budget and other personal details.[55] Eventually, if the absence persisted, the father, but again in practice the mother, had to appear before the magistrate. If the mother sent the child to school and left the baby alone she also risked prosecution if harm came to the child. Anna Martin, an active suffragist, who also worked with poorer working-class women in a settlement in Rotherhithe prior to the First World War, and who was acutely conscious of the importance of avoiding the attitude of 'ladies come from the West End to do good', described this kind of dilemma as mothers being 'ordered by law to perform the impossible and punished if they fail'.[56]

It is likely that the position of wives in respect to 'the baby difficulty' worsened during the late-nineteenth and early twentieth centuries. During the 1870s, in a pragmatic local response to the problem of absenteeism among girls, many board schools took in much younger children. Mrs Burgwin, headmistress of the Orange St School in Southwark, described this practice:

> the girls of my school have to take the place entirely of the mother of the family, the families are generally large; the woman goes out in the morning she works in a pickle house, if she is a better class woman she goes out step cleaning during the day and the little girl takes the place of the mother of the family. We were obliged to open a crèche because we found girls staying at home to look after the babies.[57]

In response to the dictates of economy and the criticisms of those acitve in the infant welfare movement, the Board of Education phased out provision for under-threes by 1904 (19,358 had been accommodated in 1875) and reduced the number of places for three- to five-year olds by almost half from 610,989 in 1901 to 332,888 in 1911.[58]

The number of places lost are sufficient to suggest that closure of these facilities would have impeded the kinds of casual work described by Mrs Burgwin, although it may well be a mistake to assume that such crèche facilities were the first choice of mothers. Margaret Hewitt suggested this was not the case for an earlier period with respect to crèches provided by factories,[59] and enough work has been done for us to know the importance of childminding earnings to elderly kin and to neighbours during this period.[60] Women active in the labour movement never called for day care, although they did support nursery education,[61] a position in line with their support for the family wage and the importance of women's position at home.

But for the purposes of the argument presented here, the main point concerns the wife's perceptions of compulsory elementary-school education. The importance of either a child's earnings, or its domestic labour to the family economy, which was controlled by the wife, was likely to lead to friction between mother and the school attendance officer. James Runciman's melodramatic tale of the poor widow reduced to misery and her children to lives of degradation as a result of the school board's insistence that the children attend school was,[62] as David Rubinstein has cautioned,[63] intended as an attack on the very existence of the board and hence, indirectly at the education of working-class children. Yet Runciman had grasped the essentials of the position of the working-class mother.

The medical inspection of school children also threatened to strain the family's scarce resources. Parents – usually the mother – were of course told what was wrong with the child, but very little provision was made for free treatment. There is little doubt but that women would have welcomed free access to medical attention for themselves and their children. Autobiographies and a collection like the Women's Cooperative Guild's *Maternity: Letters from Working Women* make this quite clear, and it is interesting that Nella Last's diary for the years of the Second World War recorded her feeling that the NHS would benefit women most.[64] Anna Martin complained that without the provision of treatment something like school medical inspection and the advice of health visitors and welfare centres on infant ailments became injunctions to 'make bricks without straw'.[65]

Many women welcomed more information regarding their children's and their own health, at least when it was freely sought, as for instance at an infant welfare centre. Hannah Mitchell recorded in her autobiography that she wished such advice had been available to her when her child had been young.[66] Infant welfare centres certainly encouraged working-class women to bring up their children according to middle-class values, often asking the impossible in terms of both the material provision to be made for the child and infant care schedules. Yet, as George Orwell noted in respect to middle- and working-class food habits in the *Road to Wigan Pier*,[67] the knowledge possessed by the middle class was often valuable, but it depended how it was passed along. At the infant-welfare centre the mother could listen or leave, could attend the baby consultations, but not the thrift club. The visitor to the home was a different matter. Somerset Maugham wrote of them in *Of Human Bondage*: 'the district visitor excited their bitter hatred. She came in without so much as a "by your leave" or a "with your leave". . . she pushed her nose into corners, and if she didn't say the place was dirty you could see what she thought right enough'.[68] Rebecca West described the health visitor in 1913 as 'an inadequate and slightly offensive substitute offered to the poor woman for the skilled service the rich can command'.[69]

Much of the antagonism towards these officials was due to the communication gulf sharply perceived by an observer such as Margery Loane.[70] Emilia Kanthack advised in her 1907 manual for health visitors that she 'always approached my East End patients with my very best manners and extended the same little courteous considerations to them that I would have served towards a lady'.[71] In practice this probably amounted to little more than at best the 'lady from the west end come to do good' and, at worst, some fairly trenchant criticism of the mother and possibly the grandmother, labelled an 'infanticide expert' by one infant-welfare activist.[72] The health visitor would also have taken her place in the mind of the working-class mother not only with parish and Charity Organization Society visitors and the inspectors of the National Society for the Prevention of Cruelty to Children (who like infant-welfare activists were too prone to interpret lack of cleanliness as neglect),[73] but also with other agents of the state, like the school attendance officer and the inspector working under the infant life-protection legislation. The latter often doubled as the poor-law relieving officer and, according to middle-class feminists, was much resented by respectable working-class foster parents.[74] Welfare provision to the working-class during the period all too often held in its train highly inquisitorial government officials. A dialogue between R. H. Tawney and one of his students, a colliery weighman, captured working-class resentment of state inspection, which was obviously viewed as a gross intrusion designed to change the way in which working-class people lived:

> Myself [Tawney]: 'Any of you read *Seems So?* Its main idea seems to be that working classes hate interference of rich – inspectors, visitors, and so on in their affairs.'
> E. Hobson [the student]: 'Well they did hate the health visitors here [Langton] at first, especially when they were single women. But they seem to welcome them now. It's a matter of habit. But the grievance is that inspection and so on does not press upon everyone equally. No inspector thinks of going into houses in _____ road. When I was at the elementary school the attendance officer would come round if I missed a day. When I went to the secondary school, no one bothered about it. People dislike that sort of interference, because it's applied to one class and not to another.'[75]

In a rather different way, the provision of school meals in 1906 also threatened the authority, although not so much the privacy, of the working-class wife. Anna Martin commented at length on the reaction of the working-class mothers she knew to school meals:

> the women have a vague dread of being superseded and dethroned. Each of them knows perfectly well that the strength of her position in the home lies in the physical dependence of husband and children upon her and she is suspicious of anything that would tend to undermine this. The feeling that she is the indispensable centre of her small world is indeed the joy and consolation of her life.[76]

The wives she knew objected to the provision of school meals on the grounds that it would undermine both their role within the family and their husbands' obligation to provide. The latter may sound suspiciously like middle-class wishful thinking along the lines of the eminent economist F. Y. Edgeworth, who quoted the advice of a social worker approvingly: 'if the husband got out of work, the only thing that the wife should do is sit down and cry because if she did anything else he would remain out of work.'[77] Similarly, liberal feminists like M. G. Fawcett opposed school meals and family allowances for fear that they would undermine parental responsibility.[78]

Certainly, just as potent a cause of opposition to school meal provision may have been the fact that the school atendance officers were often given the job of assessing eligibility for free meals. Yet, given their attitudes towards the obligation of husbands, and given the fact that food, unlike medical care, was something the wife would expect the husband to provide on a regular basis, it seems reasonable to suggest that some wives may well have shared the middle-class liberal's distrust of state paternalism.[79] Anna Martin proposed an alternative to measures like the provision of school meals. She wanted to see legislation making a proportion of the husband's income the wife's by rights. If we remember the working-class wife's concern about the husband's ability to provide, this makes sense. The proposal was, however, opposed by men acitve in the labour movement who saw it as a slur on the character of the working-class husband.

During the 1920s an interesting group was organized to protest all intervention in the working-class home on the grounds that it threatened to undermine the working-class wife's responsibility for the welfare of her family. Called the Mother's Defence League, it was led by Cecil Chesterton's wife and its arguments closely paralleled those of Hillaire Belloc (Chesterton's co-thinker) in the *Servile State*,[80] which criticized the liberal welfare reforms for sapping the independence of workers.[81] The antagonism of women like Mrs Chesterton to state officialdom sprang from philosophical considerations and a romantic regard for the working-class family and community, and was probably also allied to the strong dislike of some middle-class women of expertism, which was also exhibited in their late-nineteenth-century tirades against doctors.[82] The Mother's Defence League's blanket condemnation of state intervention would not have been endorsed by working-class wives, who were opposed chiefly to the inquisitional aspects of welfare provision, but there was some basis for an alliance. Of course, articulate working-class women's groups like the Women's Cooperative Guild disliked both state and voluntary intrusion into the home, whereas middle class observers were quite happy to welcome any voluntary effort, especially on the part of female visitors. As the Manchester Health Society pamphlet of 1893 put it: 'comparatively unfettered by the vexed relations between labour and capital, with their more ready sympathy and common interests with all other women, they would begin hopefully where men would have little chance'.[83] This admirably illustrates the middle-class hope for greater contact and communication between social classes.

Nevertheless, the fact that there were points of contact between the views of middle-class commentators and working-class women is instructive and indicates perhaps that not only is it too simple to talk of the desire to impose the male-breadwinner family model from above, but also that the perceptions of members of the working-class family need to be differentiated: those of wives may not have been the same in all respects as husbands. From the viewpoint of the working-class wife it seems that the kinds of state intervention on behalf of children looked at briefly here tended to exacerbate her financial problems and undermine her domestic authority, while ironically she was at the same time being reminded of her pivotal position within the working-class family. It may be argued that this response best describes the position of the respectable, urban working-class wife – it is difficult to say, urban almost certainly, but the evidence of Anna Martin would seem to indicate that such views were also held by poorer women. In any case, to automatically assign wives the same socio-economic status as their husbands is problematic.

Finally, it is interesting to consider the changes in working-class wives' perceptions beyond the period considered here. During the inter-war years, evidence suggests that the working-class family became more privatized and more isolated, due in part to factors such as the operation of the household means test and the development of new housing estates. There was little change in terms of the acceptance of the family wage as an ideal and of concomitant sexual divisions. But the working-class wife's activities probably narrowed as many working-class neighbourhoods fractured, and as casual work for women became both harder to obtain and less common as a result, in part, of the increase in real wages for the employed and changes in the benefit structure for the unemployed. Thus, on the one hand, everyday routines became easier and, on the other, we have the much heralded discovery in 1936 of the 'suburban neurosis'[84] (the forerunner of Betty Friedan's 'problem that has no name'),[85] which is related directly to a loss of purpose in the lives of these women. And women with less sense of purpose and with less control over the family economy may well have also changed their perception of state intervention.

But it is with the dramatic change in women's relationship to the labour force that came after the Second World War that major shifts in perceptions might be expected. School meals and day care then become welcome and the state's assumptions of female dependency with respect to social security payments made on the basis of attachment to the workforce become onerous. However, to project this latter-day perspective back and to see it as the most significant concern of the working-class wife in the early twentieth century, is problematic.

Bibliographical Notes

For background on philanthropic visiting, see Frank Prochaska, *Women and Philanthropy in Nineteenth Century England* (Clarendon, Oxford, 1980); and Anne Summers, 'A Home from Home: women's philanthropic work in the nineteenth century', in S. Burman (ed.), *Fit Work for Women* (Croom Helm, 1979). Very little has been written on state employed 'visitors' in the shape of school attendance officers or health visitors. David Rubinstein, *School Attendance in London, 1870–1904: a social history* (University of Hull, Hull, 1969,), Occasional Papers in Economic and Social History No. 1 has some useful references to the former; and J. Lewis, *The Politics of Motherhood. Child and Maternal Welfare in England, 1900–1939* (Croom Helm, 1980) has something to say about the latter. More generally on working-class attitudes towards state intervention, Pat Thane's *Foundations of the Welfare State* (Longman, 1982) is perhaps the best starting place.

For different views on the family wage, see Hilary Land, 'The Family Wage', *Feminist Review* 6 (1980); and Jane Humphries 'Class Struggle and the Persistence of the Working Class Family', *Cambridge Journal of Economics* 1 (1977), 241–58. On the interpretation of working-class husband–wife relations see, especially, Ellen Ross, '"Fierce Questions and Taunts": married life in working-class London, 1870–1914', *Feminist Studies* 8 (1982) and 'Women's Neighbourhood Sharing in London before World War II', *History Workshop Journal* 15 (1983); Elizabeth Roberts, *A Woman's Place. An Oral History of Working Class Women* (Basil Blackwell, Oxford, 1984); Trevor Lummis, 'The Historical Dimension of Fatherhood: a case study', in L. McKee and M. O'Brien (eds), *The Father Figure* (Tavistock, 1982); and Gareth Stedman Jones, 'Working Class Culture and

Working Class Politics in London 1870–1900', *Journal of Social History* 7 (1974). On motherhood more generally, see Anna Davin, 'Imperialism and Motherhood' *History Workshop Journal* 5 (1978).

Notes

I would like to acknowledge with gratitude the helpful comments offered by participants in the 'Roots of Welfare' Conference (December, 1983) at Lancaster, and especially those of Pat Thane.

1 Helen Bosanquet, *Rich and Poor* (Macmillan, 1896), p. 60.
2 J. A. Banks, *Victorian Values: Secularism and the Size of Families* (Routledge & Kegan Paul, 1981).
3 J. A. Banks and Olive Banks, *Feminism and Family Planning in Victorian England* (Liverpool University Press, Liverpool, 1964), p. 154.
4 William Ogle, 'On Marriage Rates and Marriage Ages with Special Reference to the Growth of Population', *Journal of the Royal Statistical Society* 53, (1890), 253–80.
5 Helen Bosanquet, *The Family* (MacMillan, 1906), pp. 199 and 222.
6 Brian Harrison, 'State Intervention and Moral Reform in Nineteenth Century England', in Patricia Hollis, *Pressure from Without in early Victorian England* (Arnold, 1974), pp. 289–322.
7 M. Bayly, *Ragged Homes and How to Mend Them* (Nisbet, 1860).
8 Michael Rose, 'The Crisis of Poor Relief in England, 1860–90', in W. J. Mommsen (ed.), *The Emergence of the Welfare State in Britain and Germany 1850–1950* (Croom Helm 1981), pp. 50–70.
9 Judith R. Walkowitz, *Prostitution and Victorian Society* (Cambridge University Press, Cambridge, 1980).
10 C. B. P. Bosanquet, A *Handy Book for Visitors of the Poor in London* (Longman, 1874).
11 Jane Lewis, 'Dealing with Dependency: State Practices and Social Realities, 1870–1945', in *Women's Welfare/Women's Rights* (Croom Helm, 1983), pp. 17–37.
12 Hilary Land, 'The Family Wage'; and Mary McIntosh, 'The State and the Oppression of Women', in Annette Kuhn and Ann Marie Wolpe (eds.), *Feminism and Materialism* (Routledge & Kegan Paul, 1978), pp. 254–89.
13 Davin, 'Imperialism and Motherhood', *History Workshop Journal* 5 (1978).
14 Carol Dyhouse, 'Good Wives and Little Mothers: Social Anxieties and the Schoolgirl's Curriculum, 1880–1920', *Oxford Review of Education* 3 (1977), 21–36.
15 Jane Lewis, *The Politics of Motherhood: Maternal and Child Welfare in England, 1900–1939* (Croom Helm, 1980).
16 Royal Commission on Unemployment Insurance, *First Report* (1930–1), Cmd. 3872, p. 43.

17 B. Seebohm Rowntree, *Poverty a Study of Town Life* (Nelson, 1913), pp. 166–72.

18 Iris Minor, 'Working Class Women and Matrimonial Law Reform', in David E. Martin and David Rubenstein (eds), *Ideology and the Labour Movement* (Croom Helm, 1979), pp. 103–24.

19 Cited in B. Drake, *Women in Trade Unions* (Labour Research Department, 1920), p. 17.

20 Royal Commission on Labour, *Minutes of Evidence* (1893–4), C.7063, Q.4447.

21 Peter Stearns, 'Working Class Women in Britain, 1890–1914', in Martha Vicinus (ed.) *Suffer and be Still* (Indiana University Press Bloomington, 1973), pp. 100–20.

22 Select Committee of the House of Lords on the Sweating System, *Third Report*, Cmnd 165 (1889), Q. 18010.

23 Lewis, 'Dealing with Dependency'.

24 National Association for the Promotion of Social Science, Laws Relating to the Property of Married Women (NAPSS, 1868).

25 Pat Thane, 'Women and the Poor Law in Victorian and Edwardian England', *History Workshop Journal* 6 (1978), 29–51.

26 Nancy Osterud, 'Women's Work in Nineteenth Century Leicester: A Case Study in the Sexual Division of Labour', paper given at the Fourth Berkshire Conference, Mt Holyoke, Mass., 1978. See also her contribution in the parallel volume to this, Angela V. John (ed.) *Unequal Opportunities. Women's Employment in England 1800–1918* (Basil Blackwell, Oxford, 1986).

27 Select Committee of the House of Lords on the Sweating System, *Third Report*, Q. 18010.

28 Gertrude Tuckwell, *The State and its Children* (Methuen, 1894), p. 161.

29 Mrs J. R. MacDonald *et al.*, *Wage Earning Mothers* (Women's Labour League, n.d.).

30 Departmental Committee on Sickness Benefit Claims under the National Insurance Act, (1914–16), Cmnd. 7687, *Report*, p. 80. For a fuller discussion of women trade unionists views, see Deborah Thorn's essay in the parallel volume to this, John, *Unequal Opportunites*.

31 Public Records Office, ACT 1/65, Memo by Alfred Watson on the Proposed Special Maternity Benefits, December 1918.

32 Elizabeth Roberts, 'The Working Class Family in Barrow and Lancaster, 1890–1930', unpublished PhD. thesis, University of Lancaster, 1978. See also her *A Woman's Place. An Oral History of Working Class Women* (Basil Blackwell, Oxford, 1984).

33 J. Ramsay MacDonald, *Women in the Printing Trades* (P. S. King, 1904), p. viii.

34 M. Llewellyn Davies (ed.), *Maternity: Letters from Working Women*, (Virago: 1978, first published 1915) and *Life as We Have Known It*, (London: Virago, 1977).

35 Joan Scott and Louise Tilly, *Women, Work and Family* (Holt Rhinehart, New York, 1978).

36 Humphries, 'Class Struggle and the Persistence of the Working Class

Family', *Cambridge Journal of Economics* 1 (1977), 241–58.

37 Ellen Ross, '"Fierce Questions and Taunts": Married Life in Working-Class London, 1870–1914', *Feminist Studies* 8 (1982), 578.

38 Lady Florence Bell, *At the Works: A Study of a Manufacturing Town* (Thomas Nelson, 1911, first published 1902), p. 251.

39 John Burnett, *Destiny Obscure: Autobiographies of Childhood, Education and Family from the 1820's to the 1920's* (Allen Lane, 1982).

40 Magdalen Stuart Pember Reeves, *Round about a Pound a Week (Bell, 1914)*, p. 17.

41 Nancy Tomes, '"A Torrent of Abuse": Crimes of Violence between Working Class Men and Women in London, 1840–1875', Journal of Social History 11 (1978), 328–45.

42 Henry Higgs, 'Workmen's Budgets', *Journal of the Royal Statistical Society* 56 (1893), 255–85.

43 Charles Booth, *London Life and Labour* (Williams & Norgate, 1889), vol. I, p. 147.

44 Royal Commission on Divorce and Matrimonial Causes, *Minutes of Evidence*, (1912–13), Cmnd. 6480, vol. II, Q. 20120.

45 Edward Shorter, *the Making of the Modern Family* (Basic, New York, 1975) and Michael Young and Peter Wilmott, *The Symmetrical Family* (Pantheon Bks, New York, 1973).

46 Margaret Loane, *From Their Point of View* (Arnold, 1908), pp. 26, 108, 145.

47 Roberts, *A Woman's Place*; Lummis, 'The Historical Dimension of Fatherhood: A Case Study', in L. McKee and M. O'Brien (eds), *The Father Figure*, (Tavistock, 1982), pp. 1–25; and Gareth Stedman Jones, 'Working Class Culture and Working Class Politics in London, 1870–1900', *Journal of Social History* 7 (1974) 460–508.

48 Royal Commission on Divorce and Matrimonial Causes, *Report*, (1912–13), Cmnd. 6478, p. 68.

49 Hugh Cunningham, *Leisure in the Industrial Revolution* (Croom Helm, 1980).

50 Ross, 'Fierce Questions and Taunts'. p. 578.

51 Kathleen Woodward, *Jipping Street* (London: Virago, 1983, first published 1928); and Elizabeth Roberts, *A Woman's Place*.

52 Denise Riley, 'The Free Mothers: pronatalism and Working Women in Industry at the End of the War', *History Workshop Journal* 11 (1981), 59–118.

53 The Riverside Visitor, (Thomas Wright), 'School Board Difficulties: The Baby Difficulty', *Charity Organization Review*, 14 June 1884, pp. 198–9.

54 Robert Roberts, *The Classic Slum* (Manchester University Press, Manchester 1971), p. 92.

55 Hugh B. Philpott, *London at School* (T. Fisher Unwin, 1904), p. 91.

56 Anna Martin, *Married Working Women* (National Union of Women's Suffrage Societies, 1911), p. 8.

57 Cited in Royal Commission on the Working of the Elementary Education Act, *Second Report*, (1887), Cmnd. 5056, Q. 17188.

58 N. Whitebread, *The Evolution of the Nursery-Infant School* (Routledge & Kegan Paul, 1972), pp. 64 and 50.

59 Margaret Hewitt, *Wives and Mothers in Victorian Industry* (Rockliff, 1958), p. 166.

60 See for example, Jill Quadagno, *Aging in Early Industrial Society: Work, Family and Social Policy in Nineteenth Century England* (Academic Press, 1982), pp. 80–9.

61 Rachel MacMillan, *Education through Imagination*, 1st. Ed. 1904 (Allen & Unwin, 1923, first published 1904), pp. 47 and 50.

62 James Runciman, *School Board Idylls* (Longman, 1885), pp. 21–31.

63 David Rubinstein, *School Attendance in London, 1870–1906* (University of Hull, Hull, 1969), Occasional Papers in Social History No.1.

64 Richard Broad and Suzie Fleming (eds), *Nella Last's War*, (Sphere Books, 1983), pp. 237–55.

65 Martin, *Married Working Women*, pp. 36–7.

66 Hannah Mitchell, *The Hard Way Up* (Virago, 1977) p. 102.

67 George Orwell, *The Road to Wigan Pier* (Penguin, Harmondsworth, 1970, first published 1937), p. 90.

68 Quoted by Davin, 'Imperialism and Motherhood', p. 32.

69 Cited in Jane Marcus (ed.), *The Young Rebecca: Writings of Rebecca West, 1911–1917* (Virago, 1983), p. 200.

70 This point is expanded by Ross McKibbin in 'Social Class and Social Observation in Edwardian England', *Transactions of the Royal Historical Society* 28 (1978), 175–99.

71 Emelia Kanthack, *The Preservation of Infant Life* (H. K. Lewis, 1907), p. 2.

72 Carol Dyhouse, 'Working-class Mothers and Infant Mortality in England 1895–1914', in Charles Webster (ed.), *Biology, Medicine and Society, 1840–1860* (Cambridge University Press, Cambridge, 1981), pp. 96–7.

73 George Behlmer, *Child Abuse and Moral Reform in England, 1870–1908* (Stanford University Press, A Stanford 1982).

74 Select Committee on Infant Life Protection, *Report* (1908), (99), Q. 1080.

75 J. M. Winter and D. M. Joslin (eds), *R. H. Tawney's Commonplace Book* (Cambridge, Cambridge University Press, 1972), p. 3.

76 Martin, *Married Working Women*, pp. 29–30.

77 F. Y. Edgworth, 'Equal Pay to Men and Women for Equal Work', *Economic Journal* 32 (1922), 453.

78 Jane Lewis, 'Beyond Suffrage: English Feminism in the 1920's', *The Maryland Historian* VI (1975), 1–17.

79 There are parallels here with Stephen Yeo's argument regarding national health insurance: 'Working-Class Association, Private Capital, Welfare and the State in late Nineteenth and Twentieth Centuries', in Noel Parry, Michael Rustin, and Carole Satyamurti (eds), *Social Work Welfare and the State* (Arnold, 1979), pp. 48–71.

80 Hilaire Belloc, *The Servile State* (T. N. Foulis, 1912).

81 Martin Durham, 'The Mothers' Defence League, 1920–1: A Case Study

in Class, Patriarchy and the State', paper given at the History Workshop Conference, Sheffield, 1982.

82 See, for example, Frances Power Cobbe, *Life of Frances Power Cobbe*, (n.p., 1894), vol. I, pp. 227.

83 Manchester Health Society, *Ladies Health Society of Manchester and Salford* (Richard Bell, Manchester, 1893), p. 5.

84 Stephen Taylor, 'The Suburban Neurosis', *Lancet*, 26 March 1938, p. 759.

85 Betty Friedan, *The Feminine Mystique* (W. W. Norton, New York, 1963).

Part III
The Theory and Practice
of Sex and Marriage

Karl Pearson

Maria Sharpe

5

Marriage Laid Bare: Middle-Class Women and Marital Sex 1880s–1914
Lucy Bland

To learn something about women's experiences of marital sex a hundred years ago, we are faced with a daunting task. Given that it is hard enough to grasp the meaning and experience of marriage generally for late-nineteenth- and early twentieth-century women, how much more difficult it is to arrive at any sense of their feelings about sex within their marriages. This is hardly surprising when we reflect that women find it difficult to talk or write about such experiences even today, in a time when sex is comparatively less circumscribed by taboo. We have a small amount of information on the experiences of late-nineteenth-century middle-class American women,[1] but no similar source has been uncovered for British women. However, we do have access to various types of writing which indicate the kinds of questions and problems that some articulate middle-class women, usually feminists, were raising in relation to marriage. At the heart of their dissatisfaction lay the belief that the practice of marriage was deeply immoral, particularly because of the husband's irrevocable sexual rights to his wife. In reading women's criticisms of marriage we are able, if only indirectly, to get *some* sense of the kinds of dissatisfactions and difficulties they experienced with their marriages and their sexual relationships.

In the late 1880s and early 1890s, widespread public debate on marriage raged in numerous journals and newspapers. There was, of course, also debate taking place behind closed doors and, although this is largely unrecorded, there are various sources open to us. For example, it is possible to read the unpublished minutes and letters of a certain private club, the Men and Women's Club, set up in the 1880s to discuss relationships between the sexes.[2] A key part of the

Club's discussions concerned marriage and marital sex. Although it appears that the members did not speak to the Club in any very intimate detail, the dynamics of Club discussions as well as the topics for debate indicate both the difficulties women faced in relation to marriage and sex and the contrasts between women's feelings and those of men. The 'new woman' fiction of the 1890s provides further evidence of the kind of criticisms posed and the types of strategies presented (if not actually adopted) for transforming marriage and sexual relationships.

By the early 1900s women's anger, or at least the anger of feminists, had taken a shift towards more public pronouncements on the sexual dangers of marriage. Previously confined to fiction, these claims now took a factual form. Feminists increasingly urged women to protect themselves and their children from the perils of venereal disease and licentious men. They were able to back up their arguments by drawing on the current concern with national health and the declining birth rate. Many feminists also demanded an equalization of the divorce law between the sexes as one step to establishing an equal moral standard. The few years prior to the war witnessed sharp disagreements within feminism over attitudes to sex, marriage and 'free unions'. Some feminists drew on sexology (the so-called science of sex), a new discipline whose pronouncements tended to undermine earlier feminist convictions. During the First World War and after, feminist moral gains around issues of sexuality were undermined still further. The challenge to male sexual practice evaporated.

'Speaking Out' on Sex and Marriage

By the late 1880s/early 1890s, many women were beginning to 'speak out' on many disturbing aspects of male sexual practice, including that within marriage. The criticisms of marital sex were part of a much wider attack on male sexual conduct in this period. Feminists were simultaneously confronting the sexual abuse of children,[3] men's use of prostitutes, the double moral standard and the dominant assumption that men had 'uncontrollable' (and therefore inevitable and pardonable) sexual urges. Those who 'dared' to speak were feminists, mainly middle class, both married and unmarried. According to the nineteenth-century prescriptive literature on women's role, they were supposedly 'pure': the 'sexless' spinster was assumed to know nothing of sex, and the 'angel in the home' entered

Fem Movement

marriage sexually ignorant and remained sexually passive. Women were not expected to threaten the very essence of the 'sacred hearth' by raising the unspoken, unmentionable sexual side of married life. If taboos around sex were so extensive in 'polite' society, and if most middle-class women (and many working-class ones too), were in reality entering marriage with so little sexual knowledge, what made it possible for them suddenly to question and challenge the sexual practices of married men within their marriages as well as outside them?

Feminists had been raising doubts about marital arrangements for some years. Their campaigns had led to the Married Women's Property Acts of 1870 and 1882,[4] and the 1878 Matrimonial Causes Act, which gave magistrates' courts the power to grant a separation order with maintenance to a wife whose husband had been convicted of assault upon her.[5] Women's entry into higher education, again largely accomplished through the activities of feminists, had led to a questioning not only of the marriage system but also, for some women, the necessity of marriage at all. Whereas marriage had formerly been the only respectable female career for middle-class young women, from the late 1880s onwards feminists had been active in widening employment prospects for single women.[6] The entry of women into teaching and a number of new professions, such as clerical work – in other words the possibility of economic independence for middle-class women – contributed further to challenging the inevitability of marriage. This was compounded by the fact that the ratio of women to men was steadily increasing. In the 1851 census there were 1,042 women to every 1,000 men; by 1901 it had risen to 1,068. It was therefore simply not possible for all women to marry.

Before the turn of the century there were many voices raised in support of the single woman. The *Westminster Review* wrote that she was 'a new sturdy and vigorous type. We find her neither the exalted ascetic nor the nerveless inactive creature of former days.'[7] One woman distinguished the 'old maid' from the 'glorified spinster': 'An old maid is a woman *minus* something; the glorified spinster is a woman *plus* something.'[8] As the feminist writer Sarah Grand expressed it, 'Thinking for herself, the modern girl knows that a woman's life is no longer considered a failure simply because she does not marry.'[9]

All this may explain why women were questioning marriage, but it does not explain why women were able also to start challenging dominant sexual assumptions and practices. Breaking the taboo on speaking about sex had begun in the 1870s with the feminist-inspired campaign against the Contagious Diseases Acts. The Acts, which had been introduced into a number of ports and garrisons, permitted the compulsory examination and detention of suspected prostitutes. The feminist repealers had condemned them on several grounds: they interfered with a woman's civil liberty, they gave arbitrary powers to plain-clothes police, they represented the state's condonement of vice and, above all, they stood as the apotheosis of the double standard of morality. Those involved in the repeal campaign also became concerned with what was termed the 'white slave' trade: coerced prostitution, often of juveniles. In 1885, revelations in the *Pall Mall Gazette* by W.T. Stead of the extent of white slavery led to enormous pressure for the enactment of the Criminal Law Amendment which, amongst other things, raised the age of consent to sexual intercourse from thirteen to sixteen. In 1889 Maria Sharpe, a feminist, reflected: 'Things are changed now, everything is more open, especially I think since the Pall Mall Gazette revelations, which however questionable did I believe break down a great barrier for women – after them no-one was supposed of necessity to be in ignorance.'[10]

The Men and Women's Club

The Men and Women's Club, committed to 'the free and unreserved discussion of all matters . . . connected with the mutual position and relation of men and women',[11] was set up in 1885 by the socialist and future eugenist Karl Pearson, and continued meeting until June 1889. The Club's constitution announced that it would meet monthly, consist of no more than twenty members and be composed of equal numbers of men and women. Club members were chosen carefully, as were guests, who had to receive the recommendation of at least three members. The men were largely colleagues of Pearson's with radical liberal or socialist politics and similar public school and Oxbridge backgrounds. All were employed as lawyers, doctors or university lecturers, and were further linked through membership of the same men's West End clubs. A number of the men were married but of the women members, all but two were single; moreover one of the two married women, wife of the Club's President Robert Parker, was to drop out almost immediately. Many of the women were economically independent as teachers, writers or journalists (fulfilling the image of the 1880s' and 1890s' 'new woman'); all were clearly feminists, and a number were well known. Olive Schreiner, Annie Besant, Jane Chapperton and Elizabeth Blackwell, for example, were all members or associates of the Club.

Like the men, the women were largely free-thinkers, and the Club's constitution declared its members committed to discussion of all subjects 'from the historical and scientific as distinguished from the theological standpoint'.[12] Although the Club never took marital sex *per se* as the sole subject of discussion, it was frequently referred to via other related issues. Club discussions ranged over sex instinct, morality, marriage, free unions, friendships between men and women, prostitution, family limitation and women's emancipation.

On the question of marriage reform, the men and women all appeared to agree that easier divorce was desirable and that the grounds for divorce should be equalized between the sexes. (At great expense, divorce had been available since 1857 to a husband on the ground of his wife's adultery alone, while she had to prove his adultery plus one of the following additional causes: desertion, cruelty, incest, sodomy, or bestiality.) Some women argued that men should become more responsible towards both their legitimate and illegitimate children, and objected to any idea that the state should provide financial support to mothers (referred to as the 'state endowment of motherhood') on the grounds that men's sense of responsibility would be undermined.

As for marital sex, nearly all the women and a couple of the men felt there was much need for change. One male member proposed that 'forcing the wife' (presumably he meant rape) should be treated as cruelty, though it is unclear from the Club minutes whether he was also proposing this as grounds for divorce. Mrs Walters, a guest who also sent in a paper to be read, was the only one to suggest explicitly that marriage reform, first and foremost, required the reform of the *man* – particularly his sexual behaviour. Men 'must change and become altruistic', treating marriage as 'only sexual for race ends'.[13] Once economically independent, women would refuse marriage, unless men reformed. Emma Brooke, another Club associate, made the same point. In her lengthy correspondence with Pearson, she claimed that women's economic independence would force men to learn self-restraint and 'to stop being a beast of prey'.[14] As we shall see, their views pre-figured the opinions of many feminists writing ten to twenty years later.

At one meeting Maria Sharpe read out extracts from a letter to her from a married female friend. It touched on her abhorrence at men's 'unquestioning conjugal rights':

Fem Movement

> men are . . . brought up in the tacit understanding that
> marriage secures sexual intercourse whenever *they* are the least
> inclined for it, and I am perfectly sure that most women give
> way to them for the sake of peace . . . as long as the English
> Church service remains unaltered, so long can they wield this
> against us . . . if only convocation or government would begin
> discussing it.[15]

Henrietta Muller made a similar observation: 'To many women
sexual intercourse is an unpleasant and fatiguing obligation.'[16] The
fear of pregnancy and excessive childbearing, and many women's
dislike of their husband's sexual demands, were seen by the women
as the key problems with marital sex. They tended to feel that it was
not so much that women were *less* sexual than men, but that their
experience of sexual intercourse and its consequences were generally
far less pleasant. During discussion it became clear that although all
the women were critical of marriage, they were also resolute that *for
the present*, given women's vulnerability and disadvantage, *reformed*
legal marriage was infinitely preferable to a non-marital relationship.
For example, while Henrietta Muller, possibly the most outspoken
feminist member, informed Maria Sharpe in private that she was
against marriage,[17] at the Club she argued only for legal reform.
Only in the future, *after* women were free, would alternatives to
marriage be possible.

  Although the Club had set itself up to discuss a rather 'daring'
subject for the 1880s, they were very concerned that their group
avoid being branded 'free lovers'. A number of the women had
objected to the name initially proposed for the group – the
'Wollstonecraft Club' – on the grounds of the possibly damaging
association with Mary Wollstonecraft's 'immoral' lifestyle (meaning
her free alliances), as well as its implicit inference that only women
rather than both the sexes were the object of study. Maria Sharpe,
the Club's secretary, also opposed the proposed membership of Karl
Marx's daughter, Eleanor, who was then living openly in 'free union'
with Edward Aveling. But it was not simply the women who feared
the implications of 'free lovers' in their midst. Pearson was anxious
lest the group be tarnished with the brush of 'Hintonianism'. The
late James Hinton, allegedly an advocate of 'polygamous
relationships', had a number of followers, one of whom, Hinton's
sister-in-law Caroline Haddon, was initially considered for
membership. Although she was to attend once as a guest,
membership was never granted.[18]

  However, when Annie Besant was invited to the Club to talk on 'the State and sexual relations', she argued for the advantage of free unions and birth control. She felt that in circumstances where no children were involved, state regulation of personal relationships was unwarranted. In discussion of family limitation, Besant argued for what were called 'preventive checks' (artificial methods of birth control). All the men, save possibly one, were in favour of such 'checks'. The women were split on the issue. However, even those feminists in favour of 'checks' saw them as a necessary evil, and they all seemed to agree that women were likely to 'prefer self-control and long periods of abstinence'.[19] The trouble was, it could not be assumed that men would take any notice of women's preferences. Hence, for some women, although 'checks' were 'very odious', they were preferable to continuous childbearing. To Henrietta Muller, for example, preventive checks were 'a mere *pis aller* [a last resort] till men have self-control and women have freedom.'[20] Other female members, however, felt that checks were so brutalizing – they 'vulgarized the emotions' and encouraged immorality – that they were unacceptable. Many women of this period looked on artificial birth control as a means of reducing a wife to a virtual prostitute. It was feared that once wives no longer had the excuse of possible pregnancy, they would be subjected to their husbands' every sexual demand. For example, Letitia Sharpe, although believing checks to be, for the present, a necessary evil, felt that they made women more than ever a vehicle of men's pleasure.[21]

Club members debated the differences between male and female sexuality. Pearson argued that women's childbearing potential and their strong desire for children was the fundamental distinction between the sexes. His blossoming eugenism was in evidence when he had the audacity to suggest that 'if child-bearing women must be intellectually handicapped, then the penalty for race predominance is the subjection of women.'[22] Two of the women were adamant that maternal instinct (highly romanticized by Pearson) simply did not exist for most women. On the contrary, argued Emma Brooke, married women *dreaded* rather than welcomed childbearing, and they deeply resented their lack of choice. Another area of disagreement arose when many of the men expressed the idea that women 'needed' a 'sexual outlet' to the same degree as men, and that sexual activity was therefore damaging to women and men alike. This was an argument that was beginning to circulate more widely with the development of sexology, and was to become a key way of discrediting the spinster.[23] Further, the claim that chastity was unhealthy acted to undermine the women's demand for greater male sexual self-control. All Club members treated sex as unquestionably heterosexual, but at least the women did not talk of biological 'needs'.

The women presented a view of female sexuality that was both social and evolutionary, drawing not so much on Darwin as on Lamarck, who had argued that attributes gained during an individual's lifetime could be passed on to the next generation. Thus Maria Sharpe's sister Letitia felt that 'in a state of nature' women's sexuality would probably be stronger than men's, but that as products of years of suppression by 'civilization', women's instinct was checked while men's sexuality had been encouraged. Maria Sharpe and Florence Balgarnie, Secretary of the National Society for Women's Suffrage, suggested that fear of pregnancy had checked women's sexuality still further.

In the late-nineteenth century, feminists were beginning to make direct connections between prostitution and marriage. Not only were the two institutions inextricably linked, the supposed 'purity' and sexual passivity of the middle-class woman existing at the expense of the working-class prostitute who served the sexual 'needs' of the middle-class man; but the fact of a husband's 'property' rights in his wife's sexuality led to marriage being termed 'legalized prostitution'. Prostitution haunted relations between men and women. To Maria Sharpe: 'Prostitution is . . . the great unknown subject to girls which fills them with an enquiring fearfulness . . . the region where women are possibly bodies only to men casting a dark shadow across all their own relations to the other sex.'[24] This reduction of women to mere sexual *bodies* appeared to many of the women Club members to be the key to women's subordination. To Letitia Sharpe, 'the worst disability that women suffer is the average public opinion on matters of sex. Women are still . . . judged and valued by their bodies rather than their minds.'[25]

In contrast many women, including many of the female Club members, had a vision of ideal sexual relationships which were monogamous, spiritual rather than merely physical, about love rather than lust. For a few of the women members ideal sex meant sex solely for reproductive ends. Other women, however, rejected a view of their sexuality as in essence equivalent to maternity. Either way, they wanted *women* to be the deciders of when sexual activity should occur. Further, they all objected to Pearson's view of sex as simply a physical pleasure on par with climbing a mountain. To Maria Sharpe, this put 'a taste of a strawberry and a kiss of a friend' on the same level.[26] The women members also felt that men should change and that women must believe it to be possible. For, as Florence Balgarnie argued, if women assumed that men inevitably had lesser sexual control, then they gave reinforcement to that belief. By advocating greater self-control, women did not necessarily rule out sexual pleasure for women. A number of them would certainly have agreed with Elizabeth Blackwell that if men controlled themselves, women would at last be able to express *themselves*. Some of the women were optimistic that change was already afoot. Kate Mills for example saw signs of men becoming more chaste. This was an optimism that was not to last into the next century.

On reading the Club's records, I, like the women members themselves a hundred years before, experienced a growing recognition of the men's patronizing attitude and the way in which the use of the languages of science and rationality contributed to their silencing. It was not simply that the women felt stupid, inferior, lacking in education and thereby ill-equipped to utilize the 'appropriate' vocabulary. They were also silenced by their acute experience of vulnerability in the face of the coldly calculating nature of some of the men's pronouncements. Maria Sharpe wrote later (of Parker's paper on relations among the Greeks of the Periclean Era): 'Never shall I forget the frozen impression which it left in me . . . It was the coolness with which Mr Parker seemed to treat the whole subject, showing no warmth.'[27]

A number of the women were worried lest their *personal* feelings destroyed impartiality but, faced with the men's discussion of sexuality which in effect totally denied their own experience, they felt justified in responding from a personal standpoint. Part of their reticence stemmed from their awareness that the men were only interested in what they had to say as 'woman', an alien species:

> To write as women was something like taking up the 'performing' task . . . I had however . . . come to the melancholy conclusion that it was in that light that the men chiefly valued us. That we were not trained or clever enough to do work for the Club that might be of value of itself . . . but that whatever we did as *women* . . . was something worth listening to.[28]

Despite these reservations, the women did respond to the men's papers on the Contagious Diseases Acts in terms of their personal feelings. Unlike the men, they were all resolutely opposed to the Acts. Further, they were beginning to realize the lack of an adequate language to present their feelings of horror and revulsion. Although committed to 'non-theological' discussion, some of the women acknowledged that at least religion provided a means of expressing emotions effectively prohibited by the language of scientific rationality.[29] Even Annie Eastty, in many ways the woman member most committed to a rationalistic approach to sexual relations, felt 'more and more indebted to the Club for the opportunity it has given me of discovering that I am not so completely out of sympathy with a religious element in feeling as I thought I was.'[30]

Although Annie Eastty might have felt indebted, other women felt *anger* at being silenced. Henrietta Muller finally resigned in fury. She wrote to Pearson of the last meeting:

> It was the same old story of the man laying down the law to the woman and not seeming to recognize that she has a voice, and the women resenting in silence, and submitting in silence. Even when one who is bold opens her lips, they feebly admire her courage but do not venture to follow her example because the enemy is present.[31]

Earlier, she had referred specifically to the difficulties women faced in speaking about sexuality. She noted that whenever women differed from men, their voice of protest was immediately stifled.[32] She told Pearson that she would start a rival club for women only, and 'in my club every woman shall find a voice and shall learn how to use it'.[33]

Women clearly needed a voice and language with which to confront men on all issues, but especially that of sexuality. In the years up to the First World War feminists increasingly found a voice and, selectively drawing on a patchwork of discourses – evolutionism, anthropology, eugenics, Christianity, liberalism, socialism – they attempted to develop a language of their own.

'New Women' and 'Ship-Wrecked Sailors'

In 1898 Lillian Harman wrote of a 'new martyrdom'. Harman was a prominent American feminist and sexual radical, but also President of the Legitimation League, a small British organization aiming to change the bastardy laws and to educate the public on the desirability of free sexual relationships. According to her, the 'new martyrdom' was a term used by physicians to refer to men who having been trapped into marriage by wicked 'new women', were now denied paternity. But, she wrote: 'The true cause of this cry of the New Martyrdom is that the Old Man is losing his power, and frightened by the development of the New Woman . . . Accustomed for ages to obtaining the gratification of his desires through force in marriage, and purchase outside . . . he is like a shipwrecked sailor in a strange land.'[34]

So who was the 'New Woman'? In one sense she was a journalistic and literary construction, but she also had a basis in reality. This lay in the increased opportunities for middle-class women in education and employment, the various gains made by feminism, and the public surfacing of the previously unspoken horrors of prostitution and sexual atrocity – the very reasons that it became possible for women to begin to 'speak out' on marriage and sex. The term 'new woman' was not equivalent to the term 'feminist', although a self-defined 'new woman' was likely to have held certain feminist convictions. The 'new woman' probably meant all things to all people, but she was generally thought of as a young woman of principle, drawn from the upper or middle class, concerned to reject many of the conventions of femininity and to live and work on free and equal terms with the opposite sex. Her hallmark was *personal* freedom, and her image was constructed above all in the pages of the so-called 'new woman novel'.

The 'new woman' novels had as their subject matter the doubts and dilemmas surrounding the 'new woman': her experience of work and higher education and her challenge to conventional marriage and sex. But the novels were also largely written by women who themselves epitomized the 'new woman' stereotype – women who earned their own living, travelled widely and were prepared to speak their mind. Most, if not all, of these women writers were also feminists. Several of them had been connected with the Men and Women's Club, for example Mona Caird, Emma Brooke and Olive Schreiner. The female 'new woman' fiction writers were markedly distinct from their male equivalents who included Hardy, Gissing, Grant Allen and Moore. While many of the men tended to draw on their own fantasies in focusing on the sexual freedom of a 'new woman' heroine, the women writers drew on their feminist politics and concentrated more on the sexual behaviour of men. To the female 'new woman' writers, male sexuality tended to be seen as 'alien, indiscriminate, incessant and injurious.'[35] The Men and Women's Club might have been bold in its talk of sex, but one thing it had never openly discussed was VD within marriage. However, in the 1890s a number of feminists began 'speaking out' on precisely this issue. At this stage they mostly chose to do so through the vehicle of fiction.[36]

But not all the 'new women' writers focused only on the perils of bad or diseased marriages. Some also looked to the possibilities of happier alternatives. Linda Gordon and Ellen Dubois claim that late-nineteenth- and early twentieth-century feminists can be divided into two groups: a majority focusing on the dangers of sex for women, and a small minority emphasizing the pleasures.[37] I would suggest that although early twentieth-century feminists may be characterized in this way, in the late-nineteenth century there were a number of women alert to *both* the dangers and possible pleasures of sex for women. One of these was the writer George Egerton, the pseudonym for Mary Chavelita Dunne. In her writing, Egerton clearly drew on her personal experience. She had travelled widely, earning her living in various ways. She had lived in Norway for two years with a married man who was violent and alcoholic. After his death she married a destitute Canadian, whom she was later to divorce. To earn money she began to write short stories which were enthusiastically taken up by the publisher John Lane. For a few years she was famous and sought after.

Through her heroines Egerton conveys the need for women to have fulfilling lives that relate to all aspects of themselves – their personal relationships, sexuality, maternity and work. On the one hand, some of her stories are tinged with utopianism, her heroines projected into an ideal world where women no longer face restrictions on their freedom of action and choice. For example, in the 'Regeneration of Two', the finale sees the heroine and hero setting up some kind of free union in which both can come and go as they choose. The heroine announces to the hero: 'I ask you nothing . . . for I am sure of myself, proud of my right to dispose of myself as I will, to choose.' On the other hand, some stories lay bare the unpalatable reality of the present. In 'Virgin Soil', for example, Florence, herself the victim of a terrible marriage, bitterly realizes that: 'as long as marriage is based on such inequal terms, as long as man demands from his wife as a right what he must sue from a mistress as a favour . . . marriage becomes for many women a legal prostitution.'[38] It was this kind of harsh social realism rather than the more utopian writing that typified most of the 'new woman' fiction.

In the 1880s the dire effects of women's sexual ignorance had begun to be mentioned. By the 1890s the need for a sex education that taught not only the physiological facts but also warned girls of sexual dangers was one plank in the feminist demand for transformed sexual relations. It was not new to want sex education for *boys* – for several years a number of purity organizations had been lecturing boys and young men on the evils of masturbation, the development of will-power, the desirability of chastity and the need for an equal moral standard.[39] But, until the 1890s, girls' sexual ignorance had generally been believed to provide their 'protection'. The 'new woman' fiction writers focused on some of the consequences of the silence surrounding sex. Egerton's 'Florence' believes it is the key to her disastrous marriage. She accusingly turns on her mother (though I only wish she would attack her husband with equal venom):

> 'I say it is your fault because you reared me a fool, an idiot, ignorant of everything I ought to have known . . . my physical needs, my coming passion, the very meaning of my sex, my wifehood and motherhood to follow. You gave me not one weapon in my hand to defend myself against the possible attacks of man at his worst. You sent me to fight the biggest battle of a woman's life . . . with a white gauze' – she laughed derisively – 'of maiden purity as a shield.'[40]

Demands on Men in the 1900s

Feminism in the early twentieth century is generally thought of today simply in terms of the heightened struggle for the vote. The suffrage campaign was, however, accompanied by an increasing commitment from all strands of feminism to the fight for an equal moral standard. To Louisa Martindale, 'the women's movement is a moral movement'.[41] 'There is nothing in the feminist programme about which the feminist feels so keenly as the double standard of morality', reflected Ethel Snowden; the last and greatest of the demands of the women's movement was 'a woman's absolute right over herself after marriage.'[42] These were not untypical statements from feminists of the day.

The ways that feminists now wrote about sex and marriage built directly on those ideas of the late-nineteenth century that this chapter has been describing. However, there were also definite developments and subtle changes. Feminists were more insistent than ever that men take full responsibility for their sexually immoral actions and that they *change*. As I have indicated, feminists linked the demand for sexual morality with the demand for the vote; once women had the vote, the argument went, not only would they be stronger, more independent and self-respecting, they would also be able to introduce legislation to deal with male immorality. More feminists were now also alert to the dangers of marriage. In arguing for women's and children's protection from these dangers, feminists frequently drew on the current anxiety over national health, motherhood and the declining birth rate, all products of the nation's obsession with its 'fitness' in the face of challenge from Germany and the USA to its place as an imperial power. Feminist writing refocused the blame for the supposed 'physical deterioration' of the race away from women and on to men. Women were being accused of irresponsibility in their maternity, and selfishness and degeneracy in their sterility. Feminists, however, accused men. It was men, through their sexual licentiousness, who had brought disease into marriage; this was the main cause of women's sterility and infant mortality and morbidity.

Feminists now started to present the VD issue in a *factual* rather than a fictional form. In 1908 Louisa Martindale produced the first feminist text devoted solely to the issue of VD, commissioned by the National Union of Women's Suffrage Societies.[43] But the most (in)famous feminist tract came a few years later with Christabel Pankhurst's *The Great Scourge and how to end it*, published in 1913, a compilation of articles which first appeared in the *Suffragette*. Drawing on various sets of medical statistics, she claimed that 75–80 per cent of all men were infected with gonorrhoea and 'a considerable percentage' with syphillis. Although she was accused of great exaggeration, the medical profession were themselves presenting similar figures. The effects of the prevalence of VD, Pankhurst claimed, were horrendous: 'the sexual diseases are the great cause of physical, mental and moral degeneracy and of race suicide . . . ravaging the community.' She also argued, like a number of other feminists, that 'women's diseases' were not intrinsic to the female constitution, but were rather the effects of VD surreptitiously imposed by philandering husbands on their unsuspecting wives.[44]

Frances Swiney, the feminist theosophist, saw the 'hidden scourge' as part of a wider degeneracy instigated by men. In developing her own specific theory of the cause of women's subordination, Swiney, like a number of earlier feminists, drew selectively on evolutionary and anthropological ideas. Science showed, she suggested, that women were the originators and constructors of life and the major force in human evolutionary development. But progress was being retarded by male sexual immorality. Picking up the prevalent fears of national and racial degeneracy, Swiney suggested that man was life's 'destroyer': 'The degeneracy we deplore lies at the door of a selfish, lustful, diseased manhood . . . Men have sought in woman only a body. They have possessed that body. Men have made it the refuse-heap of sexual pathology.' She also drew on eugenical and medical research concerning what were then termed 'racial poisons'. These included alcohol, tobacco and VD. Swiney added human sperm to the list, claiming that if 'limited, its power is for good; in excess it was a virulent poison'. In 'civilized' man's sexual overindulgence, including his transgression of the natural 'law of the mother' (the observance of continence during the period of pregnancy), poisonous sperm and VD took the form of retribution: 'Vices like curses . . . come back to roost.'[45] Pankhurst likewise saw VD as the punishment of nature.[46]

The actress and writer Cicely Hamilton voiced her warnings on the marital dangers of disease and male sexual excess within a wider-ranging polemic. In her witty but biting *Marriage as a Trade* (1909), she argued that through 'the narrowing down of women's hopes and ambitions' marriage was one of the principle causes of women's disabilities. Until recently marriage had been a 'compulsory trade' for women, but with the growing possibility of women's economic independence, life without marriage was becoming more possible and more desirable: 'Some of us are even proud of the fact that we have fought our way in the world without aid from any man's arm.' Like many feminists, Hamilton saw marriage as a means of enforcing obligatory sexual intercourse on the woman. Men's extreme dislike of spinsters, she suggested, was due to this 'perpetual virgin' being 'witness . . . to the unpalatable fact that sexual intercourse was not for every woman an absolute necessity.' She argued that woman's very existence was defined by men in terms of her role as wife and mother, responding: 'There are other faculties in our nature besides that which has hitherto been forced under a hothouse system of cultivation – sex and motherhood.' Further, marital sexual intercourse and motherhood not only frequently involved lack of a woman's consent, it also entailed danger to health, including the risk of VD. 'If marriage is a trade, we ought to know its risks' she remarked laconically.[47] Both Swiney and Hamilton believed that men denied women individuality; to Swiney, 'men sought in women only a body', to Hamilton, women were seen by men merely as bodies to service another, be it man or child. In her explanation for venereal disease, Christabel Pankhurst echoed Swiney and Hamilton: 'sexual disease . . . is due . . . to the doctrine that woman is sex and beyond that nothing . . . or that . . . women are mothers and beyond that nothing. What a man . . . really means is that women are created primarily for the sex gratification of men and secondly for the bearing of children if he happens to want them.'[48]

If feminists were largely in agreement about the dangers and displeasures of marriage, many also agreed over the means for eradicating them and reforming marriage. Most feminists in this period agreed that male lust was not innate. However it was not enough to know and say that men could change; men had to be made to change. Greater sexual knowledge among women seemed to be one means to this end. Swiney stressed the need for girls and women to know all the dangers of sex: 'It may be objected that this knowledge of unpleasant facts may tend to make young innocent girls suspicious of all men . . . such . . . is my intention . . . 'I would make all women suspicious of men until men live such lives as to be above suspicion.'[49]

Sex education was a long-term solution, but feminists wanted to effect a more immediate change in man's behaviour. Hamilton, Lucy Re-Bartlett and Pankhurst all declared that many women were already forcing that change by refusing either to marry, to cater sexually to men, or to bear their children. Women had been told they had a duty to the race to breed but they now responded that this same duty forbade their cohabitation with potentially diseased men – and this was part of the explanation for the falling birth rate. Re-Bartlett was certain that: 'In the hearts of many women today is rising a cry . . . *I will know no man and bear no child until this apathy be broken through – these wrongs be righted* . . . It is the "silent strike" and it is going on all over the world [her emphasis].' She saw temporary celibacy for many women as 'the first step towards a sexual love far higher', and it 'may be the only thing . . . which can call out the "new man" as well as give birth to the "new woman"'.[50] Until men had reformed, Pankhurst was convinced that: 'There can be no mating between the spiritually developed women of this new day and men who in thought and conduct with regard to sex matters are their inferiors.' It was necessary to press for 'Votes for Women, Chastity for Men'.[51]

As we have seen, feminists desired economic, political and moral changes in relation to marriage and sex. They also still wanted legal change. A number gave evidence to the Royal Commission on Divorce and Matrimonial Causes, and many feminist organizations sent resolutions. The central issues facing the Commission, which sat from 1909–12, were whether provisions should be made to enable divorce to be cheaper and more available to a wider section of

society, whether to place both sexes on an equal footing with respect
to grounds for divorce, and whether to extend those grounds. All
feminists, and all the members of the Women's Cooperative Guild
(WCG), who were certainly not all feminists, agreed that the change
crucially needed was equalization of the divorce law. This, they
believed, would raise the moral standards of men. As one WCG
member put it: 'A woman has the right to expect from a man the
same purity as he demands from her.'[52] A poll of WCG members
revealed that most members wanted cheaper and more accessible
divorce procedures through the county courts. The great majority
also approved additional grounds for divorce, such as cruelty,
insanity, refusal to maintain and desertion. Under cruelty they
included abuse of conjugal 'rights'. Some argued for divorce on
grounds of incompatibility; a number even wanted divorce by
mutual consent. Disease within marriage was also mentioned. The
fact the WCG took such a radical stand on marriage perhaps shows
the depth of female dissatisfaction with marriage, across all
classes. Rebecca West heralded the Royal Commission's report as a
feminist triumph – there was such pressure, the Commission had
'had to concede this demand of the suffragists'.[53] One of its
recommendations had been the equalization of the divorce law, but
West was also sure that no political party would bother to introduce
any of the proposed changes. She was proved right. None of its
recommendations was enacted until years later. The equalization of
the divorce law, for example, was not introduced until 1923.

From 'New Woman' to 'Free Woman'

November 1911 saw the first issue of a new feminist journal *The
Freewoman*. The term 'free woman' can perhaps be seen as a later
equivalent of the 1890s 'new woman'. Although more feminist in
orientation, it retained the stress on *personal* freedom. Dora
Marsden, the main force behind the journal, was a libertarian who
politically had much in common with the feminist members of the
Legitimation League. The League had long disbanded (in 1898),
but one or two of its former members occasionally contributed
to the new journal. Marsden had been active in the Women's
Social and Political Union (WSPU), but had recently resigned,
disillusioned with its militancy and 'obsession' with the vote.
Her dissatisfaction with suffrage politics was forcibly conveyed
in *The Freewoman* in a number of scathing attacks. However

a large part of the paper (and especially the lengthy correspondence) rapidly became devoted to the frank and open discussion of sex and marriage.

Contributors continued to raise many of the same problems that had concerned feminists over the past thirty years. There were arguments over the pros and cons of birth control, the inevitability or otherwise of prostitution, the problems with the present marriage system, the possible weapon of a birth strike by women to force the granting of the vote,[54] the demand for purity from men. Most contributors agreed that, ideally, sex was not an uncontrollable physical urge, indiscriminate in its object; most were opposed to promiscuity. All grounded their conviction in notions of the place of sex within the evolution of the human species and a woman's right to control her own body and fertility.

New to the feminist discussions of marriage and sex was a positive affirmation of female sexuality and some discussion of 'free unions' as a visible alternative to marriage. There was disagreement as to what was implied by the label 'free woman'. Dora Marsden and a number of others aligned the term with what they called the 'new morality'. The 'new moralists' stood for 'limited monogamy' and 'free unions': monogamous relationships that could be freely entered and freely left. They opposed the hypocrisy of indissoluble marriage (the 'old morality'), with the married woman maintaining her 'purity' at the expense of the prostitute.[55] Certain other women who were equally keen to see themselves as 'new women' did not like the implications of this 'new morality'. Kathleen Oliver, for example, wrote: 'I do hope . . . that the new 'morality' which will permit for women the same degrading laxity in sex matters which is indulged in by most of the lower animals, including man, will be choked and crushed . . . How can we possibly be Free Women if, like the majority of men, we become the slaves of our lower appetites?'[56]

Many women were aware of all the problems with marriage, but still feared their vulnerability in the living out of alternatives. Nevertheless, one gets the impression from reading *The Freewoman* that there were many more women and men living in 'free unions' in the years up to the First World War than there were in the 1880s, even if the numbers were still small. But there was still the same problem of male responsibility for offspring. One 'would-be Freewoman', commenting on a previous correspondent's desire 'to bear children for her own ends and . . . seek no aid from anyone', remarked 'it is what we all want.' But she faced the problem of economic dependence on her husband: 'Can any of your

Fem Movement

correspondents find a remedy for my own case? I am a clergyman's wife . . . and have a child.' How was she to be able to support herself if she broke away?[57] While some contributors (H. G. Wells, for example) argued for the state endowment of motherhood, others, like the women of the Men and Women's Club in the 1880s, thought this would let men off the hook again.

High on the agenda of the 'new moralists' was the demand for women's sexual pleasure and the destruction of the myth of female sexual passivity. They held that not only should women be allowed to be sexual, but that sex was a natural function, needing frequent exercise like all natural functions,[58] and thus as a corollary it was dangerous for women to deny or repress their sexuality. Like many feminists before them, they held that we had evolved a distinctly human and spiritual aspect to our sexual relationships: the capacity to love. It was certainly positive for women that they were seen to have an active sexuality, but this view unfortunately acted to undermine the status of the spinster.

It appears that in order to claim a sexual identity, the new moralists felt the need to lampoon those women socially labelled 'asexual'. Anti-spinster imagery was widely prevalent in society at large, but it is disconcerting to find it so repetitively on the pages of a feminist journal. For example, the spinster was referred to as 'the withered tree, the aciduous vestal under whose pale shadow we chill and whiten . . . She is our social Nemesis . . . She rules the earth . . . A restive but impotent world . . . writhes under her subtle priestly domination'.[59] Another problem with the new moralists' stress on women's sexuality was that they tended to see any problems in sexual relationships as largely the fault of the woman. This was no doubt partly due to their use of sexology. In its construction of a new language of sex, sexology did not start from *women's* experience but from men's. Once again women were defined in terms of *male* desire. The feminists of the 1880s had made the critique of male sexuality central to their analysis of women's subordination. Such a critique was unfortunately largely from the pronouncements of this new generation of 'free women'.

During the First World War, advances women had made with respect to their sexuality were undermined. There were attempts to reinstate the Contagious Diseases Acts which had been repealed in 1886; and there were extraordinary restrictions put on the movements of all women and surveillance of their sexual behaviour,[60] the 'rationale' being the troops' 'need' for protection from VD. The tide had turned, and once again women were blamed and controlled and men went free.

Conclusion

In the 1880s and early 1890s, many middle-class women appeared to have agreed that the present marriage system was immoral: it was mercenary; it was a form of 'legalized prostitution' in the sense that the wife was effectively the husband's property, including his sexual property; it frequently involved non-consensual sex and undesired childbearing; and the divorce laws backed up the double standard of morality. Change was thus needed on economic, moral and legal fronts simultaneously. The ideal, whether thought of as ideal *marriage* or ideal *union*, was seen as one of permanent monogamy based on mutual attraction, companionship, economic and social equality and, above all, love. Love was spoken of in spiritual, almost religious terms, involving not merely physical union but the union of souls.

Disagreement arose largely in relation to two connected issues: the exact nature of the ideal future relationship and the strategy for moving towards that ideal. First, there was the question of whether the ideal partnership of the future should be a state-recognized (i.e. public) contract, or a private affair between two individuals – a 'free marriage', 'free union' or 'free alliance' (the terms tended to be used interchangeably). Second, there was the question of whether for the *present*, given current inequalities, women should stick with legal marriage or attempt to live outside its confines, which required great courage. As we have seen, even the radical members of the Men and Women's Club tended to feel highly ambivalent towards those attempting to live this alternative vision. Although quite a number of women were able to say that they did not necessarily need marriage and were content to be single, it appears that not many actually wanted its abolition. While a fair number of women were able to accept the status of 'spinster', they did not wish for that of 'free lover'. If women were to have sexual relationships with men, they wanted them sanctioned by legal marriage.

In the early twentieth century, many feminists interlaced the demand for an equal moral standard with the demand for the vote. There was further 'speaking out' on the physical dangers of marriage, and the call for men to change their sexual practices became increasingly uncompromising. Yet not all feminists were happy with this approach. On the pages of the journal *The Freewoman*, feminists heatedly debated their different beliefs and practices in relation to sexual morality. A small grouping held to a 'new morality' which put forward 'free unions' as the best solution to the injustices of marriage. Although in a minority within the women's movement, their stress on an active female sexuality was a clear gain for women. Less beneficial was their denigration of the spinister and of all women who did not conform to their new image of 'natural' and vigorous heterosexuality.

After the war, the older tradition of feminism was further undermined by a flood of sex and marriage manuals attempting to recruit women into active participation in heterosexuality.[61] Sexology was gaining a hold and the feminist attempt to develop a new language had failed. It is only since the early 1970s, with the re-emergence of the women's movement, that women are again forcefully speaking out on male sexual behaviour and demanding that rape and violence be recognized as prevalent inside marriage as well as outside. This time hopefully we are *combining* this with a positive assessment of the potential of our own sexuality.

Bibliographical Notes

In thinking about questions of sexuality, Judith R. Walkowitz's work is a great inspiration. Although her *Prostitution and Victorian Society* (Cambridge University Press, Cambridge, 1980) deals with a slightly earlier period, it sets the scene for understanding discussions of sex in the 1880s and 1890s. Her article, 'Male Vice and Feminist Virtue: Feminism and the Politics of Prostitution in Nineteenth Century Britain', *History Workshop Journal* 13 (1982) deals, however, more directly with this later period and raises certain problems with feminist ideas on sexuality. Linda Gordon and Ellen Dubois, 'Seeking Ecstasy on the Battlefield', *Feminist Review* 13 (1983) is also thought-provoking on this issue.

There are several good biographies which have been helpful in thinking about the themes of this chapter. Ruth First and Ann Scott's *Olive Schreiner* (Andre Deutsch, 1980) is an obvious choice, also Yvonne Kapp's *Eleanor Marx* (Virago, 1979), vol 1 and 2; Gillian Kersley's *Darling Madame: Sarah Grand and Devoted Friend* (Virago, 1983) is fascinating, as is Sybil Oldfield's *Spinister of this Parish: The Life and Times of F. M. Mayor and Mary Sheepshanks* (Virago, 1984). A number of recent books usefully discuss the 'new woman' novel of the 1890s: see Gail Cunningham, *The New Woman and the Victorian Novel* (Macmillan, 1978), Elaine Showalter, *A Literature of their Own* (Virago, 1978) and Patricia Stubbs, *Women and Fiction: Feminism and the Novel 1880–1920* (Harvester Press, Susses, 1979). The short stories of George Egerton have recently been republished as *Keynotes and Discords* (Virago, 1983) and are an intersting read. Another welcome reprint is Cicely Hamilton's *Marriage as a Trade* (The Women's Press, 1981), first published in 1909, which is as witty and relevant today as it must have been then. Iris

Minor's 'Working Class Women and Matrimonial Law Reform 1890–1914', in D. Martin and D. Rubinstein (eds), *Ideology and the Labour Movement* (Croom Helm, 1979) is a very useful overview of working-class women's attitudes towards the law on marriage and divorce.

Notes

Many thanks for Deirdre Bland's encouragement, Ann Bottomley's legal knowledge, the helpful comments of Martin Durham, Richard Johnson, Jane Lewis, Jonnie Turpi and Zoe Wicomb and Jane's endless patience with my delays in finishing this chapter.

1 See Carl Degler, 'What Ought To Be and What Was: women's sexuality in the nineteenth century', *American Historical Review* 79 (1974), 1467–90.

2 Men and Women's Club, minutes and correspondence, *Pearson Collection* (University College, London).

3 See Sheila Jeffreys, 'Free from all Uninvited Touch of Man', in L. Coveney et al., *The Sexuality Papers* (Hutchinson, 1984).

4 See Lee Holcombe, 'Victorian Wives and Property: Reform of the Married Women's Property Law 1857–1882', in Martha Vicinus (ed.), *A Widening Sphere* (Methuen, 1977).

5 See Frances Power Cobbe, 'Wife-torture in England', *Contemporary Review* 32 (1878).

6 See Lee Holcombe, *Victorian Women at Work* (David and Charles, Newton Abbott, 1973).

7 *Westminster Review* (January 1984).

8 Frances Martin, 'The Glorified Spinster', *Macmillans Magazine* 58 (1888).

9 Sarah Grand, in *The Young Girl* (1898–9), quoted in Deborah Gorham, *The Victorian Girl and the Feminine Ideal* (Croom Helm, 1982).

10 Maria Sharpe, *Autobiographical History of Men and Women's Club* (1889), *Pearson Collection*

11 Men and Women's Club, minutes, July 1885, *Pearson Collection*.

12 Ibid.

13 Ibid.

14 Emma Brooke to Karl Pearson, letter, 14 March 1886, *Pearson Collection*.

15 Men and Women's Club, minutes, June 1887, *Pearson Collection*.

16 Ibid., 12 October 1885.

17 Sharpe, *Autobiographical History*, p.41.

18 See Ruth First and Ann Scott, *Olive Schreiner* (Andre Deutsch, 1980), pp.152–3, and Sharpe, *Autobiographical History*.

19 Emma Brooke to Karl Pearson, letter, 13 February 1886, *Pearson Collection*.

20 Henrietta Muller to Maria Sharpe, letter, May 1887, *Pearson Collection*.

21 Men and Women's Club, minutes, June 1887.

22 Karl Pearson, 'The Woman Question' (1885), in his, *The Ethics of Freethought* (Adam and Charles Clack, 1887).

23 See Sheila Jeffreys, 'The Spinster and her Enemies', *Scarlet Woman* 13 (1981), part 2.

24 Sharpe, *Autobiographical History* p.2.

25 Men and Women's Club, minutes, 10 December 1888, *Pearson Collection.*

26 Men and Women's Club, minutes, 2 June 1887.

27 Sharpe, *Autobiographical History*, p.27.

28 Ibid., p.61.

29 Men and Women's Club, minutes, 12 March, 1888.

30 Annie Eastty to Maria Sharpe, letter, 18 March 1888, *Pearson Collection.*

31 Henrietta Muller to Karl Pearson, letter, 18 March 1888, *Pearson Collection.*

32 Men and Women's Club, minutes, 13 December 1886.

33 Henrietta Muller to Karl Pearson, letter, 29 March 1888, *Pearson Collection.*

34 Lillian Harman, 'The New Martyrdom', *The Adult* (January 1898).

35 Elaine Showalter, *A Literature of their Own* (Virago, 1978).

36 See Sarah Grand, *Heavenly Twins* (Heinemann, 1893); Ellis Ethelmer, *Woman Free* (Woman's Emancipation League, Congleton, 1893); and Emma Brooke, *A Superfluous Woman* (E. F. Brooke, 1894).

37 Linda Gordon and Ellen Dubois, 'Seeking Ecstasy on the Battlefield', *Feminist Review* 13 (1983).

38 George Egerton, *Keynotes and Discords* (Virago, 1983, first published 1894), p.248.

39 See the work of the Social Purity Alliance, established in 1873 – *Annual Reports*, London.

40 Egerton, *Discords*, p.157.

41 Louisa Martindale, *Under the Surface* (Southern Publishing Co., Brighton, 1908).

42 Ethel Snowden, *The Feminist Movement* (Collins, 1911).

43 Martindale, *Under the Surface*.

44 Christabel Pankhurst, *The Hidden Scourge and how to end it* (E. Pankhurst, 1913).

45 Frances Swiney, *The Bar of Isis* (C. W. Daniel, 1907), p.39.

46 Pankhurst, *The Hidden Scourge*, p.25.

47 Cicely Hamilton, *Marriage as a Trade* (The Women's Press, 1981, first published 1909), pp.133, 35, 54.

48 Pankhurst, *The Hidden Scourge*, pp.19–20.

49 Frances Swiney, *The Awakening of Women* (William Reeves, 1908), p.220.

50 Lucy Re-Bartlett, *Sex and Sanctity* (Longman, Green & Co., 1912), pp.25–6, 33.

51 Pankhurst, *The Hidden Scourge*, pp.121, 98.

52 Women's Cooperative Guild, *Working Women and Divorce: an Account of Evidence to the Royal Commission on Divorce and Matrimonal Causes* (David Nutt, 1911), p.6.

53 West, 'The Divorce Commission', *The Clarion*, 29 November, reprinted in Jane Marcus, *The Young Rebecca* (Macmillan, 1982).

54 See Coralie Boord, *The Freewoman*, 4 January 1912, p. 130.

55 See 'The New Morality', *The Freewoman*, 14 December 1912, 28 December 1911, 4 January 1912.

56 Kathleen Oliver, *The Freewoman*, 15 February 1912, p. 252.

57 'Would-be Freewoman', *The Freewoman*, 18 July 1912, p. 353.

58 See A. B., *The Freewoman*, 1 February 1912, p. 213.

59 *The Freewoman*, 23 November 1911, p. 10.

60 See Lucy Bland, 'In the Name of Protection: the Policing of Women in the First World War', in Julia Brophy and Carol Smart (eds), *Women-in-Law* (Routledge & Kegan Paul, 1985).

61 See Sheila Jeffreys, 'Sex and Anti-Feminism in the 1920s, in London Feminist History Group (ed.), *The Sexual Dynamics of History* (Pluto Press, 1983).

Top left: A Malthusian Appliance c. early twentieth century   Bottom left: Assorted caps and pessaries c. 1920.   Right: Various contraceptive devices, including The 'Racial' suppository, sponges and caps developed by Marie Stopes c. 1920

6

Women and Reproduction, 1860–1939

Barbara Brookes

Giving birth was an experience shared by the majority of women in the years from 1860 to 1939 and, increasingly, this experience took place within marriage. As 'illegitimate' births declined in the late-nineteenth century, formal marriage became more firmly entrenched as a necessary precondition to the bearing and raising of children. Marriage patterns and rituals diverged according to class and locality but the sexual division of labour within marriage was invariably maintained.[1] The sex that bore children also raised them. The *social* norms of reproduction: that it should take place within the family unit and that it was a married woman's primary duty to care for children at home, were more firmly established. At the same time, the *individual* experience of reproduction was opened up to wider scrutiny as the state investigated maternal mortality, doctors attended more births, and middle-class women sought to inform working-class women about birth control.[2]

A number of social constraints, considered in the first section of this paper, influenced the decisions women made concerning reproduction. Foremost amongst these was the belief that childbirth should take place within marriage, an assumption that made intercourse outside marriage full of risk for women.[3] During the early twentieth century, patterns of fertility became of national concern because they seemed to suggest a decline in both the quantity and quality of births. Family limitation was clearly being practised and for a variety of reasons which both contemporaries (and recently historians), have sought to understand.

The decline in family size, the timing of which varied by class, had important implications for women's experience of marriage and motherhood. The Victorian belief that procreation was the 'primary purpose' of marriage[4] gave way to a new emphasis on companionship and sexual fulfilment. Marriage manuals of the inter-war years stressed a 'vigorous and harmonious sex life' as one of the main ingredients of an 'ideal marriage'.[5] The emotional content of marriage changed significantly, middle-class couples expected greater intimacy and could give more attention to each individual child. Childbirth (and contraception) became subject to greater bureaucratic scrutiny and medical intervention. In spite of the fact that they spent less time in childbearing, women's primary commitment continued to be defined in terms of home and family, with negative implications for any outside employment. The assumption that marriage and the family life were the bedrock of social stability remained firmly intact.

Decisions about reproduction were made within a patriarchal culture. A women's private decision to remain childless, or the method she chose to limit births, often conflicted with the public perception of women's supposed maternal nature. It is this individual decision-making that is the focus of the second part of this chapter. Individual cases allow some understanding of how and to what extent women controlled their lives, and, in turn, helped shape the broader dimensions of the demographic revolution of the late-nineteenth and early-twentieth centuries.

Finally, reproductive decisions must be considered in relation to women's autonomy/dependency within marriage, in their relations with other women, and in relation to medical professionals. The quality of the relationship between husbands and wives influenced the type and success of methods chosen for family limitation. It also determined whether sexuality was a mutual source of pleasure or an area of conflict and pain. Support outside of marriage came from female relatives and friends. Women's shared biological condition gave a basis for understanding which prompted women to assist each other with fertility control. This protective community, however, was being gradually eroded by the medical profession's assumption of authority in reproductive matters.

Social Aspects of Marriage and Reproduction

Marriage was an important social ritual in the lives of most women and constituted the legal tie whereby their subordination to men was sharply delineated.[6] Not only did it involve the transfer of legal rights and often property, it also dramatically affected the status of the participants.[7] Weddings could be elaborate or perfunctory according to material circumstances, but either way they signified adulthood and new responsibilities. Through marriage women acquired new status as a wife and potential mother, which no doubt helped to compensate for the dependency that marriage entailed. It was assumed that the family unit would include children and first births often followed the marriage ceremony quickly.

In the Victorian period marriage, sexuality and reproduction were inextricably entwined for those who aspired to middle-class 'respectability'. Within marriage the church regarded sexual intercourse as the sacred means to reproduction. If methods were employed to frustrate reproduction, or if intercourse took place outside of marriage then the sacredness of sex was profaned.[8] Women who were sexually active outside marriage were branded as 'fallen' and in need of reform.[9] Celibate spinsterhood was also derided, along with childlessness, for both thwarted women's 'characteristic function in human life' – reproduction.[10] Marriages and motherhood were regarded as socially necessary for the continuance of the 'race', and as integral to the health of individual women. Popular tracts suggested that the necessary cure for a variety of 'female troubles', including dysmenorrhoea, was marriage and children.[11] Childbearing, then, was central to the fulfilment of a woman's life and such fulfilment was only possible within marriage.

The stigma of pregnancy outside of marriage was heightened in the nineteenth century by the Poor Law of 1834, which introduced punitive sanctions against unwed mothers.[12] The assumption that the stable two-parent family was both normative and desirable pervaded poor-relief legislation, and later welfare provisions reinforced this trend. By the inter-war years payments for dependents or priority for council houses, for example, were given to 'respectable' families. The development of state benefits, T. C. Smout has noted for Scotland, literally made formal marriage pay.[13]

Whether these disincentives to illegitimacy encouraged premarital chastity is a question that remains to be answered. Whatever the underlying causes, illegitimacy declined by 40 per cent in the last quarter of the nineteenth century.[14] By the late 1930s, 'illegitimate' births, which rose during the First World War, amounted to less than 5 per cent of the total yearly births in England and Wales.[15] Robert Roberts recalled that in Salford the shame of illegitimacy was such that a pregnant single woman lowered 'not only the social standing of her family but, in some degree, that of all her relations'.[16]

Childlessness, expected of single women, became disturbingly common amongst the married in the early twentieth century. The number of childless marriages doubled from slightly over 8 per cent in the 1870s to 16 per cent in the years following 1914.[17] The decline in the birth rate began first amongst the upper classes and in under sixty years the total fertility rate was more than halved. From an average of 6 children in the 1860s, family size declined to 2.19 children born to those married from 1925 to 1929.[18] The downward trend in births was at variance with imperial ideology. By the first decade of the twentieth century, public rhetoric was loud and insistent on the need for more births for the good of the nation and the empire.[19]

Dismay at the falling birth rate was entangled with concern about the physical efficiency of the population.[20] To those who equated social standing with genetic worth, notably the eugenists, the differential in the birth rate between social classes raised the spectre of a country populated by a race of degenerates. The eugenics movement achieved institutional status in 1914 with the establishment of a eugenics laboratory in the University of London,[21] and it continued to flourish in the inter-war years. Eugenists took a selective approach to reproduction, arguing that more births were necessary amongst the upper-classes and fewer among the unfit. In fact some advocated state control of reproduction, recommending sterilization of 'mental defectives'.[22]

Reasons were sought for why the 'fit' were limiting births. Doctors and clergymen often blamed the decline in the birth rate on the 'selfishness' of middle-class women and stressed that maternity was women's highest goal. In 1920, the Conference of Anglican bishops noted the 'sinister phenomenon' of the decline in the birth rate and commended to Christian women the 'deep wisdom' of the New Testament teaching that 'she shall be saved through her childbearing'.[23] Many other similar warnings were ignored and the birth rate continued to drop so that, by the inter-war years, the previous differential between classes had evened out and the family size of all socio-economic groups was relatively small.[24]

Both contemporaries and present-day demographers and historians have puzzled over the factors that caused the crude birth rate to fall from 36.6 per thousand of the population in 1876 to 24 per thousand by the First World war.[25] In an attempt to explain the nineteenth-century middle-class decline in fertility, Joseph Banks has argued that the economic depression of the 1870s and 1880s undermined middle-class confidence in the future and encouraged the use of birth control to maintain living standards.[26] Banks assumes that it was the rational decisions made by middle-class men that led to family limitation. Thus he glosses over the differing relationship of women and men to the reproductive process.

From similiar though earlier demographic trends in America, Daniel Scott-Smith has argued that the decline in middle-class fertility offers an indication of 'domestic feminism' (the power and autonomy exercised by women within the family).[27] Women's increasing authority within the home, he suggests, enabled them to insist on abstinence or *coitus interruptus* (withdrawal) in order to make motherhood voluntary. This interpretation of family limitation raises interesting questions about the control women exercised in marital relationships. Yet it is only by looking at individual decisions rather than extrapolating from the statistics on the birth rate that an understanding of the power relationships between couples may be reached.

For working-class women, the experience of reproduction changed as infant mortality declined. Infant deaths became a much less familiar event after 1911 and women could more reasonably expect that the children they bore would reach adulthood. At the same time, compulsory education and restrictions on child labour combined to make children more of an economic liability than an asset (see chapter 3). It appears that working-class women resorted to traditional methods of fertility control with greater frequency as they sought to adjust to changes in the socio-economic system.

Women certainly had a great deal to gain from limiting births. First and foremost, the risks of death in childbirth increased with each successive birth. Maternal mortality was second to tuberculosis as a major cause of death among married women from 1911 to 1930 and, between 1923 and 1936, the maternal mortality rate actually rose.[28] Second, repeated childbearing brought health problems such as slit cervixes, prolapsed uteruses and varicose veins. A survey of 1,250 working-class wives carried out by the Women's Health Inquiry Committee in the late 1930s clearly showed that multiple pregnancies led to problems of backache, haemorrhage and lassitude.[29] Third, the emotional and physical burdens of childcare fell directly on mothers. It was only a privileged few who could afford nannies and servants to reduce domestic drudgery. Indeed many working-class women did domestic labour for others by taking in washing or doing part-time charring, thus carrying a double burden of domestic work. Although working-class men aspired to assert their 'respectable' status by having a non-working wife, many found this difficult to achieve. Married women's paid work, fitted in around family needs, was often part-time and hidden. In addition childcare was, in the words of one woman, 'hard work'.[30] The care of young children, which had formerly been the responsibility of elder siblings, fell more directly on mothers after the introduction of compulsory schooling.

Married women who worked outside the home had special reasons for wanting to limit births. Regular paid employment gave them a degree of financial autonomy and they often enjoyed the company of others in the workplace.[31] The combination of employment, marriage and children, however, was difficult not only because of the lack of child care, but also because of the claims of the growing child-welfare movement. Concern over the safety of infants in the late-nineteenth century led to attempts to regulate working-class women's factory employment. Dr George Reid, Medical Officer of Health for Staffordshire, produced figures in the 1890s to suggest that women's employment was correlated with high infant deaths. At his instigation the Factory Act of 1891 prohibited women from resuming work within a month of confinement.[32] Since the onus was on employers to implement this Act, it was unlikely to have been enforced. What was significant was the attempt to restrict women's employment opportunities with the aim of protecting infant life.

Middle-class women who wished to pursue professions such as medicine also faced difficulties when they attempted to combine career and family. In the 1920s, regulations requiring women to resign on marriage were introduced in teaching, the civil service, and in medicine. Marriage, Margaret Cole wrote in 1938, had evolved a novel purpose in that it was now expected to be a married woman's sole career, incompatible with any other employment.[33] One critic of married women teachers expressed a common view in a letter stating that 'if marriage as a profession does not appeal to a woman, she should remain single'.[34] By the inter-war years, the 'profession' of marriage for women entailed higher standards of housework and an undivided commitment to the physical and emotional needs of a small family of two or three children.

While the time women spent bearing children decreased, a new emphasis was placed on female sensuality within marriage. In 'The Sexual Impulse in Women', Havelock Ellis challenged the interpretations of nineteenth-century sexologists such as Acton and Krafft-Ebbing, who believed that the female sexual appetite was much less than that of the male.[35] Abstinence, he argued, was unhealthy for both sexes. This line of reasoning was taken up in popular marriage manuals and birth-control literature, which emphasized that 'sex union is a physiological and psychological need for the majority of virile individuals.'[36] Marriage manuals stressed the importance of satisfactory sex in giving meaning to marriage: meaning that had once been provided by parenthood. Husbands were now made responsible for their wives' sexual satisfation and the 'passionlessness' expected of the Victorian 'lady' in sexual matters was perceived as a threat to marriage, and was relabelled 'frigidity'.[37] The popularity of Marie Stopes' *Married Love*, published in 1918 and selling six editions in that year, testifies to the rising interest in sexual pleasure.[38]

Stopes was not a medical doctor and only a few in the medical profession, such as Helena Wright and Edward Griffith, authored popular marriage manuals.[39] In general, medical attention centred on the biological rather than the sexual aspects of reproduction. With increasing medical intervention, the 'naturalness' of reproduction for women receded. Birth became an event subject to notification and was more likely to be attended by a doctor than a midwife.[40] Reports on infant and maternal mortality argued that medical intervention was necessary to save infants and mothers. More attention was directed towards women's health, not in terms of their individual requirements but as 'the human casket of precious unborn life'.[41] The tie between sexuality and reproduction was loosened as women and men took measures to control births, yet women's needs remained defined solely in terms of their biological potential for motherhood.

Births, then, were declining both inside and outside of marriage and couples of all classes were likely to spend more time together alone and less as active parents by the inter-war years. In the nineteenth-century, large families were considered to provide the basis of a stable marriage while, by the 1920s and 1930s, the emphasis had shifted to the importance of compatibility between couples to provide the cement for marriage. However, it would be wrong to think of this as a seamless and smooth transition. Important differences existed between social classes. Ellen Ross has suggested that in working-class London emotional segregation between the sexes was the norm at least until the First World War.[42] In the tenements, women continued to look to children, female kin and friends for happiness and expected little emotional intimacy from their marital partners. It was amongst the middle classes that the new ideal of 'companionate marriage' took root.[43]

Individual Decisions to Control Fertility

Official statistics and public pronouncements highlighted the social dimensions of the demographic transition from high death and birth rates to low death and birth rates. What was less apparent were the attitudes and behaviour of the inarticulate women and men whose individual or joint decisions shaped the broader graph of fertility decline. By the late-nineteenth century aggregate explanations for smaller families, such as marriage rates and age at marriage were less important than the behaviour of individual married couples. The overall marriage rate varied little and the total percentage of the population who married increased slightly. Age at marriage for women rose from 22.5 in the 1860s to 25.3 in 1911 but this rise alone could not explain the halving of the birth rate.[44] The problem confronting historians, as Mary Ryan and Diana Gittins have suggested, is how to uncover the private decision-making that collectively determined the wider history of reproduction.[45] We need to understand why and how individuals limited births and what role spouses, lovers and female friends played in this process.

One way into this private sphere is through diaries and letters where literate women recorded their observations on contraception and reproduction. Jane Austen's letters, for example, contain the advice to a friend that to avoid continual childbearing she should adopt 'the simple regimen of separate rooms'. The diary of a governess records more active measures in the case of a married woman who 'took something when pregnant of her little girl, [and] intended it to fall upon the child'.[46] However detail like this, particularly because of nineteenth-century female reticence on such matters, remains tantalizingly brief.

By the twentieth century the field of sources widens a little beyond those with the leisure and self-consciousness to keep a diary. The Women's Cooperative Guild published a volume of letters entitled *Maternity* in 1915 which revealed that the idealized joys of maternity were remote from the reality of working-class lives. In these letters women discussed their reasons for family limitation. Frequent pregnancies, miscarriages, overcrowded and poor housing, bad health and sheer poverty were mentioned with distressing regularity. 'Motherhood', one correspondent wrote, was 'very nice if one has plenty to bring up a family on', but many women perceived each child as an extra 'strain on the family exchequer'.[47]

The efforts of working-class women to maintain their families on limited budgets became more visible as the state intruded into previously private aspects of women's lives. The 1918 Maternity and Child Welfare Act established local authority maternal and child-welfare committees and permitted the authorities to provide salaried midwives, health visitors, infant-welfare centres, day nurseries, and food supplements for needy infants and mothers.[48] Health visitors, district nurses and the staff at welfare centres, most of whom were female, learned of the difficulties involved in family limitation. It was soon clear that working-class women did not always use contraceptive devices to limit births. The records of one study of the health of 'artisan' families in London are instructive. During the period 1926–9 investigators found that

> the methods used [to limit family size] were very rarely indeed, contraceptive. They were methods applied not before but after pregnancy was assumed to have occurred. At this date married people were quite incredibly uninformed on the matter of birth control. Without understanding the significance of what they were doing, in the early stages of pregnancy they were using methods which, in fact, were abortifacient in action. If unsuccessful, in the later stages they frequently resorted to desperate attempts at frank abortion. The married woman was in the habit of anticipating her menstrual period by drenching herself with violent purgatives, or by resorting to any other of the reputed means for interruption of pregnancy – not only chemical, but physical.[49]

Records from the birth-control clinics that opened in the 1920s and 1930s were similarly revealing. One study of seven English and two Scottish clinics that served an overwhelmingly working-class clientele revealed that 'from a third to a half of all pregnancy losses resulted from miscarriage, natural or self-induced.' This was likely to be an understatement for the clinics did not press their clients for information on abortion. According to data collected at the Liverpool clinic, *coitus interruptus* was by far the most commonly employed method of birth control used prior to attendance at the clinic. The sheath represented a far less popular second preference, while abortifacient pills or implements ran a close third. Again the investigator was led to comment that the latter were 'known to be much more common than these figures suggest'.[50] The Walworth Women's Welfare Centre also reported that the older women who came for advice habitually brought on miscarriages 'by the use of drugs and other ways – invariably with injury to themselves, as individuals and as mothers'. The women who established a clinic in

Salford found that attempted abortion was 'almost a convention' amongst working-class women as soon as they realized they were 'caught' again.[51]

What do these reports tell us about working-class attitudes to reproduction and sexual relationships? Clearly both women and men wanted to limit births. If we classify birth-control measures in terms of male or female methods, then we may learn something of the power relationships between couples. Methods such as withdrawal or the sheath relied primarily on male initiative, though we may assume that they required a degree of cooperation to be effective. Withdrawal, for reasons of immediacy and economy, was regarded as the simplest method. Women were thankful for husbands who were 'careful'. In the words of one: 'Much depends on what kind of husband the wife has. A woman cannot possibly get on if she has a bad, worrying husband.'[52] This description of male sexual demands as a 'worry' is reinforced by Slater and Woodside's study of urban working-class marriages. They found that wives valued their husbands in 'an inverse relation to sexuality'. Praise for husbands who were 'very good' was qualified by statements such as 'he doesn't bother me much'.[53] Some husbands were prepared to practise abstinence to prevent pregnancy. Others were not so considerate. One mother of five wrote that her Catholic husband 'does not believe in stopping life by any means when I say I do not want any more he gets very nasty with me and he wont [sic] try to keep me right.'[54] In this case and in others documented by Leonora Eyles in *The Woman in the Little House*, sexual relations were a matter of 'demand and supply'.[55]

Coitus interruptus was certainly popular but, as one birth-control pamphlet warned, 'doctors consider it may be injurious'.[56] Addressing the Fifth International Neo-Malthusian and Birth Control Conference, Dr W. H. S. Stoddard stated that *coitus interruptus* could lead to anxiety, neurosis and abdominal fatigue, particularly among women.[57] Abstinence was also under attack. Marie Stopes attributed diseases ranging from neuralgia and 'nerves' to fibroid growths in women, to the practice of celibacy.[58] Traditional non-appliance methods of birth control were condemned by middle-class advocates of 'scientific' contraception. By focusing on particular contraceptive methods, the birth controllers often lost sight of some of the express reasons that working-class women gave for family limitation. They frequently underestimated the difficulties of using the cervical cap, for example, in housing that lacked privacy and running water.

The manufacture of the 'Poor Man's Friend' or condom improved in the early twentieth century. Enid Charles' study of birth-control practices amongst middle-class women concluded that 'the sheath heads the list of single methods for reliability'.[59] Condoms ranged in price according to quality. The durable and reusable 'Everlasting Sheath' cost 1/6d to 2/6d each. 'French Letters' were 4/— to 6/— per dozen, while thin 'Spanish Skins' were priced at 10/— per dozen around 1920.[60] They were therefore not always within the reach of the working-class budget and their association with prophylaxis against venereal disease made them less than respectable. The association of 'artificial' contraceptive devices with sin and vice was strong and gave them a reputation for harm. One woman claimed that the sheath her husband used 'caused' inflammation and kidney trouble. Another reported that a Harley Street specialist attributed her amenorrhoea and irregularity 'to constant use of a condom'.[61] To many, devices employed during intercourse were 'looked upon as a sin against the Holy Ghost', while it remained quite acceptable for women to exchange remedies for delayed menstruation.[62]

Women discussed birth-control methods such as soluble pessaries made from cocoa butter and quinine, cervical caps, sponges and douching. 'Both the Soluble Pessary and the Mensinga Pessary', one birth-control pamphlet claimed, had 'the great advantage that they may be used, if necessary, without the knowledge of the husband'.[63] When a follow-up study was carried out of clients from one birth-control clinic, it was found that of the 58 women visited, 4 had discontinued use of birth-control devices because of their husbands' disapproval.[64] For men who had little authority outside the home, power in sexual relationships was perhaps a means of asserting their masculinity. In these cases sexuality was clearly an area of conflict between couples.

Wives who wished to avoid conflict over birth control could resort to abortifacient measures without consulting their spouses. Women had their own networks for procuring abortion which, because abortion was illegal, were secretive and part of an oral, not a written, tradition. Insights into these networks can be gleaned from hospital and criminal records from the inter-war years. They make it clear that women took active steps to control their fertility in the face of legal and religious condemnation. The criminal records, although unrepresentative because cases only came to court when the abortion resulted in death, also gives an insight into the circumstances that led women to reject maternity.

The great majority of abortion cases involved married women. Of the 280 women admitted for incomplete abortion studied at Crumpsall Hospital in Manchester in 1938, 253 were married.[65] Often the first step a woman took when her period was overdue was to buy pills or potions 'to bring the period on'.[66] Pills containing lead or a tonic composed of oil of absinthe were among the abortifacients taken which had serious or fatal consequences.[67] Abortifacients were advertised widely in the press and in popular circulars. A typical advertisement was the for 'Rene Dubois Pilules', priced at 5/– for 'all irregularities. Guaranteed speedy and effective even in the most obstinate and unyielding cases. Act like magic, and are effective in a few hours.'[68] The author of the popular pamphlet 'The Wife's Guide and Friend' suggested using the 'Hygena' spray syringe to douche with two or three pints of hot water.[69] Soap or disinfectant were often added to the water in the hope of procuring an abortion.[70]

Syringing with quinine and soap was the method of abortion used by Millicent Fraser who came to court charged with the murder of one woman and the miscarriage of seven others in Rochdale. Married, separated and single women visited Millicent Fraser for help after learning of her skill from workmates and friends.[71] Another abortionist, May Wilson, favoured the use of slippery elm which, when inserted into the mouth of the uterus, caused it to dilate as it absorbed moisture.[72]

Previous difficult births, poor housing, and unemployed husbands were some of the reasons women gave for family limitation. Queenie Marshall's doctor 'as good as said she could not live through another childbirth'. He gave her 'certain advice' [presumably on birth control] but she became pregnant again. Her worried husband was happy to pay a Dr Devi Sasun ten guineas for an abortion. A mother of two, Eveline Judge was 'anxious not have another child for health reasons'. She paid Francis Duck seven pounds for a successful douche.[73]

Husbands sometimes assisted their wives' efforts to abort. Frank Sanderson, a bus driver, was charged with manslaughter for 'abetting Phyllis Sanderson to feloniously slay herself'. He protested that 'he had no intention of doing any harm to his wife'. Mrs Sanderson was in the habit of taking medicine when her periods were due as a preemptive measure. When it became clear that she was pregnant she tried soap and water douches and strapping across the naval in an attempt to miscarry. The Sandersons did not want another child (a previous child had died aged three), for, Mr Sanderson said, 'we were badly fixed and couldn't get a place of our own'. They shared a house with Mrs Sanderson's sister and parents.

Frank Sanderson bought a male catheter, a remedy for an unwanted pregnancy suggested by a workmate, from a surgical instrument store. The catheter, when inserted, caused Mrs Sanderson acute pain and led to her death from blood poisoning. Beatrice Kent, her sister, testified that Frank and Phyllis Sanderson were devoted to each other. Clearly, he had no intention to harm her and was horrified at her death.[74]

However, in other cases, husband's actually compelled their wives to take abortifacient measures. A postman obtained the names of abortifacient drugs from a co-worker when his wife became pregnant for a second time. The child was born in spite of the drugs and his wife conceived a third time. He 'accused her of not taking the "medicine"' and forced her to take large quantities of a drug that caused her severe illness. The husband appeared in court charged with assaulting his wife.[75]

Female friends usually took a compassionate view when a woman was faced with an unwanted pregnancy. Emma Coulter aborted Mary Mason, a professional singer, 'out of kindness'.[76] Elsie Friend, brought to trial in 1925, had been in business as an abortionist since 1913. In her view she was performing a necessary service because the women she treated 'could not afford many more children'.[77] When Maisie Roberts came to trial for the death of Betsy Hill she stated that she had 'treated 800 cases in 25 years and that Betsy was her first fatality'.[78]

Single women and widows who were pregnant sought to avoid scandal, poverty, or an unwanted marriage. In some cases they were aided by the men responsible for their pregnancy. Sarah Smedley, for example, found herself pregnant and unwed. The man responsible for her condition paid her father £130. Part of this sum, no doubt, went to pay for her visit to a shop in Villiers Street, London. The shop, ostensibly for hairdressing, carried on a business in 'regulators, medicines, pills and appliances'. After an operation there, Sarah Smedley found 'I was no longer in the family way'.[79] Sarah preferred an abortion to the scandal of unmarried motherhood while the man responsible was happy to pay her father for his part in her pregnancy rather than marry her.

Alice Smith, a widow, was assisted by her boyfriend Sydney Hamblin when she found herself pregnant. He bought various drugs and pills for her but none were successful. Alice eventually asked her friend Hannah Barrow to take her to an abortionist. After four douches over succeeding weeks Alice Smith 'took poorly' and a doctor was called. Alice refused his suggestion that she should go to hospital because 'she did not want anyone to know on account of her pension'.[80] Widows' pensions, introduced for the wives of insured workers in 1925, were dependent on the woman remaining faithful to her dead husband. Evidence of a new relationship undermined a widow's claim to support because it was assumed that the man involved would support her.

Some women preferred the risk of an abortion to that of a shotgun wedding. Gregory Kettle, a cinema operator, offered to marry Amy Kent with whom he had been 'keeping company' for eight months. She told him of her pregnancy and asked him 'to do anything to get rid of the child'. She refused to marry him 'because she did not care for him enough and he could not keep her'.[81] Ellen Mullane, pregnant by her landlady's son, also refused to consider marriage. She would not, she said 'marry a man who [sic] she was indifferent to'.[82]

Individual decisions to limit births, then, were influenced by a variety of factors including income, health and housing problems, and women's desire for autonomy. Choices about how to control births were limited by the available methods and by the quality of the relationship between partners. Husbands and wives could cooperate in the joint goal to limit births, employing foresight and care which made the use of *coitus interruptus* or pessaries, for example, more likely to be effective. When spouses failed to agree on the need for birth control, intercourse could be fraught with tension and women sometimes took the responsibility of limiting births into their own hands, often assisted by other women. Similarly, unmarried women faced with possible pregnancy turned, when their partners failed them, to female friends for help.

The information gathered at the birth-control clinics testified to the fact that methods of family limitation were well-entrenched in working-class life. However, they were not the medically approved devices that the birth controllers advocated. The comments of C. V. Drysdale of the Malthusian League were representative of the continual pleas of the birth controllers. 'I would like to express', he stated, 'the hope that the greatest care will be taken to avoid any confusion between the results of prevention of conception on the one hand and of abortion or attempted abortion on the other, as the whole subject has been seriously obscured by such confusion.'[83] In stressing the difference between contraception and abortion the birth controllers were making a new distinction in the process of conception which had previously been viewed as a continuum.

Female networks for information about and assistance with

fertility control were being undermined by medical assertions that life began at conception. Such a distinction could not be easily integrated into the circumstances of women's lives. Traditional beliefs that life began at quickening persisted with a tenacity that enabled women to procure abortion early in pregnancy without undue worry or guilt. And women knew from experience that, despite the protestations of the medical profession and the legal publicity given to fatalities, abortion was relatively safe. In 1935, 512 maternal deaths were attributed to, or associated with, abortion.[84] For the same year the demographer David Glass estimated that there were 68,000 criminal abortions.[85] There is no way of gauging the reliability of this estimate but it does suggest a mortality rate below 1 per cent. Thus abortion could be an acceptable option and one women might prefer to scandal, unemployment or family poverty. By turning to family or friends for help to 'bring on' a period, women had no thought of committing a crime and they were generally outside the purview of the law.

Autonomy and Dependency

'The modern woman', Professor Sydney Smith noted in 1932, 'had her own point of view, and that was that she had control of her own body, and if she was not inclined to go through the trouble and inconvenience of childbearing there was no moral right to compel her to do so'. To Professor Smith, this view was 'illogical' because it denied the right of the state 'to exercise control over the destruction of its future citizens'.[86] Yet for most women the problem was that the state did so little to cater for the needs of its 'future citizens'. Since all women were subsumed under the identity of the selfless mother, problems of childcare, the isolation of mothering and the drudgery of housework, were not given adequate recognition. While the needs of mothers remained unmet, women ignored the pleas of the pronatalists for more births to counter the threat of underpopulation. In light of the demands of motherhood, women made rational choices to limit births.

Whatever means of family limitation women chose, from a self-procured abortion to a medically fitted cervical cap, they were seeking to control their fertility, with or without their partner's consent. The rhetoric praising motherhood was at odds with women's experience of maternity. By the inter-war years women regarded unrestricted childbearing as akin to disease, for it undermined their health and threatened to overturn precariously balanced budgets.

Too many children also conflicted with the new middle-class ideal of companionate marriage. Leisure pursuits shared by young couples, such as a visit to the pub or cinema, ended abruptly with the advent of children. The disorganization caused by children hindered attempts to create a tranquil home. The demands of motherhood also warred against sensuality. Women, a writer in *Good Housekeeping* commented in 1938, had been convinced by Freud 'that they had sex desires and that these desires were not wicked; that to repress them was as difficult and dangerous to women as to men, and that they need no longer pretend that what they wanted was at most motherhood, when it was quite as natural for them to want loverhood'.[87] Women were now to be both sensual and maternal, roles that had previously been regarded as contradictory.

But there were clear tensions involved in attempting to divorce sexuality from reproduction. If contraceptive methods should fail, it was women who endured the stigma, if unmarried, and the extra burden of work , if married. There was now a new pressure to achieve a satisfactory sex life. Sex was something to be 'worked at'. 'Knowledge, sympathy, courage and persistence', one marriage manual advised, were 'the necessary weapons' for a successful marriage.[88] The equation of a satisfactory marriage with a satisfactory sex life put a novel element of tension into the marital relationship. Constrained within marriage by numerous social factors, many women could not accept that bad sex equalled a bad marriage.[89] Kindness and consideration remained far more important than the mutual orgasms that the marriage manuals recommended.

Women's sexuality continued to be hedged around with restrictions. There was no space for the sexually active woman who was not dependent on a particular man. 'Birth control', one popular tract promised, was the 'Charter of Freedom' for a woman, 'her real emancipation from slavery'.[90] However, it was freedom from continual childbearing, rather than the promise of women's sexual integrity, that the author addressed. Female dependency within heterosexual relationships existed within a larger framework of sexual inequality. Women's biological potential for motherhood was deemed a sufficient reason to restrict their participation in all other spheres.

The possibilities that effective contraceptive devices offered were carefully limited by policy makers. In 1930, as a result of pressure from birth-control organizations and women's groups, maternal- and child-welfare centres were enabled to give birth-control information in certain circumstances. This reluctant official sanction of contraception applied only to nursing or expectant mothers, thus it did not endanger the link between sexuality and reproduction.

In fact it was the voluntary clinics, often organized and run by middle-class women, that provided greater access to contraceptive devices such as the diaphragm. Most of the birth-control advocates (Stopes was an important exception) agreed that medical practitioners were best qualified to give birth-control advice. By doing so they narrowed the possibilities for alternative outlets. Provision of birth control in a clinical context allowed the exercise of moral control. The North Kensington Women's Welfare Centre, for example, discouraged women from using contraceptives until they had at least one child and suggested that they should have more than one.[91] Norman Himes, who conducted a number of studies of birth control usage, advocated methods such as the diaphragm, which required fitting by a doctor. To Himes, medically fitted devices were superior because they provided an 'opportunity for society to control the proper use of them'.[92] Even in the early 1970s, the Medical Defence Union advised practitioners not to fit an intra-uterine device for a woman without the consent of her husband.[93]

All the birth-control clinics restricted their advice to the married and the National Birth Control Association, renamed the Family Planning Association in 1939, widened its scope to include marriage guidance.[94] The boundaries of sexuality, therefore, remained circumscribed. The new emphasis on sexual pleasure that effective contraception gave rise to also brought the possibility that women's right to sexual pleasure could come close to being a marital duty.[95] This was the fear of opponents of birth control such as Dr Mary Scharlieb who argued in 1921 that contraception removed 'the wife's best protection against the slavery of too frequent intercourse'.[96]

The majority of women were probably most concerned about the quality of their children's lives when they decided to use birth control, a factor which their critics often overlooked. The Dean of St Paul's added his voice to the many who were disturbed by apparent population decline. Family limitation, he stated, was 'an abuse of [women's] newly won freedom' and it threatened 'to bring about a disintegration of society, and an increasing aversion from marriage on the part of men'.[97] Women's rejection of the maternal role challenged the accepted social order. Abortion amongst married women in particular threatened established boundaries.[98] It indicated that women were indulging in sex without any intention to procreate and so were detaching sexuality firmly from reproduction. Women's assertion of bodily integrity was, complained one doctor, 'feminism run mad'.[99]

The social framework within which women made their individual decisions about childbearing altered substantially over half a century. The emphasis on 'scientific' management of contraception and the birth process led to a devaluation of women's traditional knowledge and skills. Many women fought for and welcomed professional assistance which, by offering pain relief during labour, for example, had positive benefits. But the price of medical expertise was a diminution of women's control over their own bodies and a consequent loss of autonomy.

Between 1860 and 1939 the sexual division of labour dictated that total responsibility for child care fell on mothers alone. By the inter-war years, middle-class women could no longer rely on cheap and readily available domestic help, and the reduced size of the working-class family meant that women were unable to count on older children for help in the home. Moreover, domestic tasks had to reach higher 'scientific' standards in terms of both cleanliness and child care. These new demands on motherhood helped to bind women to domestic and nurturant roles, despite the fall in family size.

For most women, sexual expression and maternity continued to take place in a relationship of economic dependence with a man. What bargains and compromises were struck within relationships will never be fully known. But it is clear that, although they may have felt powerless to challenge the social conditions under which they lived, women did make individual choices as to when and how often they would bear children.

Bibliographical Notes

Jeffrey Weeks's *Sex, Politics and Society: The Regulation of Sexuality since 1800* (Longman, 1981) provides an overview for some of the themes discussed in this chapter. The issue of fertility control and the debates it aroused in the nineteenth century are analysed in Angus McLaren's *Birth Control in Nineteenth Century England* (Croom Helm, 1978). Individual women's experience of reproduction are given more attention in Jane Lewis, *The Politics of Motherhood: Child and Maternal Welfare in England 1900–39* (Croom Helm, 1982), Diana Gittins in *Fair Sex: Family Size and Structure,*

1900–39 (Hutchinson, 1982), has explored the interactions between husbands and wives, and the relations of both to kin and the workplace, in order to understand the central factors determining effective family limitation.

A full and moving account of working-class women's experience of reproduction is recorded in the volume *Maternity: Letters from Working Women* (Virago, 1978), originally published by the Women's Cooperative Guild in 1915. Letters requesting information on sexuality and birth control from a broad spectrum of the community are accessible in Ruth Hall (ed.) *Dear Dr Stopes: Sex in the 1920s*, (Andre Deutsch, 1978). Patricia Knight's essay 'Women and Abortion in Victorian and Edwardian England' in *History Workshop Journal* No. 4 (1977) discusses abortion as an aspect of the working-class 'female sub-culture'. The social, medical and legal aspects of abortion are the subject of my own PhD. thesis (Bryn Mawr College, 1982) which is at present under revision for publication.

Notes

I would like to thank Annabel Cooper for comments on the first draft of this chapter and Jane Lewis for her critical comments and helpful suggestions throughout its preparation.

1 On marriage patterns see D. V. Glass, 'Marriage Frequency and Economic Fluctuations in England and Wales, 1851 to 1934', in Lancelot Hogben (ed.), *Political Arithmetic: A Symposium of Population Studies* (Allen & Unwin, 1938), pp. 251–82, and Jeffrey Weeks, *Sex, Politics and Society; The Regulation of Sexuality since 1800*, (Longman, 1981), p. 201.
2 Roslind Pollack Petchesky has an excellent analysis of the individual biological dimensions of reproduction and the historically contingent social dimensions in *Abortion and Woman's Choice: The State, Sexuality, and Reproductive Freedom* (Longman, New York, 1984), p. 2.
3 For the risks of extra-marital sexuality see John Gillis, 'Servants, Sexual Relations, and the Risks of Illegitimacy in London 1801–1900', *Feminist Studies* 5 (1979), pp. 142–73.
4 Lambeth Palace, *Encyclical Letter from the Bishops, with Resolutions and Reports* (Society for Promoting Christian Knowledge, 1920), p. 100.
5 T.H. Van de Velde, *Ideal Marriage: Its Physiology and Technique* (Heinemann, 1956, first published 1928), p. 2.
6 Lee Holcombe, 'Victorian Wives and Property', in M. Vicinus (ed.), *A Widening Sphere: Changing Roles of Victorian Women*, (Indiana University Press, Bloomington, 1977), p. 4.
7 R.B. Outhwaite, 'Problems and Perspectives in the History of Marriage', in R.B. Outhwaite (ed.), *Marriage and Society: Studies in the Social History of Marriage* (Europa Publications Ltd, 1981), p. 11.

8 Derek Gill, *Illegitimacy, Sexuality and the Status of Women*, (Basil Blackwell, Oxford, 1977), p. 157.

9 Judith Walkowitz, *Prostitution and Victorian Society: Women, Class and the State*. (Cambridge University Press, Cambridge, 1980).

10 Lambeth Palace, *Encyclical Letter*, p. 100.

11 T.H. Reynolds, *Birth Control: Its Use and Abuse*, Collis Collection, Birth Control Ephemera, vol. 6, British Library of Political and Economic Science, hereafter C.C. BLPES), p. 23.

12 Gill, *Illegitimacy*, p. 212.

13 T.C. Smout, 'Scottish Marriage, Regular and Irregular, 1500–1940', in Outhwaite, *Marriage and Society*, p. 227.

14 R.A. Soloway, *Birth Control and the Population Question in England, 1877–1930* (University of North Carolina Press, Chapel Hill, 1982), p. 4.

15 C.L. Mowatt, *Britain Between the Wars, 1918–1940* (University of Chicago Press, Chicago, 1955), p. 515, n.5.

16 R. Roberts, *The Classic Slum: Salford Life in the first quarter of the Century*, (Manchester University Press, Manchester, 1971), p. 30.

17 Soloway, *Birth Control*, p. 8.

18 Weeks, *Sex, Politics and Society*, p. 202.

19 Anna Davin, 'Imperialism and Motherhood', *History Workshop Journal* 5 (1978), 9–65.

20 G.R. Searle, *The Quest for National Efficiency: A Study in British Politics and British Political Thought. 1899–1914* (Basil Blackwell, Oxford, 1971), p. 71.

21 D. Mackenzie, 'Eugenics in Britain', *Social Studies of Science* 6 (1979), 503–5.

22 Michael Freeden, 'Eugenics and Progressive Thought: A Study in Ideological Affinity', *The Historical Journal* 22 (1979), 666–7.

23 Lambeth Palace, *Encyclical Letter*, p. 100.

24 E. Lewis-Faning, *Report on an Enquiry into Family Limitation and its Influence on Human Fertility during the Past Fifty Years* (HMSO, 1949), p. 10.

25 Soloway, *Birth Control*, p. 4.

26 J.A. Banks, *Prosperity and Parenthood: A Study of Family Planning Among the Victorian Middle Class* (Routledge & Kegan Paul, 1954).

27 Daniel Scott Smith, 'Family Limitation, Sexual Control, and Domestic Feminism in Victorian America', in M. Hartman and L. Banner (eds), *Clio's Consciousness Raised* (Harper & Row, New York, 1974), pp. 119–36.

28 Jane Lewis, *The Politics of Motherhood: Child and Maternal Welfare in England, 1900–1939* (Croom Helm, 1980), pp. 36, 117.

29 Margery Spring Rice, *Working Class Wives* (Penguin Books, Harmondsworth, 1939).

30 Diana Gittins, *Fair Sex: Family Size and Structure, 1900–39* (Hutchinson, 1982), p. 137.

31 Ibid., p. 104.

32 F.B. Smith, *The People's Health*, (Croom Helm, 1979), p. 95.

33 Margaret Cole, *Marriage: Past and Present* (J. M. Dent & Sons, 1939), p. 198.

34 Alison Oram, 'Serving Two Masters? The introduction of a marriage bar in teaching in the 1920s', in The London Feminist History Group (ed.), *The Sexual Dynamics of History* (Pluto Press, 1983), p. 141.

35 Phyllis Grosskurth, *Havelock Ellis: A Biography* (Alfred Knopf, New York, 1980), p. 225.

36 Pamphlet, *Points for Propagandists on the Problem of Population and its Solution* (1925), C.C. BLPES, vol. 1, p. 5.

37 On 'passionless' see Nancy Cott, 'Passionless: An Interpretation of Victorian Sexual Ideology', *Signs: Journal of Women in Culture and Society* 4 (1978), 219–36. On the rise of the label 'frigid', see Sheila Jeffreys, 'Sex Reform and Anti-Feminism in the 1920s', in *The Sexual Dynamics of History* (Pluto Press, 1983), pp. 177–202.

38 Ellen Holtzman, 'The Pursuit of Married Love: Women's Attitudes toward Sexuality and Marriage in Great Britain, 1918–1939', *Journal of Social History* 16 (1982), p.39.

39 Helena Wright, *The Sex Factor in Marriage* (Noel Douglas, 1930); Edward F. Griffith, *Sex in Everyday Life* (Allen & Unwin, 1938).

40 Lewis, *The Politics of Motherhood*, pp. 117–61; Jean Donnison, *Midwives and Medical Men: A History of Inter-Professional Rivalries and Women's Rights* (Schocken Books, New York, 1977).

41 Spring Rice, *Working Class Wives*, p. 19.

42 E. Ross, ' "Fierce Questions and Taunts": Married Life in Working-Class London, 1870–1914', *Feminist Studies* 8 (1982), 575–602.

43 See, for example, Judge Ben Lindsay and W. Evans, *The Companionate Marriage*, (Boni and Liveright, New York, 1927).

44 Soloway, *Birth Control*, pp. 9–11.

45 Mary P. Ryan, 'Reproduction in American History', *Journal of Interdisciplinary History* 10 (1979), 324; and Gittins, *Fair Sex*.

46 Banks, *Prosperity and Parenthood*, pp. 143–4.

47 Margaret L. Davies (ed.) *Maternity: Letters from Working Women* (Norton, New York, 1978, first published 1915), pp. 89–90.

48 Lewis, *The Politics of Motherhood*, p. 34.

49 I. Pearse, *Observations on the Population Question*, Memorandum presented to the Royal Commission on Population, November 1944, p. 5.

50 Norman Himes, 'British Birth Control Clinics', *Eugenics Review* 20 (1928), 158–62.

51 *Eugenics Review* 15(1923), 599; 7 Cecily Mure, Charis Frankenburg, and Mary Stocks, 'Birth Control Pioneers', Documentary Transcript, *Yesterday's Witness*, BBC, broadcast 21 April 1969.

52 Davies, *Maternity*, p. 171.

53 E. Slater and M. Woodside, *Patterns of Marriage: A Study of Marriage Relationships in the Urban Working Classes* (Cassell & Co., 1951), p. 168.

54 Ruth Hall (ed.), *Dear Dr Stopes: Sex in the 1920s* (Andre Deutsch, 1978), pp. 41–2.

55 M.L. Eyles, *The Woman in the Little House* (Grant Richards, 1922), p. 37.

56 George H. Swasey, 'Large or Small Families?' (Liberator League, 1920?), C.C. BLPES, vol. 1, p. 6.

57 Dr W.H.S. Stoddard, *British Medical Journal* (BMJ) 22 July 1922, p. 133.

58 Marie Stopes, *Married Love* (A. C. Fifield, 1918), p. 107.

59 E. Charles, *The Practice of Birth Control: An Analysis of the Birth Control Experiences of Nine Hundred Women* (William & Norgate, 1932), p. 37.

60 Swasey, 'Large or Small Families?', p. 6.

61 Slater and Woodside, *Patterns of Marriage*, p. 206.

62 Roberts, *The Classic Slum*, p. 100. Claud Mullins, commenting on women's reluctance to attend birth control clinics, wrote 'contraception is not . . . considered "respectable", but harmful methods of birth control, and even abortion, are.' *Marriage, Children and God* (Allen & Unwin, 1930, p. 159.

63 Swasey, 'Large or Small Families?', p. 7.

64 N. and V. C. Himes, *Birth Control for the British Working Classes: A study of the first thousand cases to visit an English birth control clinic* (Reprinted from *Hospital Social Service* 19, 1929), C.C. BLPES, vol. 3, p. 612.

65 Ministry of Health, 71/21, Public Record Office, Kew.

66 *BMJ*, 21 July 1900, p. 201.

67 *BMJ*, 16 August 1902, p. 504.

68 Dr Ostermann, *Birth Control: Husband and Wife's Handbook* (Marble Arch Pharmacy, 1938), C.C. BLPES, vol. 10, p. 9.

69 S. Warren, *The Wife's Guide and Friend* (A. Lambert, 1927), C.C. BLPES, vol. 9, p. 10.

70 *BMJ*, 21 July 1928, p. 129; 25 February 1929, p. 328. ASSI/468; CRIM 1/408, Public Record Office, Chancery Lane, hereafter, PRO. Names from these Assize and Criminal Court records have been changed to protect the identity of those involved.

71 ASSI 52/318, PRO.

72 ASSI 52/469, PRO. The Medico-Legal Society reported in 1933 that 'slippery elm is still being used largely to procure abortion in different parts of the country.' *The Medico-Legal and Criminological Review*, 1 July 1933, p. 171.

73 CRIM 1/184; CRIM 1/408, PRO.

74 CRIM 1/187, PRO.

75 Mullins, *Marriage, Children and God*, p. 77.

76 *The Times*, 6 March 1925, p. 11.

77 *The Times*, 21 July 1925, p. 11.

78 *The Times*, 3 December 1925, p. 11.

79 CRIM 1/181, PRO.

80 ASSI 52/475, PRO.

81 CRIM 1/188, PRO.

82 ASSI 52/468, PRO.

83 Evidence to the National Birthrate Commission, National Council of Public Morals, *The Declining Birthrate: Its Causes and Effects* (Chapman

& Hall, 1916), p. 95.

84 James Young, 'The Part Played by Contraception and Abortion', *The Medical Press and Circular* 'Declining Fertility Series', 28 July 1937, p. 74.

85 This figure was based on the British Medical Association's upper estimate of 20 per cent of abortions as deliberately induced. D. V. Glass, *Population Policies and Movements in Europe*, (Clarendon, Oxford, 1940), p. 54.

86 *BMJ*, 7 May 1932, p. 844.

87 Cited in Cynthia White, *Women's Magizines, 1693–1968*, (Michael Joseph, 1970), pp. 107–8.

88 Wright, *The Sex Factor in Marriage*, p. 64.

89 Holtzman, 'The Pursuit of Married Love', p. 47.

90 Pamphlet, *Points for Propagandists*, p. 5.

91 *BMJ*, 12 January 1929, p. 76.

92 N. Himes, *Practical Birth Control Methods*, (Modern Age Books, 1938), p. 124.

93 Medical Defence Union, *Law and the Doctor*, (Medical Defence Union, 1975), p. 30.

94 Audrey Leathard, 'The Development of Family Planning Services in Britain', unpublished PhD. thesis (London School of Economics, 1977), p. 158.

95 Elizabeth Wilson, *Only Halfway to Paradise: Women in Postwar Britain, 1945–1968* (Tavistock Publications, 1980), p. 90.

96 *BMJ*, 16 July 1921, p. 94.

97 W.R. Inge, *Christian Ethics and Modern Problems* (Hodder and Stoughton, 1930), p. 286.

98 Petchesky, *Abortion and Women's Choice*, p. 78.

99 *BMJ*, 26 November 1932, p. 969.

Part IV
Compatibility and Tension in Marriage

Teaching Domestic Science at Crawford Street School 1906

7

'A New Comradeship between Men and Women': Family, Marriage and London's Women Teachers, 1870–1914.
Dina M. Copelman

We do not know what Mrs H. S. Polkingthorne, a London School Board teacher active in women teachers' affairs at the turn of the century, had to say when she gave a lecture with the above title in 1901.[1] Perhaps she was thinking of new types of relationships that women such as herself – married, full-time teachers active in the profession and, increasingly, feminist — were trying to develop.

Some 25 per cent of the women teachers in London's late Victorian and Edwardian state schools were married.[2] Whether or not a 'new comradeship' was indeed the result, the mere existence of these women who attempted to have dual-career marriages (something usually regarded as a more recent phenomenon) requires a re-evaluation of our assumptions about Victorian and Edwardian gender relations and gender ideology. This chapter attempts to do this by examining first, the family patterns among late Victorian labour aristocratic and lower-middle-class families – the social groups from which teachers in the period under consideration were recruited;[3] second, the lives of those women teachers who combined work and marriage, public and private life; and, third, their responses to attacks that were increasingly made upon their position from the 1890s onwards.

Community, Work and Family

The Victorian ideal of women as 'Angels in the House', guardians of a separate, domestic, female sphere divorced from the male, public world of work, has been put to rest. We are aware that running a home, even a middle-class one with servants, involved a great deal of work. For working-class women the ideal was even more hollow, given the cost of trying to establish it. Instead, as Elizabeth Roberts has shown, working-class women had to engage in all sorts of strategies to keep their families alive, and Ellen Ross has pointed out how married working-class women formed community networks which provided both economic and personal support.[4] In reality if not in ideology, the spheres – whether defined as public/private or work/home – were never really separate.

Yet certain assumptions persist. We still assume that the removal of women from 'productive' work was an important form of raising status and that, as Joan Scott and Louise Tilly have stated, married women engaged in paid work only if 'family finances urgently required it'.[5] The family behaviour of the labour aristocracy and the lower-middle class, however, suggest that this was not universally true.[6]

In London, the persistence of workshop production kept up the demand for skilled artisans. Even though little factory industry existed, an active construction sector and the growth of transport and trades such as printing produced a substantial stratum of skilled, regularly employed and stable workers: a labour aristocracy, for want of a better term.[7] The London economy also nurtured the growth of the lower-middle class. The expansion of local and national government, as well as London's role as a national and international financial centre required educated clerks. Similarly, the growth of large-scale retailing created a significant white-collar group of shop workers. Finally, the many local communities supported a variety of small shopkeepers – the backbone of the 'old' lower-middle class.

The hallmarks of respectability – thrift, family centredness, self-reliance – were important aspects of how both these groups defined themselves. As other scholars have recently pointed out, these values cannot be explained simply in terms of either the imposition or emulation of middle-class beliefs and behaviour.[8] Gender roles among both these groups provide an example of the complex way in which notions of respectability were negotiated. Both labour-aristocratic and lower-middle-class husbands could, for instance, often afford to keep their wives and other women in the family, out of the labour force. Yet both single and married women's work was an integral part of labour-aristocatic and lower-middle-class communities. On any high street, women could be found working: the greengrocers', the pharmacy, the corner shop, the stationers' all employed women. Often, these were family operations in which wife and children worked alongside the male 'provider'. Sometimes, women were the proprietors, as in the case of laundries and dress shops.[9] The growing arm of the state also had its working women representatives in the guise of telegraphists, telephone operators, and as teachers in the increasingly numerous Board schools. The many women commuting to work in offices and stores in other parts of the city should be added to these women employed in local communities. Finally, women engaged in a variety of economic activities inside the home, such as taking in lodgers and sewing.[10]

Lower-middle-class and some working-class autobiographies often describe a suffocating family closeness.[11] Yet the other side of that intensity was a generally greater intimacy among family members than was found among middle-class families, and a lesser attachment to Victorian gender roles. It is rare to find the frail or neurasthenic mother here. Instead, mothers waged an unceasing struggle to stretch resources and to keep up appearances, usually without the help of servants. Their toil, and the fierce passions that guided them, stand out in the memoirs of their sons and daughters; the fathers are usually rather shadowy and ineffectual figures.

Daughters also had a larger role in upper-working-class and lower-middle-class families. Although burdened with domestic responsibilities, they were brought up to be something more than household drudges or domestic ornaments. Throughout the nineteenth century, girls from these families were most likely to receive a nearly identical education to their male peers. Unlike poorer working-class girls, they were less likely to be kept out of school in order to help out at home and, unlike middle-class girls, they went to the same schools as their brothers. In those schools the boys' and girls' curriculum differed, but was still closer in content than that taught to most middle-class girls.[12]

Parents wanted their daughters to be prepared for some sort of occupation. Unlike working-class parents, they could afford to forgo their daughters' earnings for a while and allow them to acquire some skills and training. But, in contrast to middle-class parents, they did not feel they could support their daughters past adolescence, at least not if they wanted to maintain their standard of living. Therefore, among these generally stable but not affluent families, respectability was defined more in terms of maintaining an overall family income rather than keeping women out of the labour force. This is evident in the life of Helen Corke, the daughter of a conservative and status-conscious Croydon family in the 1890s. Corke's autobiography describes the strain her indecision caused the family before she settled on teaching as a career. For eighteen months after completing the highest standard in her local Board school at the age of fourteen, she tried to enjoy her freedom and dreamt of becoming a writer. However, 'as my sixteenth birthday nears I face the fact that it is essential to search for some occupation which will bring me a wage.'[13] After a trial position as a clerk for a large grocery firm, and eight months working in the local post office/newsagent/stationers' hoping to learn telegraphy and move on, she finally chose to do what had originally been expected of her and became a pupil teacher.[14]

Most women did not marry until their mid- or late-twenties, and parents were also aware that their daughters might be among the many women who never married or who had to engage in paid work after marriage. This meant that parents wanted their daughters to enter occupations that would provide them with skills, security and opportunities for promotion. For instance, testimony to an 1898 Parliamentary investigation into the training of teachers revealed that parents often preferred to send daughters into the civil service rather than teaching because of the graduated scale of promotions and the existence of a pension scheme.[15]

Parents and siblings cooperated to ensure that all the children, whether male or female, would have a chance to establish themselves in respectable, and satisfying work. Thus F.H. Spencer explained that he had turned down a much desired scholarship to stay on an extra year at Borough Road Training College because

> the domestic situation at home, with my father ageing rapidly and two younger sisters to be cared for (one of them also a teacher, not yet at College, the other a musician in great need of training), and a family income of about £2 a week was serious. How could I in any conscience take a third year at College?[16]

These young working women and men often had both considerable financial responsibilities to their families, and a considerable degree of independence, at least compared with some of their middle-class counterparts. Even Helen Corke, from her cloistered environment, joined local musical groups, and with schoolteacher friends went to the theatre, on expeditions and holidays.[17] H.G. Wells, who presented himself as a native expert on the ways of the lower-middle class, described another form of popular recreation in *The New Machiavelli*:

one evening I came by chance on a number of young people promenading by the light of a row of shops . . . the shop apprentices, the young work girls, the boy clerks and so forth . . . spend their first-earned money upon collars and ties, chiffon hats, smart lace collars, and came valiantly into the vague transfiguring mingling of gaslight and evening, to walk up and down, to eye meaningfully, even to accost and make friends.[18]

The expectation that women might have to work, and the attitude that this was a respectable undertaking also was extended to married women. A fictional example comes from George Gissing's novel *The Unclassed*. There Mr O'Gree, a miserable schoolteacher, is borrowing money to set up shop with his fiancée:

Sally's been behind the counter a good bit of late, and she's getting an insight into that kind of thing . . . Put her in Downing Street for a week, and she'd be competent to supplant the Premier! . . . We'll take a shop in a new neighbourhood, where we shall have the monopoly. The people'll get to know Sally; she'll be like a magnet behind the counter. I shall go to the wholesale houses and impress them with a sense of my financial stability . . . Who knows what we may come to? We'll turn out in the end another Crosse and Blackwell, see if we don't.[19]

The couple get married and do indeed set up shop in a new neighbourhood in South London. When visited by the friend who loaned them the money to get started, the husband proudly shows his guest through the new shop and home:

'We pass, you observe' . . . cried the ex-teacher, 'from the region of commerce to that of domestic intimacy. Here Mrs O'Gree reigns supreme, as indeed she does in the other department, as far as presiding genius goes.'[20]

A somewhat less glorious but real-life example can be found in Helen Corke's lower-middle-class family. There the mother worked periodically with the father in his shops, and at one point set up a sweet shop in her own house when the father's business failed and he took a job with an insurance company.[21] In these examples the wife/mother's work was conducted by combining family and occupational repsonsibilities, reinforcing Louise Tilly's and Joan Scott's statement that married women tried to 'find that work which conflicted least with their domestic responsibilities'.[22] However, Scott and Tilly's contention that married women worked only as a last resort must be revised in light of the patterns of married women's work considered here. Similarly, Geoffrey Crossick's conclusions that 'for [lower-middle-class] wives and children the repressive force must have been enormous. Without wider contacts of any real intimacy, with an isolated experience in a shapeless suburb where appearances had to be maintained, and entrance into the street had to be regulated for display, the tedium and frustration must have been intense' must be qualified.[23]

Work and family life were not perceived as diametrically opposed or as competing claims by lower-middle-class women. They would experience both, usually a period of work followed by marriage, but sometimes both simultaneously. Respectability, after all, meant opportunities for advancement and the ability to earn enough to maintain oneself, and often others, at a decent standard. Given this background, perhaps it is not surprising that among London teachers the work of married women, was, if not the experience of the majority, at least an accepted practice.

Who were these women who, in the words of late-nineteenth-century contemporaries 'served two masters'?[24] As young, single women teachers often already had very heavy family responsibilities. For example, Agnes Mason, teaching in Croydon during the early 1900s, was her family's 'mainstay'. The eldest in a family of eight, 'the father and mother [were] semi-invalid, partially dependent both for income and personal attention . . . More than half of Agnes' [£75] salary goes to pay . . . rent and rates.'[25] Nevertheless, though living at home and hampered by family responsibilities, Agnes probably enjoyed, like Lavinia Orton, 'some degree of independence' because of the financial and social status accorded them as teachers. This was, as Lavinia's son would later remark, 'an unusual freedom for young women' in the last decades of the nineteenth century.[26]

Teachers tended to take advantage of London's lower-middle-class cultural and social world. The activities they participated in were usually 'uplifting' in nature, but they also provided social outlets where young women teachers could mingle with men and women of their own age. In fact the London School Board expressed alarm about the activities of the Metropolitan Board Teachers' Association (MBTA) and issued warnings that it would permit the Association to hold meetings on school premises only if there was no dancing![27] Finally, summer holidays were considered essential after the hardships of the school year and teachers' newspapers abounded with travel suggestions, ranging from frugal British holidays to complicated Continental and even American itineraries.[28]

By the time women teachers married, therefore, they had considerable experience in handling work and financial responsibilities; they had cultivated social interests, had often travelled and had had the opportunity to develop close personal relationships. Those who married and chose to continue working were in all probability making a conscious decision about both work and marriage.

No doubt for some marriage involved upward social mobility and those women were probably the ones most likely to leave work. Others married 'beneath' themselves, and there is certainly evidence of women teachers married to skilled and semi-skilled manual workers and to men who were only casually employed.[29] Such cases, however, were probably the exception rather than the rule, and most women teachers married men similar to themselves both in background and occupation. Richard Church's autobiography *Over the Bridge* provides a sensitive portrait of one such marriage. His mother, Lavinia Orton, was a schoolteacher and his father, a postal clerk. The two had met at a Christmas party for people connected to a church where the father sang. At that time Thomas Church was working as a mail carrier. As would be true for the rest of their lives, Lavinia, who was five years older, took the lead in their courtship. Her son wrote that 'Mother was undeterred' by her father's opposition to the relationship (he had already driven away one suitor) and

> as often as possible she met Father when he came off duty at a branch of the South West District Office . . . The lovers would then stroll up and down the Birdcage Walk and the Mall, while she coached him in arithmetic, grammar, and the other elements required from candidates for the Civil Service examination for Post Office sorters.[30]

They were married in 1888, and from that time on

> Mother had, in addition to her school-teaching, to do the planning and take the responsibility for the family economy . . . In [Father's] eyes she could never make a mistake, either as lover, mother or chancellor.[31]

Many women teachers married other teachers. Not surprisingly male and female teachers, coming into contact at work and in their leisure time activities developed romantic interests in each other. Courtship then became a part of everyday life, as in the case of Miss Clarke and Mr Hopper, assistant teachers in the same school in 1892. As their headmaster remarked, 'Mr Hopper had of late found it necessary to give Miss Clarke the assistance of his arm to walk along Old Kent Road when coming to School.[32]

Many of the dual-career marriages resulting from the marriage of two teachers are impressive. Going down a list of 230 couples who both worked for the London School Board, it seems that an elite of the profession were married to other teachers. Of the 230 couples, 59 (25.65 per cent) were both headteachers. Some were among the most active members of the teachers' union. For instance, C.H. Heller, President of the MBTA in 1895 (and the brother of T.H. Heller, another teacher activist) was married to a teacher; J. le Manquais, an assistant teacher active in the MBTA and the National Union of Teachers (NUT) was married to a headmistress, who was also a union acitivist. This tradition continued, as demonstrated by Mrs M. E. Ridge. Married to another teacher, in 1912 she was active in both the London union and a separate feminist women teacher's union, and was secretary of the London Married Women Teachers' Association.[33] Clearly for many marriage was not an impediment but provided, instead, a context in which mutual interests could be sustained and developed.

Less dramatic than the cases above are the plentiful examples where work and personal life, intellectual interests and emotional bonds, could reinforce each other in these Webb-like partnership marriages. For instance, in 1885 Mr and Mrs Thrower, the head-teachers in a Hackney school asked 'to be allowed a month's holiday this summer as the Church-street, Hoxton school, from which they were transferred, was kept open at Christmas.'[34] This meant that they had been teaching together before, and managed to transfer together. Another couple, Mrs Harris, headteacher at Harrow-road, and Mr Harris, an assistant at the Middle Row School, asked for an extended leave in 1888 in order to go to Sweden to study Slojd, a system of teaching woodwork.[35] And at Credon-road in 1911, it was reported, disapprovingly, that Mr Hooten, a teacher in the boys' department, regularly went to the girls' department teachers' offices to have tea with his wife.[36]

In such marriages, while we can never know for sure, it is reasonable to assume that not just occupational interests were shared, but that decisions affecting the family were more likely to be taken jointly, especially in view of the financial contributions made by the wives. From the list of couples engaged by the London School Board, quite a number of women had higher positions and/or earned as much or more than their spouses (at a time when women's salaries were on average considerably lower than men's). Some women, like

Lavinia Church, were probably the dominant forces in their families, a by no means always enviable situation.

We must turn from teachers' opportunities for personal and intellectual growth to the more material consideration of incomes and family strategies as a necessary reminder that we should not romanticize their lives. For married women teachers, especially ones with children, the difficulties were daunting. Their supporters pointed out that they should

> not be confounded with ordinary working women employed from eight till eight, leaving their children to be minded by a girl not much older than themselves. No; married teachers live near their homes, and are absent three and a half hours in the morning and three hours in the afternoon. They have their evenings, also Saturday and Sunday in which to put right anything that may have gone wrong . . . [and] a child can still be nursed by a teaching mother. Most of them have a mother, or mother-in-law, or other relation dependent upon them who is thankful to manage the home in their absence.[37]

But this defence of married women teachers' work shows that in order to fulfill the responsibilities of both work and home, they had to work all day long. The life of Lavinia Church again testifies eloquently to this fact. Although a neighbouring woman took care of her two sons before they were of school age (Lavinia having returned to work soon after their birth) she ran the house by herself:

> Mother . . . was . . . exhausted by having two lives in one . . . [She did] the shopping on her way home from school. She made the beds at lunch-time . . . and frequently scrubbed the kitchen floor after the midday meal, before going to the afternoon session at school. In the evening she had the rest of the cleaning to do, the household sewing for four, the supper to get, and the rest of the tasks that usually keep the mother of a family busy from morning to night.[38]

Lavinia Church was lucky enough to work, at that time, close enough to their Battersea home to be able to go back and forth, although at midday she would come 'hurrying home, often short of breath and flushed, her eyes brighter than they need be.'[39] Her sons and husband also would provide some help, such as washing up, or heating the meals that she had prepared for them. Other women might not have been able to run such a tight ship. They had to add to their burdens daily travel to and from school, and child-care arrangements were often unreliable. Mrs. G.E. Jessman, a teacher at the Marner Street school in 1898 had to take temporary leave because her child's nurse had left. She explained that she could not 'divide her time between home and school and do justice to both, and for some time she must remain at home, but does not want to leave the Board's service'.[40] In 1911 another teacher had a different sort of child-care arrangement (reported by an unsympathetic observer). She had a 'young baby in charge of very young and inexperienced and unsuitable aunt who brought baby to school daily at midday to receive its natural nourishment (half hour journey each way)'.[41]

These cases all describe families under relatively normal circumstances. But in a time of crisis, things could be much worse and crisis – usually in the form of disease – was no stranger even to comfortable Victorian families. The School Board absence lists and requests for leaves abound with women having to nurse their families through illnesses (this was true of single as well as married teachers) and they serve as reminders that health care and medical science were very different matters a hundred years ago. One bout of scarlet fever and whole families could be wiped out. For instance, in 1892 Mr and Mrs Bailey, both assistant teachers at the Galleywall Road school, were absent because of scarlet fever in their house. Of their four children three had already died and the fourth was dying.[42] In an 1897 case, the Board was considering asking for the resignation of Mrs Andrews because she had not provided the right kind of medical certificate to explain her absences. Her husband wrote in to explain that 'she has had a great deal of worry during the past few years for in them we have had the trouble and whole expense of the illness and death of my father, her father and mother, and five of our children'.[43]

Not surprisingly women's health often broke down. Richard Church felt that his mother's health was worn out by her double service, and there were many instances of married women needing to take leave to regain their strength. But in fact there was never any conclusive proof that married women were more likely to absent themselves due to illness, whether their own or others'. What is striking is that so many teachers (married and single) suffered illness, and how tough married women must have been if they managed to continue to work.

Married women teachers seemed to accept their double burden and did not ask for special considerations. This is evident from the pattern of leaves taken for childbirth. In the 1870s and 1880s teachers continued to be paid while on leave, but they had to arrange for a substitute and pay her out of their salaries according to the substitute's qualifications. Most women took only four-weeks leave, a practice that continued into the 1890s. Between 1892 and 1894, of 315 leaves for confinements, 222 were for only four weeks after giving birth, and in another 37 cases the women absented themselves also for the week or two before their confinement.[44]

Starting in the 1890s, the mandatory maternity leave was progressively lengthened. Women were required to leave their posts sooner and stay out longer. By the First World War, a minimum of seventeen weeks' leave was required.[45] These changes originated with educational authorities, not with the women teachers. Indeed in 1907, when there was an attempt to extend the then mandated nine-weeks' leave, the London Teachers' Association Mistresses Sub-Committee argued against such a move.[46] They feared that not only would longer leaves disrupt the functioning of schools, but that they also would engender hostility towards married women teachers. For most married teachers, they felt, the old regulations were satisfactory, and if individual teachers needed more time for health reasons, they should apply for it on an individual basis.

In fact cases demonstrate that both teachers and educational authorities considered it quite normal for the mother of a young infant to be working. For example in April 1883 Mrs Vesey took a month's leave, and during that time she was appointed headmistress to the girls' department at Summerford Street, Hackney, a post she took up in June.[47] Her promotion while on maternity leave testifies that, in this period at least, married women teachers were considered valuable employees.

The economic motives behind married women teachers' determination to work need to be closely examined. Some were the sole or the main economic support of their families. However, most married women teachers, worked not to keep a family at subsistence level but, rather, to achieve and maintain a certain standard of living. For instance, when the London County Council attempted to reduce the Unattached Staff (teachers who were in the regular employment of the Council and served as replacements for teachers out ill or on leave) by dismissing the married women, Mrs Arabella Dowdell felt that 'if dismissed [from the Unattached Staff she] will be unable to help her children in the manner in which she is at present able to'. Similarly Mrs Alice Wyborn protested that she had 'contracted certain liabilities on the assumption that her engagement was permanent which she will be unable to meet if dismissed'.[48]

The income earned by women such as Mrs Dowdell and Mrs Wyborn could make a significant difference to a family. Teacher couples probably enjoyed a joint income of between £150 and £350.

Numerous contemporary and more recent estimates of late Victorian and Edwardian living costs calculate an annual income of £150 as the minimum for a lower-middle-class lifestyle.[49] Incomes of £300 might still be considered lower-middle class, but at the upper boundary. Thus, where husband and wife were both teachers, the dream of a suburban home could be realized. The family could also afford holidays, save, contribute more to benefit societies or insurance schemes and – particularly important for a working wife – afford a charwoman, or even a full-time servant, instead of having to rely on family or part-time childminders, if there were pre-school-age children.

A glimpse of what this might mean at the individual level is provided by Richard Church. The combined income of the Church family was £240 in the early 1900s, and Lavinia Church worked because she was 'ambitious to get a more substantial home together, with a house of her own'.[50] This she accomplished: first a semi-detached in Battersea then, in 1905, a £550 'Herne Hill oriental palace'.[51] Achieving these goals as well as supporting her sons until they were themselves safely established in lower-middle-class occupations (Richard's brother became a teacher and he became a clerk), and allowing the family to enjoy some other standard lower-middle-class comforts, such as a good piano and bicycles, meant that she had to impose a 'discipline of thrift' on the whole family. Her handling of the family finances was in fact all part of the way 'she loved us all with a fierceness that was desperate. It consumed her as it subdued us'.[52]

These economic motives induced many women to continue teaching, but most married women teachers also felt it important to exercise the skills acquired through long training and experience. An anonymous correspondent defended married women teachers (again, giving as an example a couple where both were teachers) by saying that 'assistant masters marry educated women, who cannot bring themselves to be household drudges'.[53] These sentiments were echoed by numerous respondents to a questionnaire sent out to married women on the Unattached Staff:[54] Mrs Annie Baldock prefered 'teaching to domestic duties'. Mrs Eliza M. Howard said 'Her home duties have not interfered with her work or her attendance at classes for improvement of qualifications, etc.; says her work is a necessity, not a pastime'.

Married women teachers were clustered disproportionately at the top and bottom of the teaching force. On the one hand, they were a substantial proportion of the women on the Unattached Staff which was where teachers whose service had been disrupted, for whatever reason, would be placed, irrespective of experience. On the other hand, a significant proportion of married women made impressive long-term careers of teaching. For instance, in 1908, 39 per cent of the women headteachers in London were married, and we have already seen that married women were among the more active leaders of the profession.[55]

Most married women, once they decided to combine home and work, stuck by their decision. And their long service was treasured. For instance, in 1911 Mrs Garlick, headteacher in the infants' department at Stanley street school, retired after more than 32 years service. Her colleagues gave her, among other things, a gold chain, a pendant, a brooch and pearls.[56] Also, if married women teachers broke down the distinctions between public and private by introducing occupational concerns into their home life, the reverse was also true. For example, personal events were often an occasion for honouring some of these teachers of long standing. In 1912 Mrs Emilie A. Smith, headteacher at Mantua Street, was given a party and presented with a silver napkin ring and silver-handled tea knives and forks on the occasion of her silver wedding anniversary.[57] These women had joined the school system when it was in its infancy and had developed along with it, some of them emerging as formidable spokeswomen for women teachers. While politically and educationally they held a wide variety of views, they all believed and ably demonstrated that marriage and careers were not mutually exclusive and, given their prominent position in the profession, it was hard to dismiss or ignore them.

Married Women Teachers and the Ideology of Domesticity

Clearly, women who decided to continue work after marriage, defined respectability more in terms of maintaining a certain standard of living, providing opportunities for their children and, in the view of some, exercising and gaining recognition for skills acquired through training and experience. Whether they hoped to achieve social mobility is unclear, but they certainly did not equate women's paid work with a lowered social status.

Evaluating the gender relations that shaped these women's lives at home and at work is more difficult. Certainly, if married women teachers managed to circumvent or bend dominant gender norms, they still had to operate under severe constraints. Their domestic responsibilities, one half of the work involved in 'serving two masters', were not reduced because they taught as well. Indeed, while on a personal level they might have had to endure exhaustion and the lack of spare time, on a public level their domestic attributes were frequently scrutinized and criticized.

When, in the period just before and after the First World War, there were movements to ban married women teachers, a constantly repeated argument was that they could not be proper wives and mothers. If they were not an invitation to 'lazy husbands' (men who would abdicate their responsibility to work and support families), then they were accused of knowing 'just as much and no more of domestic economy than the proverbial pig knows about handling a musket'.[58] Teachers' defenders responded that they *could* serve two masters, thus accepting the domestic sexual division of labour.

From the 1890s, however, bans were placed on the work of certain groups of married women and, between 1923 and 1934, on all married women teachers. This process was part of a more general decline in married women's work in the early twentieth century, accompanied by an increasing emphasis on men's duties as family providers, and 'a more elaborate domestic ideology defining the woman's role as mother and housewife rather than producer'.[59] In this new context, children were viewed differently as well, and there was more interest in 'the role of children *within* the home and family, as an enhancement of domestic and family ideals, than on their potential as future wage earners'.[60] This new attitude towards children was reinforced by greater state intervention in numerous aspects of family life which, while providing certain external supports, at the same time increased the period of children's dependency by extending their schooling, and placed a strong emphasis on mothers' responsibilities for such areas as health and nutrition.

Married women teachers found themselves in a paradoxical situation. As teachers they were a key group in spreading and carrying out these new views. As married working women they had to defend a life-style that seemed to contradict the very premises of the new domestic ideology. I would argue that in many ways married women teachers had problems defending their position because they themselves had developed some of these new attitudes to family and children. Gittins found no evidence of this domestic ideology among working-class couples where both worked full-time.[61] But this does not seem to be true of married women teachers, and perhaps the lower-middle class in general. Rather, it was concern for the quality of family life that led them to work after marriage in the first place.

The tensions inherent in their position were hard to bear in a period of direct attack on married women's work. The teaching profession as a whole and numerous other groups stood behind the rights of married teachers and London educational authorities were reluctant to ban their work, since they never found conclusive evidence that they were any less efficient than unmarried teachers. However, their position deteriorated in the early twentieth century.[62] The ideology of domesticity that already held women responsible for the home therefore also triumphed at work – it was stronger than married women teachers' attempts to innovate within its confines.

The troubles and triumphs of married women teachers at the turn of the century are hardly remote. Over half a century later we are still struggling to allow women the opportunity to have fulfilling private and public lives. Today we are questioning the institution of traditional marriage more; we have more control over whether or not to have children; we can benefit more from education and training; perhaps we have more political power. But the confusion expressed by Clara Bulcraig, a conservative single teacher and one of the *grande dames* of the profession in London, when asked her opinion on married women teachers' work in 1911 seems so immediate. She explained that

> It seemed easy enough in those old days, but, at present . . . it seems to me that the position of women generally has altered greatly during the last 40 years. The home-ties are weakening and we should be so glad to combine the English Housewife and strong home-ties with the intelligent woman who is able, without loss to the house, to take an interest in outside affairs.

But overall she realized that 'my position is somewhat contradictory and yet I am sure my intention is good and there is no lack of courage. The subject is complex'.[63] And so it has remained.

Bibliographical Notes

There is really no adequate history of teachers; the best is still Asher Tropp, *The School Teachers* (Heinemann, 1957). Frances Widdowson, *Going Up Into the Next Class* (Hutchinson 1981) provides an interesting discussion of women teachers' training, social origins and social status. For a useful account of white-collar work for women see Lee Holcombe, *Victorian Ladies At Work* (David & Charles, Newton Abbott, 1973).

Some of the most evocative sources for the social milieux from which women teachers were recruited are autobiographies. Particularly important are Margaret Bondfield, *A Life's Work* (Hutchins, 1949); Helen Corke, *In Our Infancy* (Cambridge University Press, Cambridge, 1975); and F.H. Spencer, *An Inspector's Testament* (English Universities Press, 1938). Richard Church's *Over the Bridge* (Heinemann, 1955) is an invaluable account of a married women teachers' life.

An interesting and more recent consideration of the themes explored here is Rhona and Robert Rapoport, *Dual-Career Families* (Penguin, Harmondsworth, 1971).

Notes

I would like to acknowledge the help and support of Mark G. Hirsch and the patience and editorial skills of Jane Lewis.

1 *Board Teacher* December 1901, p. 275. For other references to Polkingthorne see, among others, *Board Teacher* September 1898, p. 182 and October 1900, p. 210.

2 Figures on numbers of married women teachers are compiled from membership lists of the Metropolitan Board Teachers' Association (MBTA) and, after 1904, the London Teachers' Association (LTA), published every October in the *Board Teacher* and the *London Teacher* respectively. See also file on Married Women Teachers, 1909–23, EO/STA/2/12 (hereafter EO/STA/2/12) in the Greater London Record Office (hereafter GLRO). Most of the married teachers were not widows, see 1911 Census Tables, PP, (1913), lxxix, p. 293.

3 For teachers' social origins see Admission and Progress Register, London Fields, Hackney 1882–90, EO/TRA/5/3 and admission and Progress. Register, Hackney Pupil Teachers' School, 1890–8, EO/TRA/5/4 both in GLRO. See also Board of Education, *Annual Reports*, 1908–9 to 1913–14. Statistical evidence on teachers' origins is hard to come by, but all contemporary and more recent accounts assume that they come from upper working-class and lower-middle-class families. See Departmental Committee on the Pupil Teacher System, PP (1898), xxvi, passim; A. Tropp, *The School Teachers* (Heinemann, 1957), pp. 170, 187; and Widdowson, *Going Up Into the Next Class* (Women's Research and Resources Centre, 1980).

4 Elizabeth Roberts, *A Woman's Place* (Basil Blackwell, Oxford, 1984); and Ellen Ross, ' "Fierce Questions and Taunts": Married Life in Working-Class London, 1870–1914', *Feminist Studies* 8 (1982), 575–601. See also their articles in this volume.

5 Louise A. Tilly and Joan W. Scott, *Women, Work, & Family* (Holt, Rinehart and Winston, New York 1978), p. 124.

6 I am not adopting any particular position on the recent debate over the existence of a labour aristocratic stratum with a distinct political profile in late Victorian society. I am using the term here merely to distinguish divisions within the working class and to discuss the behaviour of those

relatively stable, regularly employed and (usually) skilled male workers and their families. See my discussion of the various aspects of this debate and of the lower middle class in, 'Women in the Classroom Struggle: Elementary Schoolteachers in London, 1870-1914' (PhD. thesis, Princeton University, 1985), pp. 27–36. E.J. Hobsbawn's 'The Aristocracy of Labour Reconsidered' in his *Workers* (Pantheon, New York, 1984), pp. 226-51 is a useful recent piece on these issues.

7 For the nature of the London labour market see E.J. Hobsbawm, 'The Nineteenth-Century London Labour Market', in his *Workers*, pp.131–51. In 'The Aristocracy of Labour Reconsidered', p. 229 he also discusses the similarities between the labour aristocracy and the lower-middle class; as does R.Q. Gray, *The Labour Aristocracy in Victorian Edinburgh* (Oxford University Press, Oxford, 1976), p. 110. Examples of such communities in London would be Battersea and Hackney. For a somewhat different interpretation see G. Crossick, 'The Emergence of the Lower Middle Class, in Britain: A Discussion', in G. Crossick (ed.), *The Lower Middle Class in Britain*, (Croom Helm, 1977), pp. 48–53.

8 On the ambiguities of respectability see P. Bailey, ' "Will the Real Bill Banks Please Stand Up?" Toward a Role Analysis of Mid-Victorian Working-Class Respectability', *Journal of Social History* 12 (1979, pp. 336–53, and Hobsbawm, 'The Aristocracy of Labour Reconsidered', pp. 238–9, 242–3.

9 See, for instance, 1901 Census Summary Tables, PP (1904), cviii, pp. 198–201.

10 See L. Davidoff, 'The Separation of Home and Work? Landladies and Lodgers in Nineteenth and Twentieth-Century England', in Burman (ed.) *Fit Work for Women* (Croom Helm, 1979), pp. 64–97, and Tilly and Scott, *Women, Work & Family*, pp. 125, 131.

11 See H.M. Burton, *There Was a Young Man* (Geoffrey Bles, 1958), pp. 27–30, 46; Helen Corke, *In Our Infancy* (Cambridge University Press, Cambridge, 1975); Richard Church, *Over the Bridge* (Heinemann, 1955); and H.G. Wells *Experiment in Autobiography* (Macmillan, New York, 1934).

12 For the ways in which popular education prepared girls for a domestic sphere see A. Davin, 'Mind That you Do As You Are Told', *Feminist Review* 3 (1980), 88–89; and C. Dyhouse, *Girls Growing Up in Late Victorian and Edwardian England* (Routledge & Kegan Paul, 1981), chapter 3.

13 Corke, *In Our Infancy*, p. 98.

14 Ibid., pp. 100–5.

15 Departmental Committee on the Pupil Teacher System, p. 46.

16 F.H. Spencer, *An Inspector's Testament* (English Universities Press, 1938), p. 153.

17 Corke, *In Our Infancy*, p. 98.

18 H.G. Wells, *The New Machiavelli* (Penguin, Harmondsworth, 1978), p. 55.

19 George Gissing, *The Unclassed* (R.F. Fenno & Company, New York, 1896), pp. 259–60

20 Ibid., p. 284.
21 Corke, *In Our Infancy*, pp. 71–9.
22 Tilly and Scott, *Women, Work & Family*, p. 124.
23 Crossick, 'Emergence of the Lower Middle Class', p. 27.
24 See, for instance, *Schoolmistress*, 25 May 1882, p. 47; Clara Collet *Educated Working Women* (P.S. King & Son, 1902), p. 121; and unsigned letter in EO/STA/2/12 received 28 February 1922.
25 Corke, *In Our Infancy*, p. 105.
26 Church, *Over the Bridge*, p. 44
27 School Management Committee Minutes (hereafter SMC), 28 April 1882, School Board for London Records (hereafter SBL), in GLRO, vol. 514, p. 451.
28 See, for instance, *Board Teacher*, July 1894, p. 147 and May 1901, p. 99.
29 See Memorandum and Return on the Reduction of the Unattached Staff, London County Council Education Committee, Teaching Staff Sub-Committee, Supplemental Agenda, 8 July 1909, EO/STA/2/48 (hereafter EO/STA/2/48).
30 Church, *Over the Bridge*, p. 91.
31 Ibid., p. 35
32 Teaching Staff Sub-Committee, Minutes (hereafter TSSC) 14 November 1892, SBL, vol. 867, p. 134.
33 Finance Committee Minutes, 15 July 1890, SBL, vol. 219.
34 SMC, 10 July 1885, SBL, vol. 524, p. 200.
35 SMC, 6 July 1888, SBL, vol. 534, p. 175.
36 File on Relatives Serving as Teachers in the Same Departments at Schools, EO/STA/2/34.
37 Letter from 'Not Personally Affected' to *Board Teacher*, March 1895, p. 63.
38 Church, *Over the Bridge*, p. 75.
39 Ibid., p. 85.
40 SMC, 24 June 1898, SBL, vol. 601, p. 93.
41 Letter from Clara Grant, 7 February 1911, in EO/STA/2/12.
42 SMC, 19 February 1892, SBL, vol. 550, p. 616.
43 TSSC, 8 February 1897, SBL, vol. 878, pp. 263–4.
44 'Absences Under Articles 120' *Board Teacher*, July 1895, p. 154. Regulations regarding maternity leave appeared in the *Annual Reports* of the School Board for London, 1888–1903.
45 Report of the Education Officer to the Teaching Staff Sub-Committee, 3 July 1912, EO/STA/2/12.
46 *London Teacher*, June 1907, p. 146.
47 See SMC for 1882 and 1883, SBL 514–17.
48 EO/STA/2/48, pp. 22, 24.
49 See Alan A. Jackson, *Semi-Detached London: Suburban Development, Life and Transport, 1900–1939* (George Allen & Unwin, 1973), pp. 46, 63; G.S. Layard, 'Family Budgets: II A Lower Middle Class Budget', *The Cornhill Magazine* n.s. 10 (1901), 657–66; and F.G. d'Aeth, 'Present Tendencies of Class Differentiation' *The Sociological Review* III October 1910), p. 270.
50 Church, *Over the Bridge*, p. 35.

51 Ibid., p. 183.
52 Ibid., p. 76.
53 Letter from 'Not Personally Affected.'
54 EO/STA/2/48, pp. 21, 22, 25.
55 Return on percentages of married teachers, 31 March 1908, EO/STA/2/12.
56 *London Teacher*, September 1911, p. 351.
57 Ibid., 8 March 1912, p. 198.
58 *Schoolmistress*, 15 August, 1907, p. 346.
59 Diana Gittins, *Fair Sex* (Hutchinson, 1982), p. 52.
60 Ibid.
61 Ibid., p. 152
62 EO/STA/2/12, passim.
63 Communication from Clara Bulcraig, 18 February 1911, EO/STA/2/12.

"WOMAN'S WRONGS."

BRUTAL HUSBAND. "AH! YOU'D BETTER GO SNIVELLIN' TO THE 'OUSE O' COMMONS, *YOU* HAD! MUCH THEY'RE LIKELY TO DO FOR YER! YAH! READ THAT!"

"MR. DISRAELI.—There can be but one feeling in the House on the object of these dastardly attacks—not upon the weaker but the fairer sex. *A laugh.* I am sure the House shares the indignation of my hon. friend who will, I hope, consider he has secured the object he had in view by raising, the question. * * * Assuring my hon. friend that Her Majesty's Government will not lose sight of the question, I must ask him not to press his Motion further on the present occasion."—*Parliamentary Report, Monday, May 18.*

Illustration from Punch 1874

8

Marriage Relations, Money, and Domestic Violence in Working-Class Liverpool, 1919–39

Pat Ayers and Jan Lambertz

Alongside measurable wage income, the average cost of living, subsistence needs, and household demography, the quality of marital relationships is crucial to an assessment of the history of working-class urban culture and gender relations. Flushing out the character and complexities of husband-wife relations remains a difficult task, however, challenging easy assumptions about intimacy, partnership and adult heterosexual commitments. The absence of marital violence, for instance, does not mean that there were no profound tensions; nor does its presence mean that a relationship was in danger of collapsing. Often we remain dependent on 'second-guessing' behaviour, speculating on what husbands assumed about their wives, and what women hid from their men. Here we have attempted to understand the quality and contradictory features of marital life in inter-war, dockland Liverpool. How did husbands and wives' roles 'complement' one another in this community? What issues of male and female power were intertwined with family survival on a low 'family wage'? Did wives objectively share power with their husbands? What was at stake in the prevailing sexual division of labour and responsibility?

Not 'making ends meet' was a fact of daily life for many working-class, dockland homes in Liverpool between the two world wars. Money problems obviously had enormous potential for creating tension between husbands and wives.[1] Yet much of this tension remained hidden below the surface, for deceit lay at the core of many successful marriages during this period. In her recent history of working-class credit and 'indebtedness' Melanie Tebbutt argues that for many households in Britain in the late nineteenth and early twentieth centuries, 'reticence over financial affairs was not confined to dealing with strangers but also dominated relations between husband and wife'.[2] In Liverpool, deception and silences between husbands and wives – especially around financial questions – seemed imperative for ensuring household survival and marital stability. Such behaviour gave rise to feelings of guilt, shame and fear in wives, who bore the responsibility for balancing the household budget. Yet, paradoxically, both partners apparently wanted and mutually reinforced this secrecy at the expense of honesty and a shared struggle for survival: there was logic to it. The struggle to live up to a particular marital ideal and the unquestioned desirability of having a marriage and raising a family can partly account for this phenomenon.

In this local study, we wish to probe more deeply into the range of factors and expectations that kept marriages intact during and despite financial strain. What did a widespread pattern of reticence over money problems mean for survival, domestic privacy, and male and female power relations? The financial difficulties which Liverpool couples almost inevitably confronted at some point entailed more than a struggle for basic necessities; they also revealed that men and women often had competing priorities. 'Mutual dependency' in marriage entailed contradictions and often hinged, first, on male claims to special privileges and men's self-interest in giving wives power to preside over the household; second, on wives' consequent fear of their husbands; and third, on unrealistic assumptions about women's work, which women did not openly challenge. Here we will broadly outline the features of how money and money problems shaped the relationships of primarily white, working-class Catholic and Protestant couples who were largely locked into the depressed Liverpudlian economy.[3]

Money and Marital Dynamics

The illusion of smoothly 'making ends meet' constituted a fundamental component in the widely understood definitions of 'a good wife' and 'a good husband' in this community. It made marriage and poverty bearable. Making ends meet as a new unit was one marital ideal that replaced the sharp thrills and suspended pleasure of premarital romance, signifying that a man and a woman were a good match and 'meant for each other'. It was an ideal, a possibility, an illusion kept afloat not only by the couple, but also exacted and reinforced by neighbours, kin, friends, and social welfare agencies in the city.

After handing some portion of their wages over to their wives, husbands largely avoided further involvement in household affairs and maintenance. In Liverpool, many working-class men appear to have made this a deliberate practice. At the same time, they lay claim to the respect and many privileges due them as breadwinners, especially if they had given their wives an unopened wage packet. These privileges included the licence to blame and abuse those wives who proved less than financial wizards in times of hardship. Taken to the extreme, this pattern of male authority and female responsibility could legitimize male violence within the home, whatever its cause. Many husbands' threats to beat their wives formed a significant undercurrent in couples' silences about money.

Wives accepted and reinforced these gender divisions. Many reasons may be suggested for a woman's quiet assumption of the responsibility for managing the household. To manage or *appear* to manage on what the 'provider' handed over, gave her credibility as a good and respectable married woman, even if the struggle to accomplish this on low wages was often fierce. Good management was crucial to married women's self-respect and identity: 'I married on the understanding that it was the wife's job to be the careful thrifty housewife and to stay at home to manage the house to the best of my ability'.[4]

Not all husbands used violence, as a means of enforcing their essential power to determine the domestic division of labour. Some reinforced their wives' responsibility for domestic management by praising and exaggerating their wives' budgeting skills. This appearance of managing went beyond the couple, involving wider social relations. The 'empowerment' of a woman through this household role – a power she often internalized – enabled her to avoid confronting certain painful realizations, such as the idea that her chosen partner might have caused the family's money problems, that he might be stingy, or that the man she 'fancied' was inadequate and could not earn a good wage. The thought that she had fallen for an apparent 'loser' could damage a woman's self-esteem. Together, these factors pulled women back and forth between pride of accomplishment in keeping their households afloat, and periods of acute guilt over 'their' individual management failures. This dynamic in Liverpool marriages needs further exploration. It often gave women gratification, while also working to the husbands' ultimate advantage. It constantly reinforced a form of 'mutual consent' to secrecy over money, and kept husband-wife conflicts at bay.

If a wife felt dubious about the amount of responsibility assigned to her, her ambivalence could nonetheless be transformed into guilt through an array of additional pressures. Hints from people surrounding the couple and active threats by the husband pushed her to acknowledge the logic of accepting 'her' duties and failures. When many neighbourhood women hid financial difficulties, the individual woman often came to the conclusion that she alone had grave or long-term money problems. Emerging family welfare agencies in the city also stressed that homes were the primary responsibility of wives and mothers. This belief clearly affected the type of advice and aid a woman could expect if she sought 'outside' help, or came into contact with voluntary and state officials and agencies monitoring the health and welfare of children. Many representatives of these service agencies appear to have believed even more strongly in the power of wives and mothers to shape their families' welfare than the women themselves.

Sharing the 'Family Wage'

Liverpool was first and foremost a port economy, and embodied certain extremes of urban life during industralization. Mass migration into the city contributed to some of the worst overcrowding in Britain during the nineteenth century. Poor housing conditions also reflected the competition for housing near dockside (the main area of male employment), and extensive family poverty in the stable population. More household economies relied on income from casual, seasonal labour in Liverpool than in many other communities, and this was of crucial importance to the way in which women worked and managed.

Men working in the large transport and shipping sector faced much greater fluctuations in the availability of work than industrial workers in other regions. Of all the insured workers on Merseyside in 1931, over half were employed in industries associated with shipping, transport, and distribution, and a further 9 per cent were employed in building and furnishing (frequently also casual trades).[5] A lack of alternative employment meant that both irregular work and extremely high unemployment rates in shipping and shipbuilding persisted well into the twentieth century. The city was particularly hard hit by the inter-war depression, but for most of the century, in fact, Merseyside suffered twice the national average of male unemployment. Because much employment in the port was of a casual nature, there was little stigma attached to being unemployed. Workers in the inter-war years often used 'continuity rules' to supplement income by drawing unemployment benefit for some days of the week. Therefore, 'signing on' did not necessarily constitute a rigid separation of workers from non-workers. The widespread experience of casual labour also meant that personal adjustment to unemployment was less dramatic for many people than might have been the case elsewhere.[6]

Erratic earnings for a large percentage of males meant that wives always had to manage money carefully. Wives' ability to rely on husbands' wages was limited, even when husbands were regularly employed workers. And even if husbands gave their wives all that they earned, steady wages often did not meet the basic financial needs of dependants. Early in the century, enquiries into Liverpool family economies by women such as the social investigator, Eleanor Rathbone, began to demonstrate that the 'family wage' received by local men in many jobs was often inadequate. Wages failed to increase proportionately as families and commitments grew.[7] Even steady income and income untouched by depression-era wage cuts could not readily accomodate sudden family emergencies and illness in a household. However, some contemporary social investigators in the 1930s observed that unemployment benefit, for instance, enabled many women to plan their budgets with comparative accuracy for the first time, although again, the regularity of such income was offset by its inadequacy.[8] The same problem also arose for dependants of men serving in the armed forces (particularly during the two world wars) and in the merchant marine.[9] The latter faced additional severe difficulties because many shipping companies did not pay out their allowances at weekly intervals.[10]

Thus, without wishing to minimize the severe hardships brought about by the inter-war depression, Liverpool's precarious employment structure and the basis of calculating wages in general had long forced women to develop survival strategies for their households that had evolved into an inherent part of daily life.[11] For instance, in a good week, they had to pay off accumulated debts in order to maintain credit-worthiness, and any surplus cash (as well as certain moveable goods) had to subsidize the poor weeks which inevitably followed. These strategies are remarkable for their diversity, and were not confined to women seeking waged work to supplement irregular male contributions.

Despite knowledge of their male kin's often fluctuating wages, most Liverpool women appear to have given up full-time waged work outside the home after marriage (and before widowhood). This was a community-wide convention, and made sense, given the existing structure of housekeeping and child-rearing. They apparently expected husbands largely to support them financially, and husbands also insisted on this. Typical 'female' jobs available locally in any case tended to be badly paid and were not remembered by Liverpool women as having brought much gratification or enjoyment.[12] Apart from domestic service, women lacked well-developed occupational opportunities before the Second World War, although the 1920s and 1930s brought some expansion of women's jobs in the manufacturing sector, notably in the food processing industry.[13] While families heavily dependent on a husband's wage probably experienced comparatively better material conditions than households relying on the income of single mothers and/or juveniles,[14] scarce resources were rarely distributed equally between husbands, wives and children, and married women often resorted to periods of casual employment.

As social investigations in Liverpool have shown, deducing a family's standard of living from the average wages of the chief earner or from the cash benefits destined for a bounded household ultimately remains problematic, although in the past many statistical analyses of poverty have done just this. Unfortunately, traditional information on 'income' has told us little about how wages in the form of food, money for clothing and leisure activities were divided among individual members of households and families. A husband could withhold some earnings and job 'perks' — as well as information about them — from his 'household manager'. Most of the older women interviewed in our study of Liverpool so far do seem to have known the amount of their husbands' flat rate earnings. Cross-checked with available data on male wages, their recollections show a high degree of accuracy.[15] However, overtime, tips, or any extras earned were considered to belong to the husband. As one woman recalled: 'He was a good man, he always tipped all his wages up and I gave him something back for his pocket — mind you, that [was] generally the same amount each week so sometimes I had more to play around with than others'.[16] Closer questioning revealed that he was also a part-time fireman and received 6d. a call-out, which was seen as his own. One man gave a more cynical view of his father's habits: 'When my dad put his wage packet on the table unopened, we all knew that he'd had a flat week. That was the only time my mother opened it'.[17]

Those men who did not turn over their whole wage to their wives generally put aside a set amount each week for housekeeping. One man boasted of his exemplary behaviour as a husband:

> We never had any trouble over money. If I wanted a drink or anything like that, I'd never touch her money. I'd take my own out. Once my own was spent, it was spent but I'd never touch her housekeeping money or anything like that — I got 35/– plus commission when I got married in 1926. I'd give her the 35/– and the commission was my pocket money.[18]

Further questioning elicited the information that 'commission' was usually about 10/– a week but might be as much as £2!

Many wives were forced to make use of credit, or earn a copper 'on the side', and apparently very much feared being discovered doing so by their husbands. Yet husbands had usually grown up in the same communities. As children, they were certainly aware of women's hidden work, and may have redeemed bundles from the pawnshop for their mothers or run errands for a penny for the gas, or gone to the corner shop for small quantities of food and tea, asking for it to be put 'in the book' (on credit).[19] Why, then, this apparent lack of knowledge and understanding when it came to their wives?

When interviewed about the inter-war period, older men frequently make a virtue of having handed all financial responsibility over to their wives with their wage packets. They boasted that they never asked their wives what they did with the money and presented this as having provided women with power over the domestic domain.[20] We wish to argue that for men, clear elements of self-interest operated in perpetuating this myth of what constituted a 'good wife', and in avoiding involvement with household affairs. The good wife was to a large degree equated with the competent manager. Financial difficulties could therefore always be blamed on her poor skills and neglect of duties. In all probability, even husbands who did not consistently give their wives their entire wage packets used similar reasoning. Psychologically, this logic enabled men to avoid confronting their inability to provide an adequate income under the prevailing work and wage systems, which in turn reinforced and maintained the widely understood idea that men were actually the undisputed family 'providers' and breadwinners. As such, husbands claimed all traditional male privileges – including sometimes substantial pocket money – without a guilty conscience or recrimination.

Writers have occasionally satirized husbands' incompetence in trying to manage households when wives and mothers were temporarily unavailable or disabled.[21] Men lacked skills and experience, or feared that their masculinity would be called into question if they performed this task well. In general, men's distance from routine housework and child-care very effectively also kept them from confronting realistic household financial needs. Wives did not resent this. The feeling that men had been 'out at work all day' and that men's work was harder made challenges or complaints less likely. Some wives were simply grateful that their spouse met at least one other major definition of a 'good husband': that he did not beat them. 'He was a good man, he never laid a finger on me', was a common attitude.[22]

The Wife's Role and Responsibilities

Even where housekeeping money was predictable, it rarely proved sufficient for highly variable or even 'average' household expenditures in the long run. We have also suggested that while a wife may have had a clear idea of her husband's basic earnings, he was far less likely to have an idea of how she used the housekeeping. The combination of strategies used by most ordinary working-class women in this community to ensure household survival shaded from the category of 'respectable' to the 'unacceptable'. The more socially unacceptable the strategies, the more reluctant wives were to reveal them to husbands. Potentially more activities became acceptable among and for women in periods of severe economic crisis. The more specifically 'male' shadow economy (including, for instance, stripping lead off roofs or using dock moneylenders) involved separate standards and value judgements largely set by men and their mates.[23]

Access to credit (indebtedness) constituted a fundamental part of numerous English household budgets in the period between the wars, as Melanie Tebbutt and other investigators have shown.[24] Even in the dockland area, the social acceptability of taking or giving credit (at least among women) varied widely and is difficult to categorize with ease. For women, gambling, playing the pools, pawning, being a bookie's 'cocky' (look-out), nicking, and accepting items stolen from the docks all fell into a grey area between legitimate and not respectable.[25] Other female economic ventures appeared generally acceptable to women, their husbands, and the neighbourhoods near the docks. Taking in lodgers fell into this category, as did co-op membership, going cleaning, sewing, hawking, flower-selling, all types of home-work, and taking in laundry.[26]

The ingenuity of some women knew no bounds in times of hardship. One Liverpool woman recalled:

> My Mam would buy sugar bags from the grocer's for a copper or so each. When she had a really big pile she would put two dolly tubs in the yard and fill one with red dye and one with blue and dye the bags. Then she'd make the blue into short pants and the red into dresses and sold them around the neighbourhood for between 9d. and 1/6.[27]

One of our male respondents also remembered this mother and being forced to wear the sugar bag clothing, the 'horrible, hairy, scratchy things that were practically indestructable'.[28] Apart from devising these lucrative tortures for children – a 'respectable' source of income – this seamstress took in sewing for a 'better' dress shop, made rag-rugs to sell, and made her own children's clothes from odd bits of clothing she bought from jumble sales. However, even some of these casual women's jobs could, under certain circumstances, become disreputable. For instance, only those prepared to sink very low in the estimation of their neighbours would take in washing from ships in port.[29]

Anticipating both disrepute in their circle of acquaintances and conflict at home, many women tried to keep quiet about their money-making activities. One woman recalled how she would take a tram ride to the (then) outskirts of Liverpool, where the Corporation was building new houses, and collect as many waste wood off-cuts as she could carry. She would bring them home, chop them up, bundle them, and hide the bundles in a yard shed. The following day she would travel to another part of the city 'where she was not known'. She explained: 'My husband would have been mortified if he'd known what I did – he always boasted what a good manager I was and I wouldn't have wanted people roundabout to know – but I just couldn't cope sometimes – the shame was something terrible'.[30]

Fighting family poverty also involved activities that were more visible in the community. Women commonly used pawnshops, and in 1929 there was almost one to a block in some dockland areas of Liverpool.[31] Mutual aid between female kin or women in neighbourhoods in emergencies and hard times was also often crucial for survival.[32] However, accounts by Liverpool women strongly imply that by the inter-war period aid was usually offered as *unobtrusively* as possible between neighbours, which suggests that the personal esteem of the woman seeking help was at stake.[33] Each woman needed to show that she was a skilled housekeeper to a wider circle around her, a projection consistent and intertwined with the image she presented to her husband.

On the one hand, women were again and again reminded that they needed each other's help at some time. But, on the other hand, the division of responsibility in the home between wives and husbands encouraged and reinforced the idea that every woman was individually responsible for her household's money problems. Thus, while all working-class women understood that need was a sensitive issue for their neighbours and friends, there were, nonetheless, definite limits on the extent to which women identified with one another's difficulties. Mental and moral distinctions were inevitably made between women who coped and women who 'failed'. Women's feelings of adequacy were intrinsically bound up in the patterns and identity created in housekeeping for husbands, and were reinforced by community attitudes.

Husbands were likely to feel their status as breadwinners threatened by their wives' pursuit of supplementary income. In a 1909 report on household budgeting among Liverpool casual labourers' families, twenty-four wives approached by investigators to keep budgets 'were, or professed to be, willing themselves to oblige [in keeping a budget, but] pleaded the disapproval of their husbands'. Several others stopped budget-keeping for the study when husbands 'dared' them to continue. Another woman stopped filling in the book provided, 'because if her husband saw how much money she was borrowing he'd "hammer" her'.[34]

For the inter-war period, evidence of women's fear of sorting out finances with husbands comes across in interviews and in discussions of why women were trapped into the grossly exploitative repayment terms demanded by moneylenders (mostly neighbourhood working-class women themselves). Local investigators, such as representatives of the Liverpool Personal Service Society, were struck by the number of women borrowing without their husband's knowledge. They described women as living in a state of daily terror, both of the lender and their husbands.[35] And the fear no doubt compounded: through subsequent loans and interest, small loans often grew in the course of a few years to a very large sum, of which the borrower had received very little. She could also scarcely pay the interest due.[36] Defaultors were threatened with exposure, and also quickly punished, sometimes by physical abuse.[37] Money secrets kept from husbands were self-perpetuating, and they also grew into new fears.

Inter-war revelations about hire purchase (HP) agreements also gave evidence as to how anxieties could mount and multiply for working-class women. A huge variety of new, mainly mass-produced and cheaper consumer durables became available between the wars, marketed with more sophisticated modes of advertising. High-pressured sales techniques (canvassers working on commission), for instance, encouraged people to enter into (HP) agreements to buy sometimes shoddy goods, which they could not necessarily afford to pay for over long periods.[38] Of course the system had appeal and fitted into working-class traditions of buying various items on credit; where money was limited, it made sense to divide large expenditures beyond the family's immediate means into small manageable weeklys sums. But goods were also more costly under HP, and their purchase often involved extremely exploitative 'agreements'. In some cases, where an article was almost paid for and an installment missed, the firm's representatives repossessed the item, using violent threats and bullying.[39] The emergence of these offers meant that women were harassed to buy (often without a full explanation of the agreement's conditions) and harassed to pay, and lived in fear of debt collectors, of repossession, and even of prosecution. They also feared husbands 'finding out', for many women apparently managed to contract large HP purchases without husbands' specific consent or involvement in the deal.[40] (Eventually, abuses by some dealers under this system led to a central government investigation, which resulted in the Hire Purchase Bill of 1937.)

Living with this anxiety resulted in seemingly contradictory behaviour on the part of working-class Liverpool women. Housekeeping demanded different tactics for different situations, including the appearance of competence and contentment, aggression, desperation and weakness. These women – and often children – had to develop the combined skills of begging, harassing, ingratiating themselves, and aggressively arguing with local pawnbrokers, shop-keepers, traders, social-welfare agencies, and sometimes even neighbours and kin, in order to keep homes together. Self-sacrifice (for example, going short of food) could only stretch the budget to a certain extent, and while wives felt reluctant to reveal their financial distress publicly, the desire to hide the inadequacy of the husband's wage from him often forced them to do so. The victimization of wives by typical moneylending arrangements and some hire-purchase deals exemplifies the paradoxical nature of successful housekeeping in inter-war Liverpool, the fragility, sacrifice, and often terror bound up in household management.

Outside Help

Seeking various forms of aid from charities and welfare agencies must be counted among the ways in which some working-class women sought to make ends meet. These alliances were not without difficulty, for while social welfare agencies provided concrete help, they also cast doubts on women's competence and intelligence as, for example, was the case in the campaigns conducted against moneylenders and against shady hire-purchase agreements. Superficially these campaigns embodied recognition for the extreme vulnerability and weak position of working-class wives and mothers. But social welfare workers of the period nevertheless managed to convey the message that women were bad, foolish or ignorant managers, who made naive budgeting decisions and drove families deeply into debt. All the same, these women had avoided the possibility of a table without dinner for a husband, and in this sense had exhibited cleverness and efficiency. Such immediate pressures often simply outweighed the search for solutions that were more 'economical' in the long run. Getting money in 'expensive' ways cannot necessarily be seen as incompatible with 'good management'.

In general, the attitudes and practices of many Liverpool social welfare agencies often blamed wives and mothers for troubles at home (such as, money, health, and children's behaviour problems), while not holding husbands and fathers accountable or pressuring them to improve household circumstances. It remains unclear whether this tendency significantly added to women's inclination to blame themselves, which was in any case triggered by husbands devolving so much household financial responsibility onto wives. Some Liverpool social workers of course realized that the root of wives' inability to budget adequately lay not in their ignorance, but in the fluctuations of income earned by husbands. Nevertheless, the advice tendered usually centred on wives' responsibility to spend 'properly', to mobilize temporary charity and welfare benefits, or to turn to modes of generating income that involved less exploitative transactions (with respect to high interest rates) and, preferably, less time spent away from home and children.[41]

Social workers had many reasons for avoiding confrontations with fathers. In daily social work practice, wives and mothers inevitably seemed to be more 'accessible' pressure points. They were also responsible for the care of infants and children, who were the focus of many new national welfare initiatives.[42] Middle-class social workers, often women, probably felt intimidated by the prospect of attempting to 'influence' working-class men, and were more optimistic about their ability to persuade Liverpool's 'tired mothers' to perform better. Working-class husbands and wives clearly had different relations to family welfare and aid organizations.

As a recognition of structural unemployment intrinsic to the port gained acceptance after the first world war, men's insecure wages were somewhat less readily attributed to personal moral deficiency, and a new understanding of men's problems as breadwinners tended to absolve them from blame. A range of social investigators had already begun to acknowledge the difficulties inherent in the concept of the male 'family wage', even where men had steady jobs. Many policymakers and investigators still feared undermining male incentives to work and provide for their families,[43] but pressure was brought to bear on men through the increasingly rationalized and impersonal social security system.

Social welfare agencies tended to deal with mothers directly and pinned disproportionate expectations on them to be 'thrifty', to stretch household budgets, and to absorb middle-class advice on 'economizing'. In an increasingly well-organized local charity and social work sector in Liverpool, mothers were treated as the key to matters of child maintenance, family stability, and even general social stability.[44] Social welfare agencies did not invent the gender-specific division of responsibility in families and its implications for women's individual sense of duty, but they strengthened this division in fundamental ways. Nascent social work agencies in Liverpool ultimately encouraged (in an abstract sense) the dependence of wives and children on the husband's hypothetical family wage, and assumed that wives had the ability to use those wages to attain adequate family maintenance.[45] Blaming women for not being thrifty or not budgeting properly could also provide a rationalization for low-cost 'solutions' to poverty and ill health, such as 'education' for mothers, rather than supplementary income and nutrition provisions.[46] Apologists for low male wages could also rely on such thinking.[47]

Liverpool wives sometimes used welfare agencies and the courts to pressure husbands for adequate maintenance.[48] It remains open to speculation whether some women also discouraged social workers from making contact with husbands. For wife-clients, such contacts must have threatened attempts to hide certain household financial transactions from their men. Seeking help from public or private welfare agencies could bring short-term benefits, but also entailed a certain amount of risk and guilt for women. Moreover, these contacts often subjected the wife's ability to manage to public scrutiny. Yet the alternative to seeking outside help was often to exact more from husbands, which remained in many ways equally uncertain.

The Thread of Violence

Some women contested the financial arrangements in their homes, 'nagging' husbands for more money.[49] But for most wives, the decision to pressure husbands directly and forcefully remained a difficult, even dangerous one. Domestic violence was a calculated risk, and partly because of it, many women opted for the strain of never explicitly airing domestic management problems. However, men also exploded for other reasons, for example, when women gave up, or when their attempts at good management crumbled, which affected both their domestic comfort and the family's reputation. Wives' pervasive and deep fear of exposing their (largely female) 'shadow economy' to husbands suggests that not merely shame, but also violence lay just below the surface in many marriages. The sexual division of labour and responsibility in the home could be backed up with the threat of physical violence. However, for many couples, the backdrop of violence was less an *explanation* for secrecy over money than an *indication* that a great deal was at stake for both men and women in financial questions. This secrecy was also about first, fundamental issues of self-worth and pride; second, potential challenges to manliness and a husband's privileges; and third, a woman's desperate struggle to keep her family housed and fed under sometimes impossible circumstances.

Links between wives who had problems with making ends meet and with violent husbands emerge at a number of levels. Firstly, a man *not* beating his wife appears to have been an important criterion of a 'good husband' in Liverpool, alongside that of being a good provider.[50] Yet several Liverpool commentators attest to the 'normality' of wife-beating through much of the first half of the century. There was a widespread assumption that the threat of domestic violence existed as a *possibility* for most women, although we can say little about its *actual* frequency. One Bootle (north end) woman recalled her marriage in 1925 to a man who was hard-drinking, selfish and demanding, saying: 'Most of the women got hidings, I was never without a black eye but no-one would interfere'.[51] Other women escaped hands-on violence, but their husbands viciously 'tormented' them and created an atmosphere heavily laden with the threat of violence, including shouted orders, dinners flung across the room, and men's heavy weekend drinking sessions.[52]

Second, men often relied on disclaimers of responsibility for problems affecting their wives. Men could claim 'ignorance' of their wives' real housekeeping expenses and difficulties because of the prevailing sexual division of labour. Likewise, men could excuse their own behaviour – including violent outbursts, for instance – by claiming that they were 'under the influence' and temporarily not in control of their actions.[53] Furthermore, the male drinking culture even claimed a certain legitimacy that wives had to accept: men used the pub to buy the foreman a drink, to hear news on ships coming in, and to keep up social contacts.[54]

Third, because women were assumed to have responsibility for, and power over, domestic affairs, they could also be accused of provoking domestic violence. The image of the empowered household manager (not weak or vulnerable) and the related assumption of provocation constituted a major reason why wife-beating was never defined as a real social problem in the inter-war period, despite its apparent prevalence. Political and social work rhetoric stressed what could be achieved by the wife-mother in the home even more strongly after the turn of the century. Twentieth-century child welfare initiatives tended to promote a more intense ideology of motherhood and, by extension, increased maternal culpability for domestic problems.[55]

Liverpool feminists, social welfare workers, philanthropists and politicians might have construed wife-beating as a large social threat in the inter-war period, had such violence actually threatened to tear apart households on a wide scale. However, paradoxically, it could create greater family 'stability' by effectively 'policing' wives. For the wife's part, the very struggles that often apparently precipitated a row and a husband's anger – around the demand for a larger piece of his wage – did not necessarily bespeak rebellion. Such struggles demonstrated, if anything, many women's commitment to holding a home together. Most women, particularly mothers, could certainly not have expected a lesser financial struggle had they left violent husbands, to set up households on their own.

For all their determination and ingenuity, 'deserting' as well as deserted working-class wives could often only hope for ill-paid work in a generally 'overcrowded' female casual labour market on Merseyside, and only limited help and living space from kin.[56] In addition, they faced discrimination in searching for alternative lodgings. Husbands also retained legal rights to property accumulated during the marriage.[57] Moreover, official separation and maintenance orders obtained through the court system had long proved notoriously weak guarantees that husbands would continue to support their families.[58] Nor did wives necessarily escape husbands' violence or threats if they moved to a different address. In the inter-war period, wives seeking advice on their rights and possible separations often ran up against a number of local welfare services, which appear to have pressured them to see the 'logic' or desirability of a reconciliation.[59] But apart from this pressure, our evidence suggests that most wives could dodge rows and violence in ways short of leaving, and women hiding money problems should be seen in this context.

Conclusion

In working-class Liverpool, a clear division of financial responsibility was crucial to the identity of husbands and wives. Men claimed to be the family providers, and women claimed to be good household managers. The structure of male employment in the port had long limited the possibility of always living up to these roles, and many men in the inter-war years still faced periods of unemployment. Yet the desire of couples to live up to the roles expected of husbands and wives remained forcefully intact. Consequently, men and women used a range of tactics to meet their obligations, in order to retain the confidence of their partners as well as self-respect. The tactics of husband and wife complemented and reinforced each other, but had quite different consequences for male and female welfare in marriage.

The persisting division of marital duties in the home testified to both male and female power. It also signified that a certain amount of anxiety was involved for both partners: a fear of revealing their perceived inadequacies, or giving up privileges. And for some, perhaps, a latent fear existed that what they saw in their partners was an illusion. A widespread pattern in Liverpool appears to have been that wives avoided discussing money problems with husbands, and as a complement to this, husbands attempted to avoid explicit knowledge of them. Ironically, husbands protected their 'manliness', their image as the breadwinner, and their extra pocket-money in this way, for wives were duty-bound to make do with what they had received. Any inquiry by men into the mysteries of wives' housekeeping could be threatening, for it could provoke feelings of guilt and even inadequacy and insecurity about their capacities as breadwinners. It could also expose them to their wives' feelings of recrimination, against which they were not always able to produce a convincing defence. Upholding the boundary between male and female responsibilities meant that couples often avoided overt antagonism and simple resentment in their marriages.

A majority of husbands appear to have insisted that the wife take the entire responsibility for 'her' duties, and violent threats were sometimes used to preserve that boundary as rigidly as possible. Some of the fear expressed by wives of husbands 'finding out' about their financial manoeuvering arose from this threat of violence. In addition, many men had unrealistic expectations of their wives, born of a lack of understanding of the strains that housekeeping in poverty entailed. Even the minority of husbands who showed an interest in the management of the household were not necessarily more 'understanding' partners, prepared to share problems at home more equally, but rather, questioned their wives' competence from beginning to end.[60]

In controlling most domestic activities, wives gained an autonomous sphere of power, even if their world revolved largely around meeting the needs of others, particularly husbands. If a wife was skilful in exercising her control over this sphere, she could gain self-esteem and win praise. Expressed in a more negative way, she could avoid criticism of her performance and even physical 'punishment' from her partner. Often confronted with situations where husbands' wages alone did not stretch far enough, Liverpool women had to make choices about whether to be candid with husbands. Women tended to take a disproportionate share of financial problems on their own shoulders, and did so as discreetly as possible. In some senses, this amounted to a trade-off of possible – although in fact often quite improbable – additional help from husbands, in exchange for continuing 'autonomy' and the continued confidence and security of their husbands. But supplementing the family income by resorting to the aid of neighbours, kin, welfare agencies, or various forms of credit meant that wives had to bear enormous physical and mental strains alone. On top of this, they suffered anxiety about the possibility of partners 'seeing through' their efforts. Finally, women simply felt much personal guilt for their family's situation; the dynamics of the male breadwinner family model, men's consequent righteousness, and community attitudes strongly encouraged them to individualize their struggles.

Many married women measured their success not only in terms of making ends meet, but also in terms of how far they were able to keep the details of household budgeting a secret from their husbands. By implication, the concept of 'good housekeeping' begs redefinition. Its true costs to women also remain literally immeasurable. The unspoken rules operating in many inter-war, dockland marriages exemplify the fact that men's understanding of the family economy differed fundamentally from that of women. Married men rarely had a sense of how women bargained in order to meet family needs or, in many cases, the scale of wives' debts. Yet this did not affect the stability of those marriages. Evidence from inter-war Liverpool suggests that wives continued to absorb large and new financial pressures, and that the logic of financial secrecy in marriage was at once resilient and durable.

Bibliographical Notes

The flavour of poverty and working-class life in Liverpool comes through strongly in Pat O'Mara, *The Autobiography of a Liverpool Irish Slummy* (Cedric Chivers, Bath, 1967, first published in 1934); and in the series of accounts by Helen Forrester, such as *Minerva's Stepchild*, (The Bodley Head, 1979), and *Twopence to Cross the Mersey*, (Fontana, 1974). Linda Grant's 'Women's Work and Trade Unionism in Liverpool, 1890–1914', *North West Labour History Society Bulletin*, 7 (1980–1), 65–83; Second Chance to Learn, *Women's History, Women's Lives*, (Printfine, Liverpool, 1982); I. Law and J. Henfrey's *A History of Race and Racism in Liverpool, 1660–1950* (Whitechapel Press, Liverpool 1981); and publications of the Merseyside Socialist Research Group, such as *Merseyside in Crisis*, (Free Press, Manchester, 1980) offer interesting short overviews of Liverpudlian work and unemployment experiences, and the surrounding political landscape. The less accessible multi-volume *Social Survey of Merseyside*, edited by D. Caradog Jones (Liverpool University Press, Liverpool, 1934), and the Pilgrim Trust's *Men Without Work*, (Cambridge University Press, Cambridge, 1938), which includes some discussion of women, are nonetheless useful, shedding very detailed and statistical light on the inter-war years.

Liverpool conditions in part inspired Eleanor Rathbone to develop a criticism of the 'family wage', and readings on this subject provide an essential supplement to discussions of work and income in the city: E. Rathbone, *The Disinherited Family: A Plea for the Endowment of the Family* (Arnold, 1924), and Hilary Land, 'The Family Wage', *Feminist Review*, no. 6 (1980), 55–77. The urban, working-class woman's 'neighbourhood economy' in the twentieth century is explored in the exciting recent studies: M. Tebbutt, *Making Ends Meet: Pawnbroking and Working-Class Credit* (Leicester University Press, Leicester, 1983), and E. Ross, 'Survival Networks: Women's Neighbourhood Sharing in London before World War I', *History Workshop Journal*, no. 15 (1983), pp.4–27. Mary Stock's comprehensive biography of Eleanor Rathbone offers some details on social work structure and development in the city, but Dorothy Keeling's autobiography, *The Crowded Stairs: Recollections of Social Work in Liverpool* (NCSSS, 1961), reveals much more about the inter-war period. Finally, two useful articles on the history of domestic violence and violence against London women are: E. Ross, '"Fierce Questions and Taunts": Married Life in Working-Class London, 1870–1914', and Judith Walkowitz, 'Jack the Ripper and the Myth of Male Violence', both in the American journal, *Feminist Studies*, 8 (1982). In addition, the review article by W. Breines and L. Gordon, 'The New Scholarship on Family Violence', *Signs*, 8 (1983), 490–531, gives an overview of the complexities underlying conflict and abuse within families.

Notes

All taped interviews below (Ayers) were conducted between 1981 and 1984, for an ongoing study of household budgets in working-class Liverpool between the world wars. The people interviewed included Catholics and Protestants, and primarily came from dock workers' families.

1 Cf. M. Tebutt, *Making Ends Meet: Pawnbroking and Working-Class Credit*, (Leicester University Press, Leicester, 1983), p.38.
2 Ibid., p.37.
3 This is not to minimize the importance of more closely examining variations in family structures and relations in Liverpool based on ethnic and/or religious differences, and how racism shaped people's lives.
4 Tape 1 (Ayers), woman, born 1902.
5 D. Caradog Jones (ed.), *Social Survey of Merseyside*, 3vols. (Liverpool University Press, Liverpool, 1934), vol. II, p.2.
6 Merseyside Socialist Research Group, *Merseyside in Crisis*, (Manchester Free Press, Manchester, 1980) pp.4, 31–2; and Pilgrim Trust, *Men Without Work*, (Cambridge University Press, Cambridge, 1938), pp.96–7. On the use of 'continuity rules', see F.G. Hanham, *Report of Enquiry*

into Casual Labour in the Merseyside Area, (Henry Young & Sons, Liverpool, 1930), pp. 88–99.

7 On the 'family wage', see E.F. Rathbone, *The Disinherited Family: A Plea for the Endowment of the Family*, (Edward Arnold, 1924); M. Stocks, *Eleanor Rathbone: A Biography* (Victor Gollancz, 1949), p. 63 *passim*; H. Land, 'The Family Wage', *Feminist Review*, 6 (1980), pp. 55–77; J. Macnicol, *The Movement for Family Allowances, 1918–45: A Study in Social Policy Development*, (Heinemann, 1980); and M. Barrett and M. McIntosh, 'The "Family Wage": Some Problems for Socialists and Feminists', *Capital and Class*, 11 (1980), pp. 51–72.

8 Pilgrim Trust, *Men Without Work*, pp. 99, 201–7; and Tebbutt, *Making Ends Meet*, p. 167.

9 On the economic hardships created by conscription to the armed forces, see S. Pankhurst, *The Home Front*, (Hutchinson, 1932), pp. 18–25, quoted in P. Thane, *Foundations of the Welfare State* (Longman, 1982), pp. 329–30; Soldiers' and Sailors' Families' Association, *Annual Report* (hereafter *AR*), (1915–16); Stocks, *Eleanor Rathbone*, pp. 76, 292 ff. Also, Tebbutt, *Making Ends Meet*, p. 139, and on no doubt more rare cases, p. 51 (the prosperous allowance recipient). Cf. Macnicol, *The Movement for Family Allowances*.

10 On seamen's family allotments, see E. Mahler and E.F. Rathbone, *Payment of Seamen; The Present System; How the Wives Suffer* (C. Tinling, Liverpool, 1911); Jones, *Social Survey of Merseyside*, vol. II, pp. 95–6; and Liverpool Personal Service Society (hereafter LPSS), *AR* (1936–37), p. 27.

11 For other examples of women's survival strategies, see E. Roberts, chapter 9 in this volume; E. Ross, 'Survival Networks: Women's Neighbourhood Sharing in London before World War I', *History Workshop Journal* (hereafter, HWJ) no. 15 (1983), pp. 4–27; and Tebbutt, *Making Ends Meet*.

12 Second Chance to Learn, *Women's History, Women's Lives*, (Printfine Ltd., Liverpool, 1982) and *The Merseyside Women's War, 1939–45*, (n.p., Liverpool, 1983); and Pat Ayers, 'The Second World War and Women, With Particular Reference to Women in Liverpool', (BA thesis, University of Liverpool, 1981).

13 Merseyside Socialist Research Group, *Merseyside in Crisis*, pp. 31–5; Pilgrim Trust, *Men Without Work*, pp. 244–63; and Second Chance, *Women's History*. On the historical background to this, see The Royal Commission on Labour, The Employment of Women, *Report* of Miss C.E. Collet on the conditions of work in Liverpool and Manchester, PP (1893–94), vol. 37, Part I, Cmd. 6894; 'Occupations of Girls After Leaving School', *Women's Industrial News*, n.s. 11 (1900), 163–4; and A. Harrison, *Women's Industries in Liverpool* (Williams & Norgate, 1904).

14 In parts of inner–city Liverpool, nearly a quarter of households lacked adult male wage earners in the early 1930s; the large-scale social survey of Merseyside at that time found a high percentage of these lived below 'the poverty line'. Employment opportunities remained comparatively limited for Liverpool women, and employers operated with the principle

that women workers needed wages which, at most, supported them alone. Jones, *Social Survey of Merseyside*, vol.III, pp.226–46, 251, 462.

15 Jones, *Social Survey of Merseyside*, vol. II, pp.25–207 *passim*; Ministry of Labour, *Standard Time Rates of Wages and Hours of Labour of Great Britain and N. Ireland at 31st August 1929*, (HMSO, 1929); and Hanham *Report of Enquiry*. However, some evidence is conflicting: interview by Lambertz with T.B., a Liverpool dock worker, about his 1940s childhood (October, 1981). For an earlier period, see Liverpool Joint Research Committee on the Domestic Conditions and Expenditure of the Families of Certain Liverpool Labourers, *How the Casual Labourer Lives*, (Northern Publishing Co., Liverpool, 1909).

16 Tape 41 (Ayers), woman, born 1908.

17 Bill Ridgway, personal communication (Ayers). A 'flat week' meant that he earned basic wages without overtime, bonuses or perks.

18 Tape 30 (Ayers), man, born 1905.

19 It remains unclear how boys were first incorporated into mothers' budgeting activities, but then evidently socialized to 'forget' mothers' or wives' struggles as they reached adulthood. See P. O'Mara, *Autobiography of a Liverpool Irish Slummy*, (Cedric Chivers, Bath, 1967, first published in 1934), pp.63–6; J. Jones, 'A Liverpool Socialist Education', HWJ no.18 (1984), p.93; and Tebbutt, *Making Ends Meet*, pp.39, 44–7, 162.

20 Tape 30 (Ayers); and Tape 39 (Ayers), man, born 1908. On working-class perceptions of what constituted a 'good' wife and a 'good' husband, see J. Seabrook, *Working-Class Childhood*, (Victor Gollancz, 1982), p.139.

21 See, for instance, the 1911 sketch (not about Liverpool) by Ada Nield Chew, 'Making It Stretch (A True Story)', in *The Life and Writings of Ada Nield Chew*, (Virago, 1982), pp.139–46. See also, E. Ross, ' "Fierce Questions and Taunts": Married Life in Working-Class London, 1870–1914', *Feminist Studies*, 8 (1982), p.588; and Tebbutt, *Making Ends Meet*, p.39, citing B.S. Rowntree, *Poverty: A Study of Town Life* (Longman, 1901) and M. Pember Reeves, *Round About a Pound a Week*, (Bell, 1913).

22 Tape 11 (Ayers), woman, born 1922.

23 S.M., Liverpool dock worker's daughter, personal communication (Ayers); cf. M. Grüttner, 'Working-Class Crime and the Labour Movement: Pilfering in the Hamburg Docks, 1888–1923', in R. Evans (ed.), *The German Working Class 1888–1933: The Politics of Everyday Life*, (Croom Helm, 1982), pp.54–79.

24 Tebbutt, *Making Ends Meet*; Pilgrim Trust, *Men Without Work*; and Liverpool Joint Research Committee, *The Casual Labourer*.

25 Various interviews conducted between 1981 and 1983 (Ayers), including numbers 7, 9, 32, 35, 40; Second Chance, *Women's History*, p.4; and Liverpool Council of Voluntary Aid, Inc., *Report on Betting in Liverpool* (Liverpool Council of Voluntary Aid, Liverpool, 1927), p.7.

26 Tapes 7, 9, 18, 26, 32, 35, 40, 41 (Ayers); interviews by Tony Lane with B.D. (April, 1978) and B.E. (April, 1978). Despite the exploitative

conditions and low income involved, a number of earlier labour investigators in the city appear to have approved of home-work for mothers, for it ostensibly allowed for more child supervision. See the Liverpool Women's Industrial Council (hereafter, LWIC), *Home Work in Liverpool* (Northern Publishing Co, Liverpool, 1909) (a study of 205 women and 13 men home-workers); and Mahler and Rathbone, *Payment of Seamen*.

27 Tape 11 (Ayers).

28 Man, born 1926, personal communication (Ayers).

29 Tape 17 (Ayers), woman, born 1917; woman, born 1933, personal communication (Ayers); and Ayers, 'The Second World War and Women'.

30 Tape 42 (Ayers), woman, born 1893.

31 *Kelly's [Gore's] Directory of Liverpool*, (Kelly's Directories Ltd., 1929).

32 See Ross, 'Survival Networks'; O'Mara, *Autobiography*; Tapes 41 and 42 (Ayers); and cf. Tebbutt, *Making Ends Meet*, pp.57–8.

33 Tapes 11 and 41 (Ayers).

34 Liverpool Joint Research Committee, *The Casual Labourer*, Case XI, p.xxxiv. Cf. Cases 4, 13, 18, and IV and VI, p.xxxiii.

35 Social and Industrial Reform Committee of the Liverpool Women's Citizens Association, *Report*, (July, 1924). Cf. Tebbutt, *Making Ends Meet*, pp.55–7.

36 LPSS (*AR* (1927), p.15; and D. Keeling, *The Crowded Stairs: Recollections of Social Work in Liverpool*, (National Council of Social Service, 1961), pp.111–12. See also, LPSS, *AR*s (1922–5); and Tebbutt, *Making Ends Meet*, pp.51–6, 130–3.

37 Interview by Tony Lane with F. B. (April, 1978). See also, O'Mara, *Autobiography*, pp.66–8; and Liverpool Watch Committee, *AR*s (1907), pp.53–5; (1908), pp.46–7; and (1912), p.19.

38 For an informative survey of the hire-purchase legislation of 1938 and the sorts of abuses that initiated concern, see A. Vallance, *Hire Purchase*, (J. Nelson & Sons, 1939). See also H. Forrester, *Liverpool Miss* (Fontana, 1982), pp.132–4.

39 For instance, see the *Manchester Guardian*, (16 September, 1937). Also, *Parliamentary Debates* (Commons), 10 December 1937, cols. 729–70, and 6 May 1938, cols. 1194–212.

40 For local discussions, see 'M.P. and Hire Purchase "Scandals" ', *Liverpool Echo* (10 December 1937); LPSS, *17th AR* (1935); N. Williams, 'Problems of Population and Education in the New Housing Estates with Special Reference to Norris Green' (MA thesis, University of Liverpool, 1938); and D. Keeling, 'Hire Purchase: An Address', *Liverpool Quarterly*, 6 (April 1938), pp.75–81.

41 This is examined at greater length in J. Lambertz, 'The Politics and Economics of Family Violence, from the late Nineteenth Century to 1948' (M. Phil. thesis, University of Manchester, 1984). On experimental classes and savings clubs for housewives, see LPSS, *AR*s (1932–39). Cf. A. Davin, 'Imperialism and Motherhood', HWJ no.5 (1978), pp.24, 26.

42 Davin, 'Imperialism and Motherhood'; and J. Lewis, *The Politics of Motherhood: Child and Maternal Welfare in England, 1900–1939*, (Croom Helm, 1980).

43 J. Macnicol, 'Family Allowances and Less Eligibility', in P. Thane (ed.), *Origins of British Social Policy*, (Croom Helm, 1978), pp.173–202; and C. Webster, 'Healthy or Hungry Thirties?', HWJ, no.13 (1982), pp.110–29. On the question of holding individual men responsible for maintenance see, for instance, M.S. Reeves, 'The Wife of the Working Man', *The Common Cause*, 5 (1914), p. 833; and 'The Obligation to Support a Wife', *Woman's Leader and the Common Cause*, 14 (1932), p. 387.

44 Cf. for instance, The [Liverpool] Mothers' Rest Association, *28th AR* (1948), p.3; C.O. Stallybrass, 'Problem Families', in Liverpool Council of Social Service, (hereafter LCSS) (ed.), *Problem Families: The Report of a Conference*, (LCSS, Liverpool, 1946); I.A. Ireland, *Margaret Beavan of Liverpool: Her Character and Work* (Henry Young & Sons, Liverpool, 1938), pp.103–12; *Liverpool Child Welfare News*, (July, 1926), pp.62–3; and The Mothers' Rest Association, *ARs* (1947, 1949).

45 See discussions in M. McIntosh, 'The State and the Oppression of Women', in A. Kuhn and A. Wolpe (eds), *Feminism and Materialism*, (Routledge & Kegan Paul, 1978), pp.254–89; and McIntosh, 'The Welfare State and the Needs of the Dependent Family', in S. Burman (ed.), *Fit Work for Women*, (Croom Helm, 1979), pp.153–72; E. Wilson, *Women and the Welfare State*, (Tavistock, 1977); and J. Lewis, 'Dealing with Dependency: State Practices and Social Realities, 1870–1945', in J. Lewis (ed.), *Women's Welfare/Women's Rights*, (Croom Helm, 1983), pp.17–37.

46 Lewis, *The Politics of Motherhood*; C. Webster, 'Healthy or Hungry?'; J. Riddell, 'A Study of the History and Development of the School Medical Service in Liverpool from 1908 to 1939' (MA thesis, University of Liverpool, 1946); Ayers, 'The Second World War and Women'; and Second Chance, *Women's War*.

47 Davin, 'Imperialism and Motherhood', p.52.

48 The *ARs* of the National Society for the Prevention of Cruelty to Children (NSPCC) and the Liverpool SPCC for the first decades of the twentieth century suggest this, as do those for the LPSS between the wars. See also, Liverpool Women Police Patrols (hereafter LWPP), *ARs* (1933, 1935), and the Liverpool Vigilance Society (Society for the Prevention of International Traffic in Women and Children), *ARs* (1919–20, 1923–24). LSPCC pressure on fathers was apparently uneven and ambivalently, and often ineffectually executed: LSPCC, *50th AR* (1932) and testimony of Ronald P. Clayton, cf. LSPCC solicitor before the Royal Commission on Divorce and Matrimonial Causes, PP, (1912–13) XX, Cd. 6481, 13 December 1910.

49 Cf. Ross, 'Fierce Taunts'; and N. Tomes, 'A "Torrent of Abuse": Crimes of Violence Between Working-Class Men and Women in London, 1840–1875', *Journal of Social History*, 11 (1978), pp.328–45.

50 Tape 11 (Ayers).

51 Second Chance, *Women's History*, pp. 15–16. On the prevalence of violence by men against their wives and lovers in the city, also see the fairly melodramatic memoirs of an inner-city detective inspector (from the early 1930s through the 1960s): W. Prendergast, *Z-Car Detective*, (John Long, 1964), pp. 19-30 *passim*, and *Calling All Z-Cars*, (John Long, 1966), p. 99.

52 Tape 75 (Ayers), woman, born 1926.

53 Suggested by O'Mara, *Autobiography*; and interview by Lambertz with M.W., former Liverpool moral welfare worker (April, 1983).

54 Tape 12 (Ayers), man, born 1913.

55 Lambertz, 'Family Violence'. Cf. Davin, 'Imperialism and Motherhood'; and Lewis, *The Politics of Motherhood*.

56 On help from kin, see O'Mara, *Autobiography*, pp. 36, 44–7; and Second Chance, *Women's History*, p. 15. On employment, Jones, *Social Survey of Merseyside*, vol. III, pp. 226–51. All the Liverpool women's job surveys preceding the first world war – by the LWIC, central government and also by independent investigators – suggest a similar employment situation. Mothers' stated occupations in their petitions for aid (for their fatherless children) to the Liverpool Seamen's Orphan Institution from the late nineteenth century up to the second world war also hint that most widows would be forced to rely on some form of badly paid casual work (analysed in Lambertz, 'Family Violence').

57 On such problems see, for instance, Rathbone, *The Disinherited Family*, p. 94 ff.; LPSS, *AR*s (1942–43); and discussions in the late 1940s in the journal of the Married Women's Association, *Wife and Citizen*.

58 Rathbone, ibid.; V.M. Shillington, 'Maintenance Grants Under Separation Orders', *Women's Industrial News*, 16 (1913), 108; *The Common Cause*, 18 (1921), p. 346; and O.R. McGregor, L. Blom-Cooper, and C. Gibson, *Separated Spouses: A Study of Matrimonial Jurisdiction of Magistrates' Courts*, (Gerald Duckworth, 1970), pp. 1–29. Inter-war organizations such as the Liverpool Women Police Patrol sometimes acted as *ad hoc* collection agencies for maintenance money: LWPP, *AR*s (1933, 1935).

59 This is suggested, for instance, by the Liverpool Diocesan Branch Church of England Temperance Society's police court work: *AR*s (1927, 1940, 1942), and in *Stewardship*, journal of the city's Anglican 'Police Court and Prison Gate Mission', no. 6 (July, 1947) and no. 8 (July, 1948). Also see, LWPP, *AR* (1935); and LPSS, *AR*s (1928,1937–8). Earlier testimony suggests that this had a long-standing basis in the city: see evidence of Ronald Clayton, Henry Goldstone, Edgar Sanders, and G.A. Solly before the Royal Commission on Divorce and Matrimonial Causes, PP, (1912–13) XVIII, Cd. 6479; XIX, Cd. 6480, and XX, Cd. 6481. However, successes were elusive and some welfare workers or police complacently accepted temporary reunifications as stable and unproblematic situations: 'A Wife's Terrible Ordeal', *Liverpool Weekly Post* (1 January 1927); Prendergast, *Calling All Z-Cars*. p. 103; and cf. NSPCC, 'A Wife Beater', *AR* (1947), p. 7. See also sceptical comments from elsewhere in 'When Mercy Seasons Justice', *Woman's Leader and*

the *Common Cause*, 15 (1923), p. 238; and 'The Police Court and Its Work', *WLCC*, 17 (1925), p. 180.

60 Cf. Rathbone, *The Disinherited Family*, p. 53.

V
The Family Economy

A woman and children making matchboxes at home c. 1900

9

Women's Strategies, 1890–1940

Elizabeth A. M. Roberts

Throughout the period under discussion, very many working-class women struggled to find the means to clothe, house and feed their families.[1] Their husbands' wages alone were insufficient for these purposes and so they had to find ways both of supplementing their incomes and of spending them as economically as possible. These various methods of balancing families' budgets may be termed 'strategies' and they included: married women working part- or full-time; relying on children's wages; exerting the most rigid control over their household budgets; using the products of their families' allotments; and borrowing both goods and cash.

For the working-class woman there was a close interrelationship between the public and private spheres of life. Their husbands, and sometimes they themselves, worked in the public sphere but the income was intended for the family and the home. The maintenance and support of these two institutions were the chief preoccupations of working-class women and the blurring of the public and private divisions in their lives was exemplified in their work. Much of it was of course domestic, unpaid and private; some of their work by contrast was in the public sphere, for example in the cotton mills. In many cases, however, they earned money, thus making themselves part of the labour market and part of the public sphere, and yet this work was nevertheless carried out in the private sphere of the home. For the women who had shops in their home the blurring of the difference between public and private spheres was complete.

The adoption of these strategies by working-class women was essential in view of the widespread poverty existing both before and after the First World War. The evidence for the existence of this poverty is very compelling, although undoubtedly historians will continue to argue about the exactness of the suggested poverty lines and the number of people living in poverty at any given time. The first, and indeed seminal study of poverty to be published in this century was that of B. Seebohm Rowntree whose work on York was published in 1901.[2] He suggested that it was possible to draw a poverty line at 21/8d for a family of four to five persons. Any family whose total weekly income was less than this was in primary poverty, that is with 'earnings insufficient to obtain the minimum necessaries for the maintenance of merely physical efficiency'.[3] It has proved difficult, in the pre-1914 period, to find labourers and unskilled men in general earning as much as 21/8d (while often having considerably more than two or three children). This large group of men and their families therefore lived in very considerable poverty. It was in these families that women were the most likely to adopt at least one and possibly two of the strategies outlined above. Further confirmation of the widespread nature of poverty before the First World War can be found in very many contemporary surveys of working-class life. One of the best known of these, and one which will be referred to in this chapter, is Magdalen Stuart Pember Reeves' work on the lives of working-class women in south London in the period 1909–13.[4] Here is vividly portrayed the endless battle women had to manage on an income of about £1 a week.

The interest felt by social observers in working-class standards of living continued in the inter-war period. There was an undoubted rise in the standards of living of many people but there still existed much poverty, especially among the unemployed and the unskilled, and notably among those with large families. A. L. Bowley and M. H. Hogg, who published their work in 1925, used, like Rowntree, a standard of bare physical efficiency. They reached the conclusion that expenditure of about 37/6d was necessary if this standard was to be achieved for a family of five (at 1925 prices).[5] The investigators in the Social Survey of Merseyside which was begun in 1928 adopted the same standards.[6] Labourers at that time were likely to earn rather more than this, i.e. about £2 a week. However Rowntree, who in 1935 repeated his survey of York, argued that an income of 53/– a week was essential for a family of five to secure the basic necessities of life.[7] If this new Rowntree standard is adopted then nearly all labourers, male textile workers and the unemployed were living below the poverty line.

It is clear from these surveys, and from the work of Margery Spring Rice in *Working-Class Wives*,[8] that there continued to be much poverty among working-class families and that as late as 1939 when Spring Rice's book was published, women were still struggling to clothe, feed and house their families.

While the widespread existence of poverty both before and after the First World War is not in doubt, it is difficult to assess which strategies were adopted by working-class women to combat it. Contemporary surveys chronicle poverty but are sometimes silent about the strategies; we do not know whether it was because they did not exist, or whether it was thought unnecessary to record them. The main evidence used in this chapter is drawn from oral testimonies. One hundred and seventy old people from the three northern towns of Barrow, Lancaster and Preston were extensively interviewed about many aspects of working-class life in the period 1890–1940. The group was divided almost equally between men and women and questions were asked about both their own and their parents' lives. The evidence used here relates either to their mothers' experiences or their own or their wives'.[9]

Each town in the survey had a different economic base. Barrow, a new town in the 1860s, relied on engineering, iron and steel, and shipbuilding. Lancaster had a mixed economy based on manufacturing (oil-cloth, linoleum and furniture) and on services (hospitals and various other instituions). Preston was predominantly a textile town; in 1911 by far the largest group of workers (over 40 per cent) were involved in the manufacture of cotton while well under 10 per cent, the next largest group, were in engineering. It is clear from the oral evidence that women adopted a range of strategies to combat poverty: this has also been borne out in other regional oral history surveys, for example in Kent and in Greater Manchester.[10]

There must be reasons for the tantalizingly limited references to women's activities in the printed surveys, but without being able to question the people who undertook them, it is impossible to know what they were. It must be stressed therefore that there is not sufficient empirical data at this stage to make possible generalizations about women's strategies on a national scale.

It would seem from what evidence *is* available that the range of strategies undertaken and the number of women involved in them varied both from town to town and from family to family. Within an area the most striking differences are observable between the wives of unskilled men, whose wages throughout the period were below both of Rowntree's poverty lines, and those of skilled men, whose wages were comfortably in excess of those lines. These women and their husbands were clearly influenced by the domestic ideology and middle-class ideal of domesticity of the nineteenth century. Men were seen as the sole wage earners and women as housewives and mothers. Many poorer women also shared the male-breadwinner family model as an ideal to aim for (see chapter 4). They worked, not because they saw work as a liberation or an emancipation from household imprisonment, but because they needed the money. It would be misleading, however, to make too clear a division between wives of labourers and those of skilled men. The latter were still obliged to keep a tight control of their spending, and if a skilled man was unemployed, or ill or, indeed, if he died then his wife, like her poorer sisters, was obliged to adopt various other strategies in order to survive.

It will be observed that the assumption made so far is that working-class women controlled the household finances. This appears to have been widely true whether in York in 1900, in Lambeth just before the First World War, or in the North-West throughout the fifty-year period under consideration. Helen Bosanquet writing in 1906 described what appears to have been a general division of responsibilities and separation of roles:

> But there is one most important brand of industrial co-operation which still prevails in the great majority of society: it is that which assigns to the wife the functions of manager and spender of the family income and the care of the home and children, while the husband and adult children take responsibility of providing the income . . . Generally speaking they (i.e. the women) expect to have and they get the entire management of the family income, in many cases determining even the amount which the wage earners, husbands, son and daughter alike may reserve for their own use.[11]

Although Helen Bosanquet refers to 'all ranks of society', one may presume she is writing particularly of working-class families both because of her reference to 'wage-earners' and because of the context of the rest of her book. Mr Richards, from Lancaster, spoke thus of his mother in the 1890s (the word 'schemer' has somewhat changed its meaning): 'This is how they had to do it, they were schemers and providers in them days, but I'm sticking up for the woman. The provider had a little wage and it was the women who were the schemers. There was always something on our table and they always had a supper.'[12] Mrs Harrison, growing up in Preston over thirty years later, had the same view of her mother: 'My father gave my mother all the money . . . he left the money to mother because she was the manager and he knew that she used every halfpenny of the money. He didn't interfere.' She also recalled her father (who was active in local politics and his trade union) discussing the state of the nation in the late 1920s and saying, 'The country would never have been in such a state if mother had been over the Bank of England!'[13]

One of the most obvious ways of coping with an inadequate family income was for women to earn money on their own account. It is quite probable that over the nation as a whole we shall never be able to make even an approximate estimate of how many married women had paid work within this fifty-year period. Both Richard Wall, and Michael Anderson, after working extensively on the census returns, argue that the amount of wage-earning work done by married women has been grossly underestimated.[14] I would agree with them. The census returns for 1901 and 1911 give the following percentages of married women and widows in full-time work in the local area. Barrow, 6 and 7 per cent; Lancaster, 10 and 11 per cent; Preston 30.5 and 35 per cent.[15] A different way of looking at married women's work is to consider it over a life-time. From my local survey (see Table 9.1), one could argue that approximately twice as many married women worked full-time *at some point during their married life* as is indicated in census returns for any particular year.

Census returns also underestimate the amount of paid work carried out by married women because they ignore casual part-time jobs. Table 9.1 shows how widespread was paid part-time work among respondents. The table does require, however, some

TABLE 9.1   PERCENTAGES OF MARRIED WOMEN IN WORK, 1890–1940

	Mothers of respondents		
	In full-time work at some point in married life	*In part-time work at some point in married life*	*No paid work at any time in married life*
Barrow	13.5	46	40.5
Lancaster	25	40	37.5
Preston	55	41.5	23
	Respondents or wives of respondents (excluding unmarried respondents and respondents married after 1940)		
Preston 71	28.5	19	

explanation. It was not possible to do any meaningful calculations for respondents and/or their wives in Barrow and Lancaster because the research project concentrated mainly on their parents' generation and their own younger lives (up to 1930). There is, of course, evidence about married women's wage earning for the inter-war period. This is used to illustrate certain points but is not present in sufficient quantity to make even tentative statistical calculations. It will be seen that in all cases except for the mothers' generation in Barrow the figures added up to more than 100 per cent. This was because some women did both full-time and part-time jobs at different points in their married lives. (Barrow women however appear to have worked either part-time, or full-time or not at all.) It would, however, be most unwise to read too much significance into these figures for they cannot begin to estimate the *amount* of work done by married women, or indeed their earnings. Some women worked for a few hours a week for only a short period, while others worked long hours for many years. It all depended on their circumstances and their perceptions of their families' needs.

In my local survey, over 40 per cent of the mothers of respondents had had part-time work at some point in their married life. And yet it is difficult to assess how widespread, through the nation as a whole, this practice was. The only way of women earning money which is mentioned several times in *Round About a Pound a Week* is that of taking in lodgers (a woman would rent a house and then sublet part of it to help out with the rent).[16] Margery Spring Rice records that only 34 out of the 1,250 women replying to her questionnaire had paid work. This low percentage may have been the result of the wording of the questionnaire, the relevant question being 'What paid work if any do you do *outside* your home?',[17] thus ignoring the possiblity of doing paid work inside the home. It could also be that women who ran a house, family and who also worked for wages, did not have the time to fill in questionnaires. It has been suggested that the absence of evidence regarding paid employment in Pember Reeves' survey was because her interviewers visited women who were about to have, or who had recently had a baby and that this would prevent them working. Interestingly, many Preston women in a similar situation were in full-time work with their babies and small children in the care of a childminder. The apparent absence of a neighbourhood network of childminders may also have contributed to the absence of references to women going out to work in Lambeth.

Rowntree's findings for York at the turn of the century were rather different. He calculated the average sums contributed by wives to family budgets, as shown in table 9.2. These figures illustrate that in the *poorest* families (which in York, according to Rowntree, were usually those where there was no male breadwinner) the woman's financial contribution was of more significance than in the rather more prosperous ones. In the local survey women had wage-earning jobs where there was a perceived financial necessity to do so. They might have been widows, but more usually they were the wives of low-wage earners. As so many said, 'we worked because we had to'. This was true whether the women worked full- or part-time. They may have enjoyed their work or hated it but their reason for working was their need for money. As the Inter-Departmental Committee on Physical Deterioration (1904) said of wage-earning wives, 'The one wage was insufficient to keep the family in the standard of life they expect'.[18]

TABLE 9:2   MARRIED WOMEN IN YORK. AVERAGE CONTRIBUTIONS OF WEEKLY INCOME IN THE 1890s

Weekly family wage	Women's weekly average earnings
Under 18s	5s. 8½d
18s–21s	2.7½d
21s–30s	1.5½d
Over 30s	1.3d

Source: B. S. Rowntree, *Poverty: A Study of Town Life* (Longman, 1901), p. 102.

Whilst it is perhaps obvious that very many poor women believed that they had to work in order to feed their families, it is less clear what women regarded as an adequate income. Perceptions of what was necessary for a family's well-being differed considerably from individual to individual. Consequently some women felt it essential to earn more money than did others, although their husbands' wages may have been identical. Even when the basic needs were satisfied some women still saw compelling reasons for working, such as to buy a house, or to improve one, or to educate the children.

Mr Pearson's mother in Barrow bought and sold goods in the auction rooms so that eventually not only she but her six children could buy their own homes. She bought her first house about 1900 and was therefore presumably earning rather more than the 'average' woman in Rowntree's survey (her husband at that time earned 18/– a week, but was frequently out of work).[19] Mrs Morris's mother, in the 1890s, opened a shop in her parlour so that she could pay for her children to have a secondary education. She did this for four out of five (the fifth being of a more practical inclination) and they all became teachers. Her husband was a shipwright and earned a reasonable wage, possibly as much as £2 a week, but there was much industrial unrest in Barrow during that period and he was often unemployed.[20]

These two women are not only illustrative of the difference in women's perceptions of what constituted a family need, they also show how women worked not for themselves but for their families; familialistic concerns were of abiding importance, individualistic ones were not. Indeed women throughout the period demonstrate an interesting attitude to 'liberation'. Whilst there was no shame in working, other non-working women feeling pity rather than contempt for those who *had* to work, it remained the ambition of the great majority of working women to give up paid work as soon as it was possible. The influence of the domestic idyll of the wife staying at home managing the home and family and the husband going out to work to earn the family living was very strong.[21] So too was the idea that a woman staying at home was more respected than one going out to work. It is interesting that these conclusions, which were reached after a close look at the empirical evidence for the North West of England were also suggested by Tilly, Scott and Cohen for a much wider group and a longer time-period. They have stressed the importance of familialistic concerns rather than individualistic ones: 'British women [in the nineteenth century] tended to give up work outside the home, or moved in and out of the labour force when necessary. This demonstrates that women married and single were motivated to work by economic necessity and not by desire for "liberation".'[22]

The nature of employment for married women appears to have varied considerably from area to area and from generation to generation. They were as affected as other workers by the law of supply and demand: women in both Magdalen Stuart Pember Reeves' survey and that of Margery Spring Rice very often did not have access to a proper water supply and washing facilities and it would be difficult to see them therefore as washerwomen. Women in Preston were much more likely to be in full-time work, because of the mills, than were women in Lancaster, where there were only a few mills, and particularly more than women in Barrow, where there were none. Childminders were much more common in Preston because full-time working mothers created a demand for their services.

One of the most interesting divisions between the women who earned money was between the women who were in effect self-employed, the washerwomen, shop-keepers, childminders, lodging-house keepers and so on and those who worked for someone else, most notably the full-time cotton worker and the part-time charladies. The self-employed have been described as 'penny capitalists'. Using a wide range of evidence, John Benson in *The Penny Capitalists: a study of nineteenth century working-class entrepreneurs* argues that penny capitalism did not decline before 1914. (He suggests that as many as 40 per cent of all working-class families at any time were involved in some form of part-time penny capitalist activity.)[23] My own survey would support this view for the end of the nineteenth century and for the Edwardian period. It is interesting and perhaps significant however, to see from table 9.1 for Preston the increase in those engaged in full-time work (almost inevitably as employees) and a decline in those in part-time work (mostly self-employed) between the two generations of Preston women. Some reasons for these apparent changes are suggested below.

The work of part-time women penny capitalists is examined first. Some women took in washing: this was easier in this area than in others because most women had the necessary equipment (boiler, tubs, dolly legs or possers* and mangle) and the essential water supply in the home and/or washhouse. However, not all women had equipment and as being a washerwoman was deemed a good way for a widow to make a living, help was often provided by the community. Mr Darnley reported that in Preston 'If a woman's husband died they used to buy a mangle if she was hard up and had a big family so she could earn a living doing washing for other people.'[24] John Benson reveals similar help in Fife: 'Widows of Fife miners killed in the pit were sometimes provided by the coal-owners with a "large mangle" so that customers could get their washing mangled at so much a bundle.'[25] In the local survey both widows and wives of men on low incomes were washerwomen. It is clear that it only provided a small income.

Mr Richards' mother was left a widow with six small children; try as she might as a washerwoman, and with the help of the extended

*Dolly legs were short sticks with three legs at the end, used for 'beating' the washing in the tub. A posser was a stick with a metal dome on the end.

family, she could not manage adequately to care for the children. Eventually she placed them in a local private orphanage where they stayed during term time, returning home for the school holidays.[26] The income from washing is difficult to assess; there were no fixed prices and women worked different numbers of hours. It was, of course, very hard work: water was lifted in and out of boilers and tubs, dolly legs or possers pounded and twisted the clothes, heavy wet clothes had to be lifted and mangled and then ironed with very heavy irons when dry. It is surprising that as many women took in washing as they did, about 11.5 per cent of Preston mothers, 4 per cent in Barrow and 14 per cent in Lancaster. It was a very unpopular activity with their families who did not like their homes filled with wet washing. Mrs Nixon of Lancaster, whose husband was a labourer and who had eight children, took in washing in the inter-war period, doing three baskets a week and charging 2/6d a basket: 'I daren't have them round the fire when dad [her husband] came home. I used to hurry up and get them washed and dried and ironed and back at night. That half crown helped us for the rest of the week.'[27]

Mrs Nixon represents what appears to be a declining group of women workers; no Preston respondent or wife of a respondent took in washing and there were fewer among younger Barrow and Lancaster women. One can only speculate about the reasons: possibly customers with larger orders were turning to commercial laundries, perhaps in the belief that they did a 'better job'. It is difficult to know about relative costs as washerwomen varied them so much. In Preston, older washerwomen had mostly done the washing of women in the mills: perhaps the next generation of mill workers with much smaller families to wash for and more time in which to do it (mill hours were reduced in 1918) preferred to do their own.

There were advantages in working at home, – a woman could control the hours worked, the pace of work, and could oversee her own family at the same time. Perhaps most importantly she was not at the beck and call of an employer. In her own home a woman could be a provider of personal services (taking in lodgers, childminding), a manufacturer (dressmaking), or a retailer. No one was interviewed who remembered women of their family working as sweated labour, or as outworkers. Undoubtedly their accounts of working at home might have been more disturbing and rather less glowing if they had done.

Taking in lodgers who were strangers was not all that usual. Only

4 per cent of the Barrow mothers, 8 per cent of Lancaster ones and 5 per cent of those in Preston had lodgers who were strangers to the family. On the other hand very many women had relatives living with them; in fact several women who are listed as having no paid occupation did in fact have co-resident relations. The reasons that they are classified as not having a wage-earning job is because respondents did not categorize taking in relatives in this way. Indeed, young or old, or sick relatives constituted a drain on the family resources rather than representing a profit. However, children grew into wage-earning adults and older relatives with employment or an employed spouse always paid a sum of money for rent and board, thus representing a 'hidden' income for many women.

There were many more family than non-family lodgers because of ties of affection, feelings of obligation and because of practicality. It was much easier to get a relation to share a family bedroom, indeed a bed, than a stranger. The most common period during which strangers were lodged was during the two world wars. This was not always because of a desire to do one's patriotic duty. Mrs Burns in Lancaster had her husband in the army and found it very difficult to feed herself and her two small daughters on her army allowance. Like many other women she was tempted to the munitions works by the high wages (in this case Gillows who made aeroplanes) but, before finally committing herself, discussed it with a neighbour: 'She said "Oh don't leave little Minnie and Emily . . . I'll tell you what Sally, I've two lodgers from the Projectile (another munitions works) . . . they call them Polly and Cissy and they belong to Wigan. They would like to come to live if you'd let them." I said "Are you sure? I've got the front bed room." That was how I never went to Gillows!'[28]

Taking in sewing was another form of penny capitalism. The woman provided the labour and the machinery and the client provided the material. Six per cent of Lancaster mothers, 6 per cent of those in Barrow and 7 per cent of those in Preston took in sewing. The majority of working-class homes had sewing machines, it was often the only piece of technology in the working-class home. Women altered clothes and ran up things for the family but were usually quite reluctant to sew for anyone outside the family circle. Most dressmakers catering for clients had in fact served their apprenticeship and were very competent. Like other forms of work undertaken at home, sewing could cause conflict. Seeing their wives working for money may have upset some men's pride by reminding them that their wage on its own was insufficient to provide for the family. Others disliked their wives being overworked, underpaid and generally exploited. Mrs Mulholland's mother was a remarkable woman. She had sixteen children of whom only three reached adulthood. She found time to be active in the socialist movement and also to earn money in a variety of ways. Until 1914 her husband earned only 18/— a week. She enjoyed sewing and took in dressmaking. Mrs Mulholland said: 'Sometimes she never got paid and she never charged much when she did get paid but often she never got paid. M'dad used to worry with her having all the babies and he'd see her sewing and sewing. One time he picked it up and put it on the fire because it got him down so much.'[29]

One of the most profitable jobs a woman could do in her own home was child-minding. This occupation was only possible of course where there were large numbers of mothers in full-time work and they are conspicuously absent in the Rowntree, Pember Reeves and Spring Rice surveys. Not surprisingly in view of the very low percentage of married women in full-time work, no Barrow respondent or her mother was a childminder; in Lancaster, 4 per cent of respondents' mothers were childminders; but in Preston the figure was 11 per cent. For the period before the First World War weekly payments of between 3/— and 10/— per child have been quoted. This would include a charge for the child's food but it is clear that a woman who was prepared to take three or four children and to charge the top rate had a very comfortable income.

The most difficult group of penny capitalists to write about are those involved in retailing. It can be said with confidence that all the women in this category were self-employed (if that includes working in their family shop) but, after that, meaningful generalizations are impossible, except possibly to say that it was the most usual way, apart from mill work, for women to earn money on their own account. John Benson wrote that 'retailing long remained a most popular form of penny capitalist activity.'[30] In Barrow, 17 per cent of mothers, 6 per cent of those in Lancaster and 18 per cent of those in Preston, and 12 per cent of Preston respondents and/or wives were involved in retailing. However, these figures cover a very wide range of experiences. At one end of the spectrum was Mrs Pearce's mother who, on being left a widow, became a hawker – selling laces, buttons and general haberdashery in the villages round Preston, trudging the lanes in all weathers for many years. (She could not work in the town because of the competition from shops who undercut her prices.) As soon as her four children were all wage earners she understandably refused to work any more, relying on the children for both wages and housekeeping.[31]

At the other end of the spectrum was the mother of Mr Cartwright who, when unmarried, opened her own confectioner's shop. She continued to run this after marriage and through ten pregnancies. By the time her sons had grown up (and she was dead) the business had become very large and of regional importance.[32] In between these two extremes come a number of respondents' mothers, respondents and/or their wives. Some worked part-time like Mr Maguire's mother who made pies in her back kitchen, while others helped in their husbands' shops, or opened and ran shops on their own account whilst their husbands worked (or failed to) elsewhere. Three women ran public houses. Mrs Phillips' mother had a shop in Preston which opened at 6 a.m. and closed at midnight. Undeterred by the example of her mother's unremitting labour, Mrs Phillips opened her own pie shop when still very young: '1929 I started in an empty room and waited for my first customer. I went round all my mother's wholesalers and asked them if they would give me credit . . . And they did. From there I worked the shop up and after three years I sold it for £250. My husband was out of work.' She opened another shop which was very successful and it is clear that she ran the shop and her husband helped.[33]

These women retailers are difficult to categorize. Some remained very poor and unmistakably working-class, others began as poor and working-class and became prosperous and middle-class, while some lost their money and sank down the social scale. The motives of women retailers for working are also difficult to generalize about. Women working in other occupations did so because of perceived financial needs. Certainly, many retailers worked for the same reasons and often stopped work when those needs were satisfied. But others worked at retailing because they enjoyed it, and perhaps hated housework like Mrs Phillips' mother. Some enjoyed the prestige of being a shop-keeper and, indeed, the power it conferred when deciding on whether or not to grant credit. Mrs Phillips remarked; 'We thought we were better than the rest but we didn't show it.'[34] As John Benson has remarked, 'The shop met social as well as economic needs,' and 'Shopkeeping appeared to possess all that was lacking in other working-class jobs; comfort, security, independence and status.'[35]

Whereas some women possibly had a strong preference for working at home and being self-employed, others appear not to have minded, or perhaps more accurately, did not feel they could afford the luxury of choice: they worked because they had to and sought work wherever it could be found. Mrs Mulholland's mother, like several others, was both self-employed (as a dressmaker) and an employee: she went round houses decorating rooms, charging from 2/– to 2/6d each. Mrs Stott's mother was a washerwoman at home; but Mrs Stott herself went out washing in the inter-war period. (Her husband was a labourer, and she had one child.) Her employers were Morecambe boarding-house keepers. She started with forty sheets and progressed to the smaller items, receiving 3/6d a day. Sometimes she took in washing at home and charged 1/– for a dozen items of any size.[36]

The most usual part-time job away from home was domestic and/or office cleaning. In the inter-war period a woman could earn between 3/– and 3/6d for a long morning. In Barrow, 10.5 per cent of mothers, 18 per cent of Preston mothers, 18 per cent of Lancaster mothers, and 21.5 per cent of Preston respondents or their wives went out cleaning or washing or both.

The women who worked full-time were mostly involved in the production of cotton. The minority who were not thus employed were full-time shop-keepers or domestic workers. Both Lancaster and Preston had cotton mills and women had worked in them since the beginning of the nineteenth century. By the beginning of the twentieth century, according to the census returns of 1901 and 1911, Preston had about one-third of all its married women in work and the great majority of those were in textiles. The whole subject of full-time working wives and mothers is both interesting and complex and can only be touched upon here.[37] The women's reasons for working were complicated. To the economist they appear to have worked because of the demands of the local labour market, since cotton mills had always relied extensively on a labour force comprising large numbers of women and young people. The women themselves and their relations always say simply that they worked because they had to: they needed the money.

Women who chose mill work expected to increase their family income substantially: to this end they sacrificed control over a substantial part of their waking day, leisure, and much of the day to day upbringing of their children (who went to child minders). Their expectation of a substantial improvement in the family wage is easy to understand. Before 1914, a four-loom weaver could earn about £1 a week which was in excess of what an unskilled husband might earn. In reality, the women were nothing like as well off as the arithmetic suggested. Cotton wages were notoriously erratic, one good week could encourage a woman weaver to keep on working through many bad ones when the looms kept breaking down or new beams (warp threads) failed to arrive. Weavers were paid by the piece and their wages varied widely from week to week. Childminders had to be paid, even when they were relatives. Washerwomen also had to be paid. Before 1914, women arrived at the mill at 6 a.m, and left at 5.30 p.m., which left them little time and energy for a lot of heavy housework. Convenience foods – fish and chips, cold cooked meats, pies, bread, – all had to be bought at greater expense than the more traditional food which took time both to prepare and to cook. The burden of work carried by married textile women was colossal, far worse than anything described for Lambeth wives in *Round about a Pound a Week,* and was one very good reason why the great majority of women gave up full-time work as soon as they were financially able to do so; that is when their husbands got 'better' jobs, when their children began to earn, or when they themselves found part-time jobs. (Among the Preston respondents this move from full-time to part-time work was much more usual among the mothers than among the respondents themselves who tended to work full-time and then give up all paid employment to become 'ladies'.) Although the costs of working in both financial and physical terms were very high, the women *did* make a profit and the money made an important difference to their budgets, often raising them above the poverty line.

The final irony about married women's work in textile areas is that while women believed they had to work because their husbands' wages were low, what they did not realize was that by working they were helping to keep those wages low. It is clear from the Board of Trade Enquiry (1908) that labourers' wages in the building and engineering trades were lower in the textile towns than in the non-textile towns of Lancashire.[38] In the cotton trade itself a large female workforce kept down men's wages. The Board of Trade Report for 1931 gave the average textile wage (for men and women) as £1 14 6d, [39] which was below any of the inter-war poverty lines. The Pilgrim Trust suggested that in the textile towns employers had always paid unskilled men (in whatever trade) low wages on the understanding that their wives worked, the man's wage alone being insufficient to feed a family.[40] It is not, of course, argued that individual women could have increased their husbands' wages by stopping work. If *all* women had ceased working in the mills then mens' wages might have been increased, but even this is debatable because of the tradition of low wages in the textile industry.

Oral evidence gives many additional and vivid illustrations of the price these textile women paid in order to keep their families fed and clothed. Mrs Williams' husband was a caretaker and she worked most of her married life: 'Then when I had the baby I went right back to work because I had to do for the money . . . I would be washing at 1 o'clock in the morning and getting up at 5 o'clock to go to work.' Mrs Williams always had a lot of help in the house from her husband.[41] So too did Mrs Hudson whose husband was a roadman:

> Jack used to go at half past six . . . I used to get up at 7 and have a bit of breakfast, wash and dress Emily and put my sandwiches up for work, and I would take her down to auntie on the way. You hurried home at night . . . on Monday night we washed. Dad (i.e. her husband) used to light the boiler . . . he would have the water boiling and ready and he would have the first lot of whites in by the time I got home. I would cook the tea and we would finish washing. And it would be bed-time. Tuesday night I was ironing and every night something – bedrooms . . . cleaning the sitting room . . . I still used to manage to bake every week . . . we used to have one night out a week and it was Saturday.[42]

Eventually Mrs Hudson gave up full-time work and became a part-time cleaner because her husband could not cope with the double burden of housework and a full-time job.

In general a working-class woman regarded 'emancipation' as a move away from work towards staying at home. They welcomed, understandably, the lightening of their burden of work. Once they left full-time work they very rarely returned, the main exception being the widows. The widows in my survey managed well, none having to call on poor relief. Some had help from their extended family – Mr Mawson's mother in Barrow went to live with her widowed father and bachelor brother and kept house for them, receiving in return a home, income and support for herself and her three small children. Other widows managed without such extensive family support, keeping themselves by part-time or full-time work, and/or relying on the wages of their older children.

One of the most successful widows, in financial terms, was Miss Turner's mother. Her husband, a bleacher, died in 1921 aged 37 leaving her with four children, the eldest of whom was thirteen. She went weaving and was joined by her two older daughters and eventually by Miss Turner herself. Everyone shared the housework and all worked immensely hard. They gradually became more prosperous, affording holidays in the Isle of Man, and eventually the mother was able to buy, in the late 1920s, a new house complete with gardens and bathroom, all previously unknown luxuries.[43]

There were, of course, many women who did not earn money on their own account and yet they still adopted a variety of strategies in order to balance their budgets and provide for their families. About a third of the families interviewed had children earning money before they left school. These young earners were almost entirely boys and could be found in many branches of the retail trade, working at as young an age as nine years (before and after school, at weekends and holidays). They were paid in both cash and kind and both they and their mothers were very proud of their contribution to the family budget.

A common feature in all the surveys so far mentioned is the overwhelming evidence of working-class woman's ability to spend carefully, to know the price of everything and to allocate her funds (however small) between the various essential items in her budget, – food, rent, heating and clothing. Anyone reading Rowntree, Pember Reeves and Spring Rice, and the oral history transcripts cannot fail to be impressed by the budgeting skills of virtually all the women. Some were, however, more successful than others in making their money stretch. Margery Spring Rice wrote rather controversially: 'It is noticeable that the Scots and women of the North of England were better managers than those in the South'.[44] It is impossible to make a similar claim but it is clear that women in the northern towns I studied were very good managers. Except for those in very straitened circumstances, they kept a tight hold on their spending and avoided debt wherever possible. They were adept at making something out of nothing. Sacks were made into doormats, boxes into furniture, adults' clothes into children's clothes, nothing was ever thrown away unless it was truly rubbish. Thin clothes were made into patchwork quilts, thick clothes cut up for rag or peg rugs, made by most of the family as a winter evening's occupation. Food was never thrown out. Mr Pollard, one of nine children, said, 'There was no bread wasted, it was toasted up . . . if she did have any crusts that had got too hard, she'd let them soak overnight, take them out, put them in a big basin, put a few currants in and bang it in the oven. Then put sugar and a little drop of milk. That was a sweet and it was beautiful.'[45]

Whilst it is clear from the evidence, first, that working-class women knew how much they had to spend on food, housing and clothing; second, that they tried very hard to avoid debts; and, third, that they knew down to the last farthing the price of everything, there were criticisms of their performance in perhaps the most critical area of all, that is in the selection, purchase and cooking of their families' food. Margaret Hewitt in *Wives and Mothers in Victorian Industry* chronicles the almost endless criticisms of working-class womens' abilities in this respect.[46] Rowntree added to them: 'It must also be remembered that at present the poor do not possess knowledge which would enable them to select a diet that is at once as nutritious and as economical as that which has been adopted as the standard'.[47] Margery Spring Rice did not find much general improvement forty years later: 'It is possibly true that better nourishment would be possible even with the income she has if the housewife exercised a more scientific choice of food . . . and if there were greater knowledge about the cooking and preparation.'[48]

There are some observable similarities in working-class diets throughout the period and probably throughout the nation; housewives everywhere included a lot of bread in their diets and when meat was eaten it tended to be of the cheapest variety. But it is impossible to trace those who ate the 'typical' working-class diet described so confidently in the Inter-Departmental Committee on Physical Deterioration: 'A diet of bread and butter for breakfast, potatoes and herrings for dinner and bread and butter for tea, enlivened by some cheap cuts of meat on Sunday and purchases from the fried fish shop during the week when funds permitted are the normal working-class diet'.[49] Despite some similarities it is clear that there were regional differences in diet, which persisted until after the Second World War. There were variations too between groups of housewives.

With the exception of full-time working mothers who, on the whole, had to buy expensive and monotonous convenience foods, other Lancashire wives appeared to feed their families nutritiously and economically, and with more *variations* than one can see in the other surveys. Women's skills in doing this can be regarded as one of their most successful strategies in ensuring their families' healthy survival. The basis of all local working-class diets was bread. This was true in all other geographical areas and throughout the period. Most observers would echo Pember Reeves who wrote, 'without doubt the chief article of diet in the 20/– budget is bread'.[50] Locally this was almost exclusively home-made until the inter-war period. Its true nutritional value is now realized; no doubt women in the past did not know its value, but by giving it to their families, they were feeding them well. As far as can be ascertained local people were eating approximately the same amounts of bread as the national average for 1900, that is 6–7 lbs per head per week.[51] Mrs Sharp had ten brothers and sisters:

'How often would you bake bread?'
'We had to start buying the bread because do you know how
many loaves we had and this is the truth. They were two for
4½d and they were big loaves and we used to have eight one day
and nine another. If my mother baked she had to bake a stone
of bread every day and so sometimes she baked it and
sometimes she bought it'.[52]

There are mentions of vegetables in the other surveys of diets but
one has the impression that rather more of them and a much wider
variety were eaten in the North-West – potatoes, carrots, cabbage,
leeks, onions, peas, beans, tomatoes, lettuce, sprouts, cauliflowers,
turnips, swedes, parsnips, beetroot are all mentioned. Nearly half of
the respondents' families had allotments at some time and these
provided vegetables not only for the owners but also for friends,
relatives and neighbours, both as presents and as cheap purchases. It
is unlikely that local greengrocers would be able to charge high
prices for their goods in the face of this competition. Working-class
women probably served meat and two vegetables as their Sunday
dinner, but during the week vegetables could well appear as part of a
broth or soup. These were very popular and contained a bone, or
sheep's head, cereals and vegetables. This is Mrs Askew's memory
of her mother's broth:

Very often sheep's head broth. Mam used to get it and there
we'd see it with its glassy holes for eyes looking at us out of a big
dish, soaking getting the blood out of it in salted water. Mam
used to take the brains out and cook those for m'dad. The
tongue she used to cook separately and the sheep's head was
boiled and boiled and made into jolly good broth, barley and all
the lot. Pot herbs they used to call them . . . carrot, turnip, and
a bit of leek, a bit of parsley, bit of onion, sometimes a bit of
celery if it was the season, she used to put in lentils and barley.
We had that soup and that was the whole meal.[53]

(The tongue would have been pressed and used cold in sandwiches.)
There are very many examples of cheap, nutritious and very
economical dishes which give the lie to the accusation that working-
class women were not skilled in the selection and cooking of food.
   Earning money on your own account, careful budgeting and
skilful cooking were all strategies of which women were justly
proud. They were especially proud of being self-reliant. But they
also cherished ideals of co-operation and another strategy was to
borrow goods (or much more rarely, cash) from neighbours. It was
understood that the loan was always paid back in kind (i.e. a cup of

sugar for a cup of sugar) and that in any case, a borrower was able to offer loans herself when necessary. Women were proud of having a surplus to lend and not so proud of needing to borrow, but all valued a system of neighbourhood support. Help from relations was of a different kind; there gifts were more usual than loans and relatives knew that they could not expect to be repaid for some long-term service. Helping was part of the family's duty as understood in working-class mores and an enormous amount was given and received almost as a matter of course.

Some strategies were necessary for some families but were not regarded as desirable, either by those using them or by working-class people in general. One of these was seeking credit. When there were weeks with a very low income because of unemployment, underemployment, holidays or sickness, then the working-class woman had to seek credit. A small minority lived on credit but the majority did not and preferred not to ask for it. Respondents were aware that the credit system could be abused by both sides. Mrs Hesketh came from a very poor family in Preston and they frequently had to ask for credit. She said this of her local shop: 'They [the customers] were robbed hand and foot because they never checked up on them. It was written down in the book and you would take the book . . . and it was ever so much at the end but there was never any checking up on it . . . they would add things you hadn't had.'[54]

It is of course impossible to check this kind of statement but it is repeated by various respondents. If it is true it does suggest that, however necessary, seeking credit at the corner shop (which in any case tended to have high prices) was not a very successful strategy for the honest housewife to undertake. But for the dishonest, living on credit could be very successful. Mr Thomas came from a very poor (but honest) family growing up in the 1890s. 'Hundreds of shopkeepers have been done with little bits of what people owed . . . some people lived for that purpose, they owed so much to this man and so much to the milk man and so much to the grocer and butcher. Then when he goes for his money he would find they had moved somewhere else.'[55] (Moving was easy when a hardcart usually carried most families' belongings.) Even more unpopular with the mass of working-class people was the idea of going to the pawnbroker, and yet it was essential for many. Some of those on low incomes adopted it as a regular strategy, others only in dire emergencies. Rowntree has only one reference but he claimed it was an important part in the life of the people in class B (those with a family wage of between

18/— and 21/— a week).[56] It is difficult to know why it was not mentioned in connection with the even poorer families in class A. Mrs Hesketh's mother used the pawnbroker regularly but, like most women, would not go herself. Many areas had a runner:

> 'This old lady . . . she was the runner. She would go from one neighbour to another on a Monday morning. The poor husbands didn't know. They had to be out by Friday and God help you if they found out it had been there. I don't remember my mum being found out.'
> 'What would she send?'
> 'A man's suit or overcoat.'

The old lady was paid a few coppers for taking the clothes and Mrs Hesketh remembered her mother getting 3/6d which went towards the rent.[57] Given the interest rates charged and the cost of paying the 'runner', taking goods to the pawnbroker was not an economical strategy to adopt. Working-class wives realized this, which is one reason why pawning was undertaken only by women who could think of no other ready alternative.[58] Most of the women in my survey who spoke of using the pawnbroker were already employing other strategies, notably part-time work and strict budgeting, but still needed more help, usually because of their large families.

There were undoubted improvements in working-class standards of living in the inter-war period, compared with those of pre-1914.[59] Real wages rose and, perhaps more importantly, family sizes fell dramatically. Most working-class women had more money to spend on fewer people than did their mothers. But there were still many women in the 1920s and 1930s who had to adopt one or more strategies either because their husbands had a low wage, or were unemployed or because their families were large. So, within a geographical area like the North West of England, it is possible to see elements both of continuity and of change. It is much more difficult to compare this area with others in Britain. There are glimpses, as has been seen, of women's lives in other places but there is not enough to make reasonable generalizations about lives of working-class women. More oral history investigations would be helpful.

I am sometimes asked what women themselves 'got' out of their lives. It has been remarked that they gave to their families much more than they received in return. These questions and comments would not have been asked nor made by the women themselves. Their own individual concerns were of little importance to them.

They appeared to have found their chief satisfaction in running their homes economically and seeing their children grow up. Their major preoccupations were (throughout the period) feeding, clothing and housing their families. It is, of course, difficult to know how successful the women were in their use of the various strategies in the war against poverty. There were so many variables which affected a family's well-being as well as women's strategies, such as men's wages, unemployment, sickness, family size, the availability of an allotment, or the help offered by neighbours and relatives. However, although quantification remains impossible, it is clear from the available sources that the ingenuity, resourcefulness, and physical toughness of so many working-class women played a very significant part in their families, survival and, more particularly, in maintaining and improving their standard of living.

Bibliographical Notes

Various contemporary surveys of working-class standards of living have been quoted in this paper. B.S. Rowntree, *Poverty, a Study of Town Life* (Longman, 1901) was a detailed survey of the poor in York and concentrated particularly on the budget and life-styles of twenty-six families. Helen Bosanquet, as a member of the Charity Organisation Society, was a pioneer of social-work case studies through her inside knowledge of working-class life in *The Family* (Macmillan, 1906). Magdalen Stuart Pember Reeves drew together evidence collected from working-class wives by the Fabian Society Women's Group in *Round About a Pound a Week* (Bell 1913). For the inter-war period, contemporary accounts include A.L. Bowley and M.H. Hogg's *Has Poverty Diminished?* (London, 1925): D. Caradog Jones (ed.), *The Social Survey of Merseyside* (P.S. King, Liverpool), 3 vols; and Rowntree's social study of York, *Poverty and Progress: A Second Social Survey of York* (Macmillan, 1941). Margery Spring Rice's *Working Class Wives* (Penguin, Harmondsworth, 1939) has been referred to several times. The book contains evidence collected from 1,250 questionnaires filled in by working-class wives. The survey was principally concerned with the women's health.

Almost all the points made in this paper are further examined in Elizabeth Roberts, *A Woman's place, an oral history of working-class women, 1890–1940*, (Basil Blackwell Oxford, 1984). Rickie Burman has a valuable article on Jewish women as retailers in 'The Jewish Woman as Breadwinner: the varying value of women's work in a Manchester immigrant community', *Oral History* 10 (1982). Ellen Ross considers ways of women helping neighbours in 'Survival Networks: Women's Neighbourhood Sharing in London before World War I, *History Workshop Journal* 15 (1983).

Notes

1 For another approach to these problems using different material see Roberts, *A Woman's Place, an oral history of working-class women, 1890–1940* (Basil Blackwell, Oxford, 1984), chapter 4.

2 B.S. Rowntree, *Poverty: a Study of Town Life* (Longman, 1901).

3 Ibid., p.86.

4 M.S. Pember Reeves, *Round about a Pound a Week* (Bell, 1913).

5 A.L. Bowley and M.H. Hogg, *Has Poverty Diminished?* (P.S. King, 1925), p.37.

6 D. Caradog Jones (ed.), *Social Survey of Merseyside* (P.S. King, Liverpool, 1934), 3 vols.

7 B.S. Rowntree, *Poverty and Progress: A Second Social Survey of York* (Macmillan, 1941), pp.28–9.

8 Margery Spring Rice, *Working-Class Wives* (Penguin, Harmondsworth, 1939).

9 The oral material used in this essay is taken from two projects. The first investigated working-class social and family life in Barrow and Lancaster 1890–1930. This was supported by a Nuffield Small Grant in the period 1972–4; and an SSRC grant from 1974 to 1976. The second was a similar project in Preston for the period 1890–1940, and was funded by the SSRC for 1978–81. They were carried out under the aegis of the Centre for North West Regional Studies at the University of Lancaster, where the indexed transcipts are available for the use of the public.

10 Michael Winstanley's oral history project *Everyday Life in Kent before 1914*, funded by SSRC. The archive is kept in the university of Kent at Canterbury. Manchester Polytechnic also has a large collection of oral history interviews undertaken by a variety of people.

11 Helen Bosanquet, *The Family* (London 1906), p.199.

12 Mr R.3.L., born 1890, father a woodcarver, mother a nurse before marriage who had two children; Mr R. became a woodworker and had 6 children; p.54.

13 Mrs H.7.P., born 1916, father a railway worker, mother a carder with six children; Mrs H. became a weaver and had no children; p.14 & p.5.

14 Michael Anderson, unpublished paper, Urban History Conference 1983. Richard Wall, Workshop in Household and Economic Arrangements, University of Essex, 1984.

15 Census of 1901, County of Lancaster, table 35a; Census of 1911, County of Lancaster, table 25.

16 Pember Reeves, *Round About a Pound a Week*, p.77.

17 Spring Rice, *Working-Class Wives*, p.23.

18 Inter-Departmental Committee on Physical Deterioration, PP (1904), Ap.V, p.125–6.

19 Mr P.1.B., born 1900, father a labourer, mother a jute worker before marriage and auction room dealer after, with six children; Mr P. became a fitter and turner, with 3 children.

20 Mrs M.3.B., born 1886, father a shipwright, mother a cook before

marriage who afterwards ran a parlour shop, with ten children (five died); Mrs M. was a pupil teacher with no children.

21 Carol Dyhouse, 'The Role of Women from Self-Sacrifice to Self-Awareness' in Laurence Lerner (ed.), *The Victorians* (Holmes and Meier, New York 1978), p.175.

22 L. Tilly, J. Scott, M. Cohen, 'Womens' Work and European Fertility Patterns', *Journal of Interdisciplinary History* VI. (1976), 462.

23 John Benson, *The Penny Capitalists, A Study of Nineteenth Century Working-class Entrepreneurs*, (Gill and Macmillan, Dublin, 1983), p.129.

24 Mr D.2.P., born 1910, father a professional soldier, mother a domestic servant before marriage, took in sewing and charred after; with nine children (two died); Mr D., a cabinetmaker, had three children.

25 Benson, *Penny Capitalists*, p.73.

26 Mr R.1.L., born 1894, father a driver, mother a washerwomen before and after marriage, with six children (one died); Mr R., a builder, had one child.

27 Mrs N.1.L., born 1899, father a painter, mother a slubber before marriage, took in washing and went out cleaning afterwards, with eight children; Mrs N. was a slubber and washerwoman and had eight children; p.8.

28 Mrs B.1.L., born 1888, father a labourer, mother a weaver before and after marriage, with five children; Mrs B was a weaver before and after marriage and had four children; p.42.

29 Mrs M.6.B., born 1896, father a labourer, mother a dressmaker before and after marriage with sixteen children (thirteen died); Mrs M. was a professional drummer before and after marriage and had one child.

30 Benson, *Penny Capitalists*, p.98.

31 Mrs P.1.P., born 1899, father a blacksmith, mother a doffer before marriage, a hawker after, with five children (one died); Mrs P. was a weaver before and after marriage and had six children (two died).

32 Mr C.6.P., born 1903, father a baker/confectioner, mother ran a bakery and confectionery business before and after marriage and had ten children; Mr. C. worked with family business and had one child.

33 Mrs P.2.P., born 1907, father a sketching-master in the mill, mother a weaver before marriage, kept a shop after, had six children (two died); Mrs P. was a weaver before marriage, kept a shop after, had one child.

34 Ibid., p.30.

35 Benson. *Penny Capitalists*, pp.126 and 117.

36 Mrs S.4.L., born 1896, father a gravedigger, mother a washerwoman before and after marriage, with nine children; Mrs S. was a weaver before marriage, taking in washing and going out washing afterwards, and had one child.

37 E. Roberts, 'Working Wives and their Families', in T. Barker and M. Drake (eds), *Population and Society in Britain 1850–1980* (Batsford Academic Press, 1982).

38 *Cost of Living of the Working Classes: Board of Trade Inquiry into Working Class Rents, Housing and Retail Prices in the Principal Industrial Towns (HMSO 1908)*, Cmd.3864.

39 Ministry of Labour, *21st Abstract of Labour Statistics in the U.K.* (1919–33) HMSO Cmd. 4625, p.104.

40 Pilgrim Trust, *Men Without Work* (Cambridge University Press, Cambridge, 1938). pp.85,235.

41 Mrs W.1.P., born 1899, father a stoker, mother a weaver before marriage (died young) but had nine children (one died); Mrs W. was a weaver, then ring spinner before and after marriage and had two children; p.8.

42 Mrs H.8.P., born 1903, father a clogger, mother a winder, childminder after marriage, with twelve children (four died); Mrs H. was a weaver before marriage and a cleaner afterwards, she had one child; p.25–6.

43 Miss T.4.P., born 1912, father a mill labourer (bleacher), mother a weaver before and after marriage, with five children (one died); Miss T. was a weaver.

44 Spring Rice, *Working-Class Wives*, pp.164–5.

45 Mr P.2.L., born 1899, father a labourer, mother a confectioner before marriage with nine children; Mr P. was a labourer with two children; p.19.

46 Margaret Hewitt, *Wives and Mothers in Victorian Industry*, (Rockliff 1958), pp.75,78–80.

47 Rowntree, *Poverty, a Study of Town Life*, p.105.

48 Spring Rice, *Working Class Wives*, p.156.

49 Inter-Departmental Committee on Physical Deterioration, PP (1904), Cd. 2175, xxx, p.11.

50 Pember Reeves, *Round About a Pound a Week*, p.94.

51 D.J. Oddy, 'Working-class Diets in late Nineteenth Century Britain,' *Economic History Review*, 2nd ser., xxiii (1970), 314.

52 Mrs S.2.B., born 1895, father a labourer, mother took in sewing and went out nursing, with ten children; Mrs S. was a tailoress and had four children; p.4.

53 Mrs A.2.B., born 1904, father a labourer, mother went out cleaning and took in washing, and had four children; Mrs A was a domestic servant, then shop assistant and had one child; pp.34–5.

54 Mrs H.4.P., born 1903, father a fitter, mother a weaver before and after marriage, with ten children (two died); Mrs H was a weaver, then domestic servant and had two children; p.18.

55 Mr T.3.P., born 1886, father a labourer, mother doffer before marriage, washerwoman afterwards, with seven children (two died); Mr T was a spinner, shuttleworker, and insurance collector, and had three children (one died); p.14.

56 Rowntree, *Poverty, a Study of Town Life*, p.59.

57 Mrs H.4.P., p.18.

58 Melanie Tebbutt, *Making Ends Meet. Pawnbroking and Working-Class Credit* (Leicester University Press, Leicester, 1983).

59 John Stevenson, *British Society 1914–45*, (Viking, London 1984).

Sorting sheepskins at the C. W. S. Mills, Buckfastleigh c. 1930

10

Marital Status, Work and Kinship, 1850–1930
Diana Gittins

The three spheres of marriage, work and kinship form the socio-economic context within which women live out their lives. They are not, however, rigidly separate spheres, but ones which intertwine and overlap in a changing and complex web of obligations, opportunities and restrictions. The patterns that emerge vary according to social class, time period, geographical location, household circumstances and individual life-cycle. Too often the explanations offered by historians and social scientists concentrate on only one of these spheres, to the relative neglect of the others. This chapter will attempt to show how it is essential to examine the relationships between all three if we are to make sense of the various dimensions of women's lives. It will focus in depth on one geographical area, a small town in Devonshire, over an eighty-year period, and will be primarily concerned with working-class women, although the boundaries of class were in some ways quite fluid.

Marriage and marital status have usually been treated as a bridge between the world of work and the world of family and kinship. This approach is based on the assumption that 'work' is synonymous with wage labour and that, except in unusual circumstances, women who are married will tend not to 'work'. Such an assumption totally ignores the salience of the vital unpaid work women perform within households as well as the important economic links that exist between households. It also ignores the ways in which women often move between different types of work according to their household economy and the local economic situation.

Recent research has shown clearly that analysing women's work involves understanding both work carried out in the labour market and work carried out within and between households.[1] Marxists have persistently attempted to fit this ambiguity into an appropriate paradigm.[2] While it is now generally accepted that such paradigms have been inadequate, there remains a strong tendency to separate the two 'types' of work, usually arguing that domestic work is 'private' and produces use-value, while wage labour is 'public' and produces exchange-value.[3] This type of model presupposes an isolated family household and ignores the possibility that domestic work can produce both use-value and exchange-value. Moreover, it fails to acknowledge the importance of an exchange of work and services and, not unusually, also of people *between* family households and individuals. These exchanges are frequently, although by no means always, based on kinship and informed by marital status.

While the laws on women's property, and women and children *as* property, were altered in the late-nineteenth century, the notion of women as dependants of men, and of men as responsible for 'their' women has remained an essential cornerstone of women's position in society generally.[4] These assumptions are imbued in the concept of patriarchy.[5] Women's patterns of dependency have been mediated, above all, by marital status. Thus a single women who lived with her parent(s) owed her primary allegiance to, and was by law dependent on, her father (or mother or brother or uncle, depending on circumstances) and the dictates of that family household. Her work might involve caring for kin within or outside of the parental household. She might be engaged in wage labour full-time or part-time, or might work for a member of the family in their workshop or business for no payment at all. Which strategy of work she participated in would depend on the 'needs' of her family household, its resources in terms of family labour power, skills, space, time, the local economic conditions and opportunities for wage labour, and so on. Whether and what sort of work she was involved in was determined and decided almost invariably by her father, or other relative who was head of her household.

Marriage shifted a woman's primary allegiance from her father (or mother or brother) to a husband and the needs of his/their family household. The needs of a woman's parents and kin for the use of her labour power, in whatever sphere, and the needs of a potential husband for a wife's labour power have often created very real and powerful tensions and conflicts. These have focused primarily on daughters and their entry or non-entry into marriage.

As Rubin and Ross have shown,[6] this conflict is also one between notions of loyalty to kin and community generally, and loyalty to husband and children. The relative importance of each has varied by social class, parity, household and local socio-economic conditions. Generally speaking, the more economically insecure the household, the greater will be its reliance on community and kin, the greater its needs for children's labour power, and thus the more conflict there will be about daughters' marriages.

The growth of the state since the middle of the nineteenth century has been an important factor in altering this tension and giving legal and ideological primacy to the needs of husband and children via marriage at the expense of parents, kin and community.[7] This has been achieved, to a considerable extent, by loosening the bonds between parents' rights to children, especially daughters, and their labour power, while strengthening the duties and responsibilites of parents, and especially mothers, to dependent children. Enforced dependency itself, of course, has been considerably prolonged by law, through compulsory education. Thus obligations to children have been reinforced, while the once reciprocal obligations of grown children to parents have been weakened.

To understand some of these relationships better it is important to emphasize that there have been *two* economies and two labour markets which, to varying degrees, overlap and interact. The formal economy and labour market are of obvious importance and are well-examined. But there have also been an informal economy and labour market where work and services have been exchanged and negotiated. Exchanges have been carried out between women of different social classes, notably between middle-class women and working-class domestic servants; between men and women, usually of a similar class position but not always, by means of marriage and cohabitation; and between women, and in some cases, men and women, in similar class situtations through care of each others' children, lending and borrowing services, goods, money and one anothers' childrens' labour power. These exchanges have also gone on between parents and children, particularly mothers and daughters, but also brothers and sisters, grandparents and grandchildren, uncles and nieces.[8]

The informal economy has been largely, but not entirely, a woman's economy and an economy of poverty. It has been much influenced by notions of kinship and kinship ties, at times *creating* kinship as a consequence of such economic relations.[9] These socio-economic relations are crucial in understanding patterns of women's participation in the formal labour market, the marriage market and the relative importance of ties between households, kin and neighbours. By way of illustration I would like, therefore, to examine some of these forces in detail by focusing on a number of individual case histories.

The cases come from work carried out on a small textile town in Devonshire between 1850 and the present day. The town is on the edge of Dartmoor and its population has fluctuated around 2,500 since the early nineteenth century. It was dominated by the woollen industry from medieval times until the 1970s. Unlike the West of England as a whole, the woollen industry here did not collapse when that of Yorkshire gained dominance from the eighteenth century onwards.[10] Cottage industry prevailed until the middle of the nineteenth century, when rapid mechanization resulted in a growing consolidation of capital and a proletarianization of the workforce. The process of proletarianization, however, was not gender-neutral. It was quite markedly a process of *feminization* of the workforce as well. As women's labour was both cheap and plentiful and, in this area particularly, generally lacking in opportunities, it resulted in extremely high profit margins for the local capitalists, and accounts to a large extent for the industry's survival in this area. The local woollen industry was not unionized until the 1920s, at which time it was also taken over by the Co-operative Society.[11]

Detailed work has been carried out on individuals and family households for the whole town using the census enumerators' books for the years 1851, 1861 and 1871, in conjunction with parish records of births, marriages and deaths, legal records, and workhouse records where available. In-depth interviews were also carried out with women who were born between 1895 and 1910.[12] By analysing the whole population from the enumerators' books over three census years it has been possible to trace the households and work patterns of many individuals over time, often filling in gaps from other records.

This has enabled analysis of links between households and kin that would not have been obvious had a percentage sample of the population been analysed instead. For instance, some who were listed as 'lodgers' in one census year appear ten years later in circumstances which indicate that the earlier household situation was in fact based on kinship. Census data, marriage records and interviews have also indicated that kinship relations permeated a very large portion of the town. Reconstructing individuals' circumstances has made it possible to gain some idea of how economic changes affected both individuals and households, and how these in turn affected economic changes.

The demise of woolcombing as a skilled and well-paid male craft in the mid-nineteenth century resulted in many men simply leaving the area altogether in search of work elsewhere. Many left behind pregnant lovers and wives. There was a dramatic increase in illegitimacy at this time. The percentage of illegitimate baptisms (and, as such, highly likely to be a considerable underestimate of illegitimate births) rose from 4.3 per cent of all baptisms in the period 1841–50, to 6.3 per cent during the priod 1851–60, and then to 10.8 per cent in the period 1861–70. Women left behind became a pool of cheap labour, which enabled the local capitalists to cheapen labour costs, de-skill and proletarianize the workforce. Thus in this area (which in many ways was *not* typical of other areas such as Yorkshire), proletarianization was largely a female experience. But individuals altered their occupations, their household arrangements and, it would seem, their links and exchanges with kin and neighbours as a means of coping with new economic circumstances, both in terms of the formal and the informal labour markets. Above all else, the out-migration of large numbers of men resulted in increasing instability of the local marriage market for women, and this decline in marriage as a source of economic security made more women dependent on work in the formal labour market *and* on informal networks between kin and neighbours.

Some women worked in the formal economy until they married, then withdrew and worked full-time in the informal economy as wives and mothers, often entering the formal economy for a period, or part-time, when economic circumstances within the family-household necessitated it. The death or departure of a husband usually meant re-entering the formal economy full-time, often doing two jobs because of appallingly low wages. Some women never entered the marriage market at all and worked full-time in the formal economy all their lives, but because of poor wages had to organize their households and their inter-household relationships in a way that would supplement their meagre earnings. It was not unusual for women to move geographically if economic circumstances and household circumstances were unfavourable. There seems to have been, for instance, a small stream of women who moved between jobs in the local textile industry during times of relative prosperity, and then worked as prostitutes in nearby Plymouth during periods of recession in the textile industry.[13]

As mentioned earlier, illegitimacy rates were quite high in the town, and rose during the period of proletarianization. Fairchild has argued that it is possible to see a large proportion of illegitimacy as a result of 'frustrated marriages' which seems to fit the conditions of this town quite well.[14] However, it could be argued that many women in difficult economic circumstances may have welcomed children as a means of investing in the future, providing future wage earners who could help them to survive when they were older. Theories of *marital* fertility have for a long time used just such arguments for explaining why married people have wanted children.[15] As marriage was not, at least until the late-nineteenth century, by any means as important economically or socially for the poorer sectors of the working classes as it was for the more skilled sectors and the middle classes, it seems reasonable to suppose that some of the reasons for unmarried women wanting children (and, indeed, few have even considered that unmarried women may have *wanted* children at all) may have been similar, if not identical, to those of the married.

Consider, for example, the case of Elizabeth Memory. She was born locally and in 1851 was recorded as aged twenty-two, single, working as a weaver and living with her unmarried brother, William, who was thirty-five and working as a woolcomber. Also living with them was their sister, Charlotte, aged twenty-eight, who was single and worked as a dressmaker; five-year-old John, illegitimate son of their sister, Grace Mayne; Grace Mayne, who was twenty-five and described herself as a tin miner's wife; and Elizabeth's own illegitimate daughter of one. The following year Charlotte married William Petherick, aged twenty-two, who worked as a woolcomber, and they set up their own household nearby. Presumably Grace had done the bulk of the domestic work and childcare, being the only one without an occupation, though Charlotte probably worked at home as a dressmaker and would also have taken on a fair amount of the domestic work.

In 1861 Elizabeth Memory was still unmarried and worked as a weaver. Now, however, she was living with her mother, Mary, who was a widowed midwife of sixty-eight. Also living with them were Emma Parsons, aged eight, and Mary Langmead, aged four, both Elizabeth's illegitimate daughters. The eldest illegitimate daughter was not present, nor was she recorded as having died. Probably she was working and living in another household as a servant. Lodging with them was Louisa Gruit, aged twenty-one, who was single and worked as a weaver. The Gruits and the Pethericks were kin. Grace, the miner's wife, and her children are not in the town at all and are not recorded as dead. Miners were extremely mobile at this time, and it is likely that she had left to join him elsewhere. Charlotte and William now had three small children, although Charlotte was still working as a weaver, while William had become a foreman in one of the woollen mills. They, too, had a lodger, In 1865 their mother, Mary, died; then in 1870 Elizabeth's daughter, Mary Langmead, died at the age of thirteen.

We find Elizabeth in 1871 still unmarried, aged forty-two, but now heading her own household while continuing to work as a weaver. Two more illegitimate children, Elizabeth, aged eight, and John, aged six, also lived with them. With Emma able to earn as well as Elizabeth, the latter is able to head her own household independent of other kin, although their standard of living was undoubtedly low.

It is impossible to know for certain why Elizabeth never married, whether through force of circumstances or lack of inclination. It might well be argued, however, that her access to a wide variety of kin with whom to live and share domestic responsibilities and pool incomes may have meant that she was less dependent on marriage for reasons of economic security. Elizabeth appears to have been what Laslett has referred to as a 'bastard bearer'[16] but there is no way of knowing whether she and her kin and neighbours regarded this as in any way undesirable. The fact that she happily gave the census enumerator the paternal names of all her illegitimate children suggests that she may not have regarded it as anything particularly reprehensible. It is certainly possible that at this time, in a community that was experiencing rapid economic changes, general instability and disruption, women may have seen children as a positive asset, whether they were legitimate or illegitimate.

It is interesting to note that while Elizabeth's marital status remains constant, as does her occupational status, the households in which she lives, and the kin with whom she lives, change. First she lives with her brother and sisters and their illegitimate children. Grace, the married sister, is not employed in the formal economy and was almost certainly responsible for the bulk of childcare and domestic work. Later, she lives with her widowed mother and her own illegitimate children plus a lodger. Finally she heads her own household with her children. Her household mobility is thus quite marked, although the ratio of breadwinners to dependants remains similar, that is, the structure of the households is almost identical over time, although the actual individuals co-residing, and their relationships to one another, change.

In Elizabeth Memory's case, her strategy for survival in adverse economic circumstances was achieved through work in the formal economy throughout, and a sharing and exchange of resources and work between kin within her various households. Had she not had a plentiful supply of kin, not least of whom in later years were her own illegitimate children, she might well have been more anxious to enter the marriage market as a means of economic security.

While women tended to be reliant on both the formal and informal economies to survive, men's mobility and tactics of survival were more directly related to the formal economy. To a large extent, of course, their ability to do this rested on the situation of women. When woolcombing was mechanized in the town, male woolcombers had several strategies for survival. Unionization, however, was not one of them. Some changed occupations and went to work as agricultural labourers (there was a lot of good agricultural land in the vicinity) or as miners or quarriers (there were a few tin mines and a limestone quarry nearby). Some, mostly the younger men, migrated to Yorkshire to find work in the woollen industry there; others emigrated to North America. A few, overwhelmingly older men, accepted more menial jobs in the local woollen mills. Though by no means non-existent, women's geographical mobility was much less, and so was their occupational mobility within the formal economy, largely because there were far fewer occupations open to them. Their mobility was a far more complex one than men's, involving a relationship between wage labour, marriage and domestic work within and between households.

An interesting example that illustrates the variety of strategies often adopted is that of Eliza Arscott. In 1851 Eliza was twenty years old, single, and worked as a serge weaver. She lived with her mother, Elizabeth, who was sixty, widowed and described as a grocer. Her 26 year-old brother, Philip, also unmarried, was listed as a woolstapler employing three men. Her sister, yet another Elizabeth, aged twenty-eight and also unmarried, lived with them and worked as a woolsorter. It is interesting to note that in this one household there was a range of occupations entailing ownership of capital as well as wage labour. The mother and brother both owned some capital (presumably inherited from the father/husband), while Eliza and Elizabeth were wage labourers, although it is quite possible that they were, in fact, working for their brother and not being paid wages.

In 1855 Eliza married John, who was twenty-four and worked as a woolcomber. He moved in with Eliza's family household. By 1861 Eliza and John were still living there, Eliza was the only married sibling and continued to work as a serge weaver. The mother was listed as head of the household and was described as a landed proprietor. Philip, thirty-five, remained unmarried and was working as a woolstapler employing four men. Elizabeth was now thirty-seven, single and working as a woolsorter. Eliza and John had two daughters, aged five and two, and John was working as a woolcomber. The following year mother died.

In 1871, after rapid and dramatic changes in the local woollen industry, Eliza and John continued to live in the same household with Eliza's unmarried brother. Philip, however, had apparently sold his woolstapling business and had invested the capital in the mother's previous grocery business, expanding it into a bakery as well. Elizabeth was not listed as having any occupation, nor had she married. Eliza was also listed without an occupation. One or both may well have been working at least part-time in Philip's business, although with two of John and Eliza's children working in the labour market, Elizabeth and Eliza may have been concentrating most of their effort in domestic tasks. John had changed his occupation from woolcomber to farm labourer. Of Eliza and John's children, one was sixteen and working as a weaver, one was fourteen and employed as a spinner, while the three younger ones were at school.

This family household is an interesting example of three economic strategies rolled into one. Philip was always engaged in the formal economy as a small-scale capitalist. His ability to do this, however, rested to a very large extent on the command he had over his mother's capital and his sisters' labour power, both in his business in the formal economy and within the informal economy of his household. The two, of course, were by no means separate. It also meant that he did not have to enter the marriage market or employ domestic servants. His sisters, nieces and brother-in-law worked in the formal economy, as wage labourers, when the household economy necessitated. Only one sibling ever married – Eliza. Why this was so we can never know, but it is possible that given that some ownership of capital was attached to the family household, there may have been concern with producing heirs, or Philip may have welcomed extra labour power in the household at a time of economic severity. It is also highly likely that Eliza was pregnant by John and that they came to some kind of arrangement with Philip so as to have a roof over their heads.

How exactly the household labour was divided cannot be known for certain either, but in all probability it would have been the responsibilty of one or some of the co-resident women, probably shifting from the mother in the early years when the daughters were in the formal economy to one or both of the daughters in the later years when Eliza's daughters were working in the formal economy. It is interesting, too, to note the persistent co-residence of three siblings over a long period of time. Eliza and Elizabeth could have set up their own separate household at some point, or John and Eliza could have done so after their marriage. Presumably their standard of living as a family household was maximized by staying together, although there must also have been strong emotional, and perhaps sexual, reasons for choosing to live together most of their lives. They are an excellent example of the dangers of generalizing about either 'the family' or 'the working-class family'; their family household combined different class situations, marriage strategies and economies under one roof and between close family relations.

Many women were able to survive quite well through more 'conventional' channels of marriage, re-marriage and domestic labour. Take for example, Elizabeth Furneaux, who in 1851 was nineteen years old and lived with her parents and five brothers and sisters. She, like Eliza Arscott, worked as a serge weaver. Her father worked as a labourer in the local paper mill and was fifty-three; her mother was forty-five and had no listed occupation. Her eldest brother, Thomas, was eleven and worked as a farmer's boy. The other siblings were still at school.

In 1855 Elizabeth's father died, and in 1856 she married Richard Routley, who was twenty-five and worked as a carrier. In 1861 they had their own household and three children aged four, two and two weeks. Richard continued to work as a carrier and Elizabeth was described as 'carrier's wife'. A wet nurse of thirty-three was living with them, presumably temporarily to nurse the infant, as well as a male lodger of fifty-two who worked as a farm labourer. Lodgers were, of course, an important supplement to household income.[17] Elizabeth's mother, Mary, lived nearby and worked as a schoolmistress. Elizabeth's brother, Joseph, was living with Mary and working as a farm labourer. He was seventeen. Margaret, fifteen, also lived with their mother and Joseph and worked as a spinner. The older brothers, Richard and Thomas, were not recorded as living anywhere in the town, and had presumably moved to find work elsewhere.

Elizabeth's husband, Richard, died in 1865. Her mother died in March 1867, and then in August Margaret, the youngest sister, married. In 1869 Elizabeth married again, to James Vile who was from Somerset. In 1871 Elizabeth was thirty-nine and was living with her new husband, who was thirty-four, and had taken over her first husband's business as carrier. Elizabeth's children by her first marriage all lived with her and James; the eldest was fourteen and worked as an apprentice wheelwright, the second, aged thirteen, was a woolsorter, and the rest were at school. Elizabeth's brother, Joseph, was unmarried and now lived with them. He was twenty-six and described as a 'general servant', presumably helping James with the business. There were also two lodgers – a married couple. Elizabeth's elder brother, Richard, now lived next door to them with his wife and seven young children. Richard was also listed as a carrier, and it is likely that Elizabeth and James had set him up in business, either independently or with James.

Through marriage, widowhood, remarriage and keeping lodgers Elizabeth survived without working in the formal labour market. She was also able to help two of her brothers. With both parents dead, all of the children either moved away or married, with the exception of Joseph. Elizabeth's participation in the economy should not be underestimated, as it was vital to her, her children, husbands and brothers. Since her first marriage, however, it was always carried out in the informal economy and the marriage market. Crucial to her ability to do this, of course, was her inheritance of Richard's business/capital which, however small, put her in a strong position in the marriage market.

For women who became widowed and did *not* inherit anything, the situation was potentially dire. Compare Elizabeth Furneaux's history, for example, with that of Elizabeth Knowling. In 1851 Elizabeth Knowling was seventeen years of age and lived with her parents and four brothers and sisters. Neither she, nor her mother, was listed as working, and her two youngest siblings were at school. Her father, aged fifty-four, worked as a farm labourer and her twin brothers, Henry and John, ten years old, worked as farmers' boys. Like most farm labourers in the area at that time, her family had moved around a great deal: her father was born in Chagford, her mother in Ashburton, she herself in South Brent, her twin brothers and one sister in Staverton, and only the youngest child of four was born locally. Although they had been moving within an area of some twenty miles, they had no close kin living in the town itself.

In 1853 Elizabeth married William Harvey. She was nineteen, and pregnant, and William was twenty-seven and employed as a farm labourer. In 1858 her father died. In 1861 Elizabeth and William had their own household, William still worked as a farm labourer and Elizabeth had no recorded occupation. They had two children, aged eight and six. Elizabeth's widowed mother, Mary, lived nearby and worked as a charwoman. Her three unmarried sisters also lived with

Mary. Charlotte, twenty-four, was working as a weaver, as was Susan who was nineteen. Harriet, aged fourteen, worked as a spinner. The twin brothers had left the town. The mother died in 1869, and two months later William died.

Elizabeth remained a widow in 1871, by which time she was thirty-eight years old and heading her own household. She worked as a labourer in the wool mill, as did two of her daughters – Mary, aged eighteen, and Millia, fourteen. The youngest children, aged six and eight, were at school. Their incomes as labourers would have been extremely low, and even with three of them working full-time, their standard of living would have been very poor. With both parents dead as well as her husband and with all her siblings having left the town, Elizabeth had nothing but her own and her daughters' labour power to sell in the formal labour market as a means of economic survival. With no capital and two dependent children, her chances of a second marriage were very poor indeed. With no skills, she was forced to take the worst paid jobs available. With no kin locally, she had no viable alternatives in the informal economy. Lacking kin, capital, husband and skills, women like Elizabeth Knowling were the poorest of the poor, those who if ill or injured had to resort to the workhouse or, in times of economic slump, prostitution. Elizabeth's only salvation was her own children.

It is, of course, impossible to know how these women interpreted their life situation. Interviews with their descendants, however, gave some insights into similar experiences in the same town at a later date when, nevertheless, the economic structure remained remarkably similar to what it had been in the latter half of the nineteenth century.

Lizzie J., for instance, was born in Liverpool in 1898 and was the youngest of four children. Her father had been born in the town studied, but had moved to Liverpool as a young man to work as an engineer. He came back again for health reasons when Lizzie was a small girl. His parents were present in the 1871 census in the same house which Lizzie described in the interview. Her grandfather had also been an engineer. Lizzie's father died when he was only fifty and her mother was left to bring up the children as best she could:

> My mother she was only forty, she was ten years younger than he, an' there was nothing then, you know, in they days, no pensions or nothing. She had to go out to work to keep us – washin' an' cleanin'. Then as we got a little bit older she took on cleanin' in the schools, with the help of me two brothers and me elder sisters, 'cause I was too young to go helpin', you see, real hard work.

The help Lizzie's brothers and sister gave their mother must have been a real boon to her. Both brothers left the household, however, in their late teens. One emigrated to the USA and never returned, which was a very common experience of families in the town from the 1850s onwards. The other brother joined the army. Her elder sister married the local postman when she was twenty-nine, after having worked as a woolsorter. Lizzie herself also worked as a woolsorter as well as caring for her mother.

When Lizzie was thirty-four, however, her brother who had joined the army and then settled in London became widowed and was left with a young son. He asked Lizzie to move up to London to look after them. She was not overjoyed at this prospect:

> I didn't feel too good about it. No, well I didn't want to leave mother, 'cause I was the one that was left with her, see, and what was going to become of mother, and she wouldn't be with me always, see. Didn't know what to do about it, but went in the end any rate. Then she come up to London to live with us. She used to go forward and back. She'd come up to us for perhaps a couple of months, then she'd down here again with my sister, perhaps for the rest of the time. Then we'd come down on holiday, then she'd come back with us. An' she used to do that, see?

The fact that she had to give up her work as a woolsorter in the formal economy did not seem to bother any of them. Lizzie's dilemma was not one of conflict between her own interests and those of her family, but between which member of her family needed her care and attention most. She still lives with, and cares for, her brother now.

The expectation that a sister should be available to look after brothers as well as elderly parents seems to have been common. Lizzie's best friend did the same thing for her own brother:

> She used to look after her brother, see, and also go in the factory to work. An' her brother – stayed at somebody's house where there was a young lady an' got in with this young lady an' he married her. She said she was glad really that her brother got married, becase she was havin' to cook all meals an' do all the work an' everything.

The interviews showed clearly how youngest daughters in particular were expected to 'be on call' to care for parent or brother in times of need. They were usually also expected to work in the formal economy if household circumstances necessitated, but were discouraged from entering marriage and the marriage market, which would have meant that their first duty would have been to their husbands rather than to their parents or brothers.

Lizzie J. made it clear that she and her elder sister were treated differently by their mother: 'Mam didn't mind, her never minded my *sister* pickin' up, you know. She had a couple of chaps. The only one she had really was the one she married. Mam used to tell me sometimes not to get married, she didn't think I was strong enough.' Yet her mother thought she was strong enough to work full-time in the mill until she was thirty-four, in addition to looking after her and, later, her brother and young nephew. Convincing youngest daughters from an early age that they were too weak and/or infirm to consider marriage was a common tactic used by parents in their bid to retain their daughters' labour power within the informal economy of the family household.

Lizzie J.'s life in London with her brother and nephew was, in fact, quite similar to married life anyway, and she did not indicate any feelings that by renouncing marriage to care for her mother and brother she had missed out on some 'fantastic' experience. When asked if she ever wished if she had married, she replied: 'No, no. Well, I always really done what I like, haven't I? He (her brother) would always give me his wage packet. I never went short of money. You got the best of it – 'aint got no worries, an' the children, bring them up an' they leave you.' Her implicit definition of marriage is that of economic security; in her case she was able to achieve this, as she saw it, through caring for her brother and nephew, with the added bonus of avoiding the 'worries' of children and perhaps also sexuality and childbirth. The interview is also interesting in the way it shows how she decided that her first loyalty was to her brother rather than her mother; the question of sibling ties is one which is too often neglected in studies of families and family relationships.

Overall, the interviews revealed that the women did not perceive marriage as a major dividing-line in their lives in the way in which we have arguably come to see it. Rather, the most salient and persistent attitude to work and families was the overall and overriding sense of responsibility they felt towards parents, brothers and children. This responsibility might or might not involve wage labour, marriage, and unpaid domestic work, although there was *always* some of that in whatever situation they lived and worked in. Most frequently it involved mobility in and out of each, often engaging in two simultaneously, depending on individual, household and economic circumstances generally, and mediated by ties of marriage and kinship.

Charlotte B., for example, was born in the town in 1902. Her mother's family was local and her mother had worked as a weaver. Her father, also local, was a gardener. Charlotte was an only child and during her childhood she and her parents lived with her mother's parents. Her mother's brothers and her father's brothers had all emigrated to the USA or Canada, and consequently her mother was responsible for both sets of Charlotte's grandparents (which may have been an important factor in their having only one child themselves). Then: 'When I was twenty-one my mother died, an' I was left with my father and grandfather. 'Cause, you see, you had to look after your parents in those days.' At the time, she was working full-time as a shop assistant, having previously worked as a domestic servant. She was also engaged to be married to Tom, but then he:

> lost *his* mother eighteen months before I lost mine, and he was left with his father. 'Course then I was left with mine. We couldn't get married. For me to have four men to look after – we would've been his father, my father, me gran'father an' me husband! So, he said, I can't let you have all that. So he went to Australia and we were parted for nearly nine years.

Tom's father was put into lodgings, but Charlotte continued to care for her own father and grandfather as well as working full-time. When Tom eventually returned (she was by then thirty-one) and they married, she continued to look after her father, although their houses were separate and some distance away. She did, however, cease full-time work in the formal economy. Marriage in her case meant the ability to leave the formal labour market, but it did not mean abrogating familial responsibilities and, of course, it meant taking on new ones for her husband and their household. With the decline of working-class family size in the early part of the twentieth century, more and more women were put in the position of having no, or only one, sibling with whom to share responsibilities for ageing parents and, as in Charlotte's case, even grandparents. This has been made worse by the increase in longevity which has occurred since the middle of the nineteenth century. Whereas in the past more women renounced marriage to care for family members, now more women marry while their parents are still relatively young, and then take on the cares of ageing parents when they are middle-aged themselves. Similarly, smaller families have meant that while, in the past, all children would work in the formal labour market except one who remained as the 'carer' at home, increasingly women such as Charlotte, because they were only children, have had to combine full-time wage labour with caring for parents and, not infrequently, with the demands of marriage and their own children and husbands as well.

Historical, anthropological and sociological evidence all indicate that, in one form or another, it is overwhelmingly women who care for dependants. Often a group or network of women have taken collective responsibility for child supervision and share resources and tasks between households, as Ellen Ross has shown.[18] In both the past and the present grandmothers, sisters, daughters and aunts have taken much responsibility for children and care of parents and brothers, uncles and grandfathers. Women's general perceived responsibility for children, men and household work – that is, work in the informal economy – has meant that 'work' for women *always* has the potential implication of such responsibilities, regardless of their positions in the formal economy or their marital status. Patriarchal ideology imputes to women the primary responsibility of care for others as defined by ties of kinship and marriage. The situation of women in a family household is a crucial determinant of their work in both the formal and informal economies and of their occupational and household mobility.

In many families, but particularly those with large numbers of children, older daughters have generally been regarded as responsible for care of young siblings and have been expected to take a large amount of work within the household during their adolescence. As younger daughters get older, so the eldest have been 'released' into the formal economy and/or marriage. Youngest daughters, on the other hand, experience older parents and no, or few, young siblings. They have therefore been held responsible for the care and support of their parents. This may or may not involve work in the formal economy, depending on family household circumstances. For many it has meant the renouncing or deferral of entering the marriage market. The interviews revealed clearly that these expectations and responsibilites were almost wholly accepted by women, and none of them expressed any resentment that their brothers were able to get better jobs, migrate, emigrate and abrogate all responsibility for parents or siblings. All of them indicated that their role as carer (whether of siblings or of parents) was essential and that other occupational choices, whether marriage or work in the formal economy, were secondary to their family household-related work.

Paid work, unpaid domestic work and marriage were three interrelated and often overlapping occupational spheres for women which might more appropriately be conceived of in terms of strategies for survival, but survival for the family household generally rather than for the individual women. Which strategies were adopted at a given point in time depended on the circumstances of others within the family household, age and parity of family members, and economic circumstances both within and outside the household. Understanding women's position in society necessitates an understanding of the often complicated ways in which work, marriage and kinship are woven together in a perplexingly intricate tapestry.

Bibliographical Note

One of the most interesting recent debates on the household has been that initiated by Miranda Chaytor's article 'Household and Kinship: Ryton in the Late Sixteenth and Early Seventeenth Centuries', *History Workshop Journal*, 10 (1980). There is an interesting and useful collection of articles on the historical aspects of marriage in B. Outhwaite (ed.), *Marriage and Society: Studies in the Social History of Marriage* (Europa Publications, 1981). See, too, S. Burman's collection, *Fit Work for Women* (Croom Helm, 1979); M. Vicinus (ed.), *A Widening Sphere* (Indiana University Press, Bloomington, 1977). Diana Leonard's *Sex and Generation* (Tavistock, 1980) has useful background material on marriage. For a more theoretical discussion of the economic aspects of marriage (although not historically) see N. Sokoloff *Between Money and Love: The Dialectics of Women's Home and Market Work* (Praeger, New York, 1980), and K. Young, L. Wolkowitz and R. McCullagh (eds), *Of Marriage and the Market* (CSE Books, 1981).

Notes

1 Notably, Miranda Chaytor, 'Household and Kinship: Ryton in the Late Sixteenth and Early Seventeenth Centures', *History Workshop Journal* 10 (1980); and Ellen Ross, 'Survival Networks: Women's Neighbourhood Sharing in London', *History Workshop Journal* 15 (1983).
2 Wally Seccombe's 'The Housewife and Her Labour Under Capitalism' *New Left Review* (Jan/Feb. 1979), was the catalyst in this debate.
3 For more detailed discussion of this controversy, see H. Hartmann (and others) in Z. Eisenstein (ed.), *Capitalism, Patriarchy and the Case for Socialist Feminism* (Monthly Review Press, New York, 1979); N. Sokoloff, *Between Money and Love: The Dialectics of Women's Home and Market Work* (Praeger, New York, 1980); K. Young, L. Wolkowitz and R. McCullagh (eds), *Of Marriage and the Market* (CSE Books, 1981).
4 See Lee Holcombe, 'Victorian Wives and Property: Reform of the

Married Women's Property Law, 1857–1882' in Martha Vicinus (ed.), *A Widening Sphere: Changing Roles of Victorian Women* (Indiana University Press, Bloomington, 1977).

5 Patriarchy is a much-contended and discussed concept. Classic discussions and definitions can be found in books such as Kate Millett, *Sexual Politics* (Ballantine, New York, 1970); Juliet Mitchell, *Psychoanalysis and Feminism* (Penguin, Harmondsworth, 1975); and Veronica Beechey's article, 'On Patriarchy', *Feminist Review*, no. 3 (1979). The most useful discussion to emerge recently is that of Judy Lown in 'Not So Much a Factory, More a Form of Patriarchy' in Eva Gamarnikow et al. (eds), *Gender Class and Work* (Heinemann, 1983). Lown argues that the essence of patriarchy lies in the twin concepts of women's and children's dependence on, and service due, to older men.

6 Lillian Rubin *Worlds of Pain* (Basic, New York, 1976); Ross 'Survival Networks'.

7 For a full discussion of this see Jane Lewis *The Politics of Motherhood* (Croom Helm, 1980); Diana Gittins *Fair Sex: Family Size and Structure 1900–1939* (Hutchinson, 1982) and *The Family in Question: Changing Households and Familiar Ideology* (Macmillan, 1985).

8 Michael Anderson *Family Structure in Nineteenth Century Lancashire* (Cambridge University Press, Cambridge, 1970) is a classic discussion of these types of exchange.

9 See Leonore Davidoff and Catherine Hall, 'Marriage as an Enterprise: the English Middle Class in Town and Countryside 1780–1850', paper presented at the American Historical Society Meeting, Washington DC, 1982. For a contemporary discussion, see Carol Stack, *All Our Kin* (Harper & Row, New York, 1974).

10 W.G. Hoskins 'The Rise and Decline of the Serge Industry in the South-West of England', unpublished MSc. thesis, University of London, 1929.

11 There had been occasional attempts by members of Yorkshire unions to unionize here in the late nineteenth century, but none were successful.

12 These were carried out by Anthea Duquemin.

13 This observation was a result of personal discussion between Judith Walkowitz and myself. See J. Walkowitz, *Prostitution and Victorian Society: Women Class and the State* (Cambridge University Press, Cambridge 1980).

14 Cissie Fairchild, 'Female Sexual Attitudes and the Rise of Illegitimacy: a case study', *Journal of Interdisciplinary History* VIII (4) (1978); U. Henriques, 'Bastardy and the New Poor Law', *Past and Present* 36 (1967); Françoise Ducrocq, 'De la loi des pauvres à la loi de la jungle: Londres 1850–1870', in Marie-Claire Pasquier et al (eds), *Strategies des Femmes* (Tierce, Paris, 1984).

15 For a synopsis of theories of marital fertility see Gittins, *Fair Sex*.

16 See P. Laslett, K. Oosterveen and R. Smith (eds), *Bastardy and Its Comparative History* (Arnold, 1980).

17 Leonore Davidoff 'The Separation of Home and Work? Landladies and Lodgers in Nineteenth and Twentieth Century England' in S. Burman

(ed.), *Fit Work for Women* (Croom Helm, 1979).

18 Ross 'Survival Networks'.

Index

abortion and miscarriage 17, 19, 157, 159–63, 165–6
Acorn, George 87
Acts of Parliament
  Contagious Diseases Act 10, 16, 126, 131, 141
  Criminal Law Amendment Act 126
  Elementary Education Act *1870* 101
  Factory Act *1891* 154
  Married Women's Property Acts *1870,1882* 101, 104, 125
  Maternity and Child Welfare Act *1918* 157
  Matrimonial Causes Act *1878* 125
age of consent 126
All Change Here (Naomi Mitchison) 36, 43
Anderson, Michael 227
anthropology 1–2
armed forces 199
Austen, Jane 156
autobiography 12, 15, 28–44 *passim*, 87, 111, 178–87 *passim*

Baby: The Mother's Magazine 79
Balgarnie, Florence 130, 131
Banks, J.A. 7, 17, 99, 152–3
Barrow 225–43 *passim*
Bayly, M. 100
Bell, Lady Florence 107
Belloc, Hilaire 113
benefits and pensions
  maternity 79
  national insurance 102, 106, 151, 163, 199
  separation allowances 88
  widows' 162
Benson, John 231, 234–5

Berdoe, Edward 83
Besant, Annie 127, 128–9
Beveridge, William 5, 101
birth control 12, 17, 129, 149–66 *passim*
birth control clinics 157, 162, 165
birth rate 3, 12, 17, 76, 99, 124, 138, 149, 151–2, 155
Bjura, Janet 19
Blackwell, Elizabeth 127, 131
Blake, Jex 14
Bloom, Ursula 35
Board of Trade 237
Booth, Charles 107
Bosanquet, Charles 101
Bosanquet, Helen 99, 100, 226
Bowley A.L. 224
Branca, Patricia 7, 8
breastfeeding 93*n20*, 94*n32*
Brittain, Vera 36–7, 40, 41, 42, 44
Broadhurst, Henry 103
Bulcraig, Clara 189
Bunting, Evelyn 78
Burnett, John 107
Buss, Frances 37
Butler, Josephine 10

Campbell, Beatrix 20
capitalism 231–6, 252
celibacy 138, 151, 158
census returns 5, 18, 76–7, 125, 227, 252–3
chainworkers 104, 105
Chamberlain, Joseph 9
Charity Organisation Society 7, 112
Chesterton, Ada E. 113
childbirth, *see* pregnancy and childbirth
childhood
  accommodation 29–30

child abuse 83
childcare 4, 11, 53, 79–80, 85, 105
childminding 34, 85, 109–10, 154,
    228, 231, 234
  contribution to family budget 56–61,
    86–8
  discipline 85–6
  gender differences 34, 58–60, 63–5
  gender socialization 49–67, 87–8, 101,
    134–4
  help with housework 14, 52–6, 61–4,
    85, 109–10, 188, 262
  mealtimes 33–4
  pocket money 56–7, 60
  see also education and training; family
    life and marriage; health and
    medicine; infant mortality;
    pregnancy and childbirth
Chorley, Katherine 31, 33, 38, 39, 41, 43
Church, Lavinia (née Orton) 181–4, 186
Church, Richard 181–4, 186
civil service 154, 177, 178
cleaning 236
  see also housekeeping and housework
clerks 176
Cohen, M. 230
coitus interruptus 153, 158
Cole, Margaret 154
commuting 31–2
condoms 159
consumer action 19
cooks 29, 32
Corke, Helen 178, 179
cotton industry 236–8
credit 201, 202, 242
Crook, Rosemary 19
Crooks, Will 87
Crossick, Geoffrey 180
cruelty to children 83
Cunningham, Hugh 108
Curtis Brown, Jean 34, 38–9, 40, 43

Darwinism 2
Davidoff, Leonore 9–10, 40
Davin, Anna 101
Degler, Carl 9, 15
Departmental Committee on National
    Health Insurance *1914* 105
diaries 15, 36–7, 42–3, 111, 156
diet *see* food and diet
Dinnerstein, Dorothy 13
division of labour by gender *see* family
    life and marriage

divorce and separation 103, 107–08, 124,
    125, 127, 138–9, 208, 210
doctors *see* health
domestic technology 3, 7, 11, 55, 231–2,
    233
domestic work *see* housekeeping and
    housework
dress 59, 86
dressmaking 233–4, 203
Drysdale, C.V. 162
Dubois, Ellen 134
Duquenin, Anthea

Eastty, Annie 132
Edgeworth, F.Y. 113
education and training 2, 99
  absenteeism and conflict with home
    responsibilities 87, 88–90, 109–11
  compulsory education 74–5, 125, 153
  gender differentiation 30, 37–8, 101,
    177
  see also school; teaching
Egerton, George (Mary Chavelita
    Lunne) 134–5
Eliot, George 12
Ellis, Havelock 154
employment 18, 103–6, 175–89, 200,
    203, 223–44
eugenics 109, 136, 151, 152, 163
Eyles, Leonora 158

Fabian Women's Group 80
factory inspectors 104
Fairchild, Cissie 253–4
Faithfull, Lilian 29–30, 34, 43
family life and marriage
  division of labour by gender
    attitudes 1–3, 5–6, 11, 17–18,
      99–100, 106, 149
    changing attitudes 114, 166
    children's learning of 49–67
    labour movement's acceptance 105
    Liverpool 197, 204
    skilled workers and shopkeepers
      176–8
    social welfare agencies 207
    teachers 187–8
  family income and budget, *see* wages
  family wage, *see* wages
  marriage attitudes 5, 15, 150–1, 250–1
  mutual aid 19, 86, 107, 183, 203–04,
    233, 241–2, 250–65
  parental authority and discipline 51,
    60, 67, 85–6, 112–13

relationships
  brothers/sisters 30, 63–5, 177, 262
  fatherhood 6, 14, 27, 30–2, 51, 67,
    251
  husband/wife 15–18, 84–5, 99–100,
    106–08, 123–43, 150–5, 164,
    182, 195–212, 250
  mother/baby 84
  mother/daughter 14–15, 34–6,
    38–45, 49–67
  mother/schoolchild 88–90
  motherhood 5–6, 10–11, 13–4, 53,
    73–90, 91*n*3, 99, 251
  state intervention 8, 11, 99–115,
    206–08
family planning, *see* birth control
Family Planning Association 165
Fawcett, M.G. 10, 113
feminist movement 1–3, 16, 41–2,
    124–43
fertility, *see* birth rate; birth control
Fifth International Neo-Malthusian and
    Birth Control Conference 158
Flint, Elizabeth 89
Florence (George Egerton) 135
Foakes, Grace 80
food and diet 8, 78, 86, 237, 239–41
  mealtimes 33–4
  school meals 112–13, 115,
  see also breastfeeding
Freewoman, The 139–42 *passim*
Friday, Nancy 13

Gay, Peter 15
gender differentiation, *see* childhood
gender socialization, *see* childhood
Girls' Public Day School Trust 37
Girouard, Mark 29
Gissing, George 41, 179
Glass David 163
Good Housekeeping 164
Gordon, Linda 134
Gorham, Deborah 9, 28, 35
Grand, Sarah 125
Great Scourge and how to end it, The
    (Christabel Pankhurst) 136, 137, 138
Griffith, Edward 155

Hamilton, Cicely 15, 137, 138
Harman, Lillian 132
Harrison, Brian 100
health and medicine

doctors 2,7,83
  mothers' treatments 83–4
  nurses 78
  state intervention 103, 105, 109–12
  vermin 53–4
  womens' 4, 8, 153, 155, 184
  see also abortion and miscarriage;
    birth control; infant mortality;
    pregnancy and childbirth; venereal
    disease
health visitors 101, 111–12, 157
Hewitt, Margaret 110, 240
Higgs, Edward 18
Higgs, Henry 107
Himes, Norman 165
Hinton, James 128
hire purchase 205
Hogg, M.H. 224
holidays and leisure 3, 28, 87, 108, 180
homework 177, 203, 231–6
hosiery industry 104
Hot Bread and Chips (Elizabeth Flint) 89
housekeeping and housework 4, 7, 27–9,
    32–3, 50–65, 68*n*3, 101, 107–08, 153,
    166, 176, 250
  see also childhood; help with
    housework; domestic technology;
    servants
housing 3–4, 7–8, 28–9, 79, 84, 114–15,
    158, 186, 198, 230
Hoxton Childhood (Arthur Jasper) 80, 84
Hufton, Olwen 19
Hughes, M.V. 35, 43
Humphries, Jane 106

I Have Been Young (Helena Swanwick)
    34, 38, 40–1, 43
illegitimacy 5, 18, 104, 149, 151, 161–2,
    253–4
In Our Infancy (Helen Corke) 178, 179
In the House of my Pilgrimage (Lilian
    Faithfull) 29–30, 34, 43
infant mortality 3, 13, 77–83, 94*nn*27,
    29, 30 153, 155
infant welfare movement 11, 102,
    105–06, 110, 111, 154, 157
Interdepartmental Committee on
    Physical Deterioration *1904* 229, 240

Jasper, Arthur 80, 84

Kanthack, Emilia 111
kinship, *see* family life and marriage:
    mutual aid

Kitzinger, Sheila 73–4
Knowles, Josephine Pitcairn 41

labour movement 11, 19, 105
Lady's Child, A (Enid Starkie) 30, 32, 43
Lancaster 225–43 *passim*
Last, Netta 4, 111
Legitimation League, The 132, 139
leisure, *see* holidays and leisure
Liverpool 198–212, 214*n14*, 224
Liverpool Personal Service Society 204
Loane, Margaret 108, 111
lodgers 232–3
London Child of the 1870's A (M.V. Hughes) 35, 43
London Married Teachers' Association 182
Lummis, Trevor 108
Lunne, Mary Chavelita, *see* Egerton, George

MacArthur, Mary 105
MacDonald, Ramsey 105
Manchester Health Society 114
Manchester Made Them (Katherine Chorley) 31, 33, 38, 39, 41, 43
Mann, Tom 103
Markham, Violet 7
Marriage as a Trade (Cicely Hamilton) 137
marriage guidance 165
Married Love (Marie Stopes) 155
Marsden, Dora 139–140
Martin, Anna 109, 122–13, 114
Martindale, Louisa 135, 136
Marx, Eleanor 128
Mary Oliver (May Sinclair) 44–5
maternal deprivation 6,13
maternity, *see* family life and marriage; pregnancy and childbirth
maternity benefit 79
maternity leave 184–5
Maternity: Letters from Working Women, *see* Women's Cooperative Guild
Maugham, Somerset 111
meals *see* food and diet
mechanization 252
medicines 83–4
 see also health and medicine
Medical Defence Union 165
Men's and Women's Club 123–4, 126–32, 142
menstruation 35–6, 151, 159

merchant navy 199
Metropolitan Board Teachers' Association (MBTA) 180
migration 253, 256, 261
Minor, Iris 103
Mitchel, Hannah 11, 111
Mitchison, Naomi 36, 43
moneylenders 204
motherhood *see* family life and marriage
Mothers' Defence League 113–14
Muller, Henrietta 128, 129, 132
munitions 233
My Mother Myself (Nancy Friday) 13
My Part of the River (Grace Foakes) 80

National Association for the Promotion of Social Science 104
National Association of Schoolmasters 18
National Birth Control Association, *see* Family Planning Association
National Society for the Prevention of Cruelty to Children (NSPCC) 83, 112
National Union of Womens' Suffrage Societies 136
New Home, The (C.S. Peel) 29, 32–3, 34
New Machiavelli, The (H.G. Wells) 178–9
'new woman' 124, 132–5, 139–41
 see also feminist movement
Nield Chew, Ada 11
novels 41, 44–5, 124, 133–5, 179

Of Human Bondage (Somerset Maugham) 111
Ogle, Dr William 100
Oliver, Katherine 140
oral history 12, 18, 49–67, 105, 108, 225–45
Orton, Lavinia 181–4, 186
Orwell, George 111
Osterud, Nancy 104
Over the Bridge (Richard Church) 181–4, 186
'overlaying' 82–3, 94*n32*

Pall Mall Gazette, The 126
Pankhurst, Christabel 136, 137, 138
Parr, Joy 85
patriarchy 27, 51, 264
 see also family life and marriage: fatherhood

pawnbroking 201, 202, 203, 242–3
Pearson, Karl 126, 129, 130
Peel, C.S. 29, 32–3, 34
Pember Reeves, Magdalen Stuart 7, 107, 224, 228, 230, 237, 240
Penny Capitalists; a study of nineteenth century working-class entrepreneurs (John Benson) 231, 234–5
Peterson, Jeanne 7,9
Petty, Florence 85–6
philanthropy 10, 39–40, 100, 101
Pilgrim Trust, The 237
pocket money 56–7, 60
Poor Law 5, 100, 107–08, 112, 151
population figures 75–6, 156
    see also birth rates; census returns
Poverty: a Study of Town Life (B. Seebohm Rowntree) 102, 224, 229, 240, 242
poverty line 224
pregnancy and childbirth 8, 75–9, 128, 150, 153, 155, 163–4, 184–5
    see also birth control; infant mortality; maternity leave
Preston 225–43 *passim*
Price, Marion 16
proletarianization 252–3
prostitution 126, 130
protective legislation 102, 104–05, 154

Ragged Homes and How to Mend Them (M. Bayly) 100
Rathbone, Eleanor 199, 213 *bibliography*
Regeneration of Two (George Egerton) 134
Reid, Dr George 154
rents 8
    strikes 19
retail trade 176–7, 179, 223, 230, 234–5, 242
Road to Wigan Pier (George Orwell) 111
Roberts, Robert 109, 151
Rosaldo, Michelle 2
Rose, Phyllis 12, 17
Rosenberg, Carol Smith 8
Round about a Pound a Week (M.S. Pember Reeves) 7, 107, 224, 228, 230, 237, 240
Rowntree, B. Seebohm 102, 224, 229, 240, 242
Royal Commission on Divorce and Matrimonial Causes *1912/13* 107–08, 138–9

Royal Commission on the Factory Acts *1876* 104
Royal Commission on Labour *1894* 103
Royal Commission on Unemployment Insurance 102
Rubin, L. 250
Rubinstein, David 110
Runciman, James 110

Saint Pancras School for Mothers 78, 79, 82
sanitary conditions 35, 79, 230
Scharlieb, Dr Mary 165
school
    attendance officers 11, 101, 109–10, 112, 113
    Boards 74, 87, 180
    inspectors 83
    meals 112–3
    see also education and training; teachers
Schreiner, Olive 127, 133
Schwartz, Cowan R. 7
Scott, Joan 106, 176, 179, 230
Scott Smith, Daniel 153
seasonal work 198
Select Committee of the House of Lords of the Sweating System *1889* 104, 105
servants 3–4, 9, 18, 28–9, 32–3, 153, 166, 251
Servile State, The (Hilaire Belloc) 113
sex and sexuality 9, 15–7, 149–66
    age of consent 126
    feminist movement 123–43
    husband/wife relationship 107
    parental discipline 60
    sex education 35–7, 134–5
    state involvement 101
Sexual Impulse in Women, The (Havelock Ellis) 154
Sharpe, Letitia 129, 130
Sharpe, Maria 126, 127–8, 130, 131
shipping and shipbuilding 56, 198–9, 230
shop workers, *see* retail trades
Shorter, Edward 13
Sinclair, May 44–5
single women
    attitudes to 5, 125, 141, 151
    employment 1, 18, 200, 210
    family responsibilities 19, 62–3, 180, 250, 261–2

illegitimacy 161–2
  see also widows
60 Years of Home (Ursula Bloom) 35
skilled workers 103–04, 176, 225–6
Slater, E. 158
Smith, Sydney 163
Smout, T.C. 151
Snowden, Ethel 135
social investigation 99–115 *passim*
  199–206 *passim*, 224–44 *passim*
social life
  'at home' 39
  calling 10, 11, 38–9
  'coming out' 39, 40, 42–3
  etiquette 27
  mealtimes 33–4
  see also philanthropy
Somerset, Lady Helen 39
Spencer, Herbert 2
Spencer, F.H. 178
Spring Rice, Margery 4, 224–5, 228,
  230, 239, 240
Stacey, Margaret 16
Starkie, Enid 30, 32, 43
Stead, W.T. 126
Stedman Jones, Gareth 108
Stoddard, Dr W.H.S. 158
Stokes, Esther 32
Stopes, Marie 155, 158
suffrage 10, 19, 21*n*2, 135, 139
Suffragette, The 136
Swanwick, Helen 34, 38, 40–1, 43
sweated trades 103
Swiney, Frances 136–8

Tawney, R.H. 112
teaching 18, 154, 175–89
Tebbutt, Melanie 196
Testament of Youth (Vera Brittain) 36–7,
  40, 41, 42, 44
textile industry 1, 236–8, 252–65
Thane, Pat 104
Tilly, Louise 106, 176, 179, 230
To the Lighthouse (Virginia Woolf) 45
Tomes, Nancy 17
trade boards 10
Trade Union Congress (TUC) 103
trade unions 18, 103–05
Tuckwell, Gertrude 105

Unclassed, The (George Gissing) 179
unemployment 198–9, 207
Upholstered Cage, The (Josephine

Pitcairn Knowles) 41
venereal disease
  Contagious Diseases Acts 10, 16, 126,
    131, 141
  feminist attitudes 124, 136–8
  fiction 133
  protection against 159
  World War I 141
Victorian Girl and the Feminist Ideal, The
  (Deborah Gorham) 9, 28, 35–6
Virgin Soil (George Egerton) 134–5

wages
  equality 1
  family income and budget
    children's contribution 49, 56–61,
      86–8, 178
    cost of new baby 78–9
    mothers' control of 8–9, 49, 51, 75,
      113–14, 195–212
    women's contribution to 185–6,
      223–44
  family wage 103–06, 198–202, 207
  poverty 102
  rise in 3
  teachers' 182–3, 185–6
  textile workers' 1
Wages Councils 10
Wall, Richard 227
washing 55, 108, 231–2, 236
Webb, Beatrice 9, 19
Webb, Sidney 9
welfare 19, 53, 102, 109–15, 206–08
  see also benefits and pensions
welfare centres 157–8, 165
  see also infant welfare movement
Wells, H.G. 178–9
West, Anthony 13
West, Rebecca 13, 111, 139
Westminster Review, The 125
Whichelo, Lily 34
widows 18, 161–2, 229, 238–9, 259–61
wife-beating 17, 85, 101, 107, 197, 202,
  204, 208–10
Wilson, Stephen 13
Wives and Mothers in Victorian Industry
  (Margaret Hewitt) 110, 240
Wollstonecraft, Mary 128
Woman in the Little House, The (Leonora
  Eyles) 158
Women, Power and Politics (Stacey and
  Price) 16

Women's Cooperative Guild 16, 19, 114, 139
  Maternity: Letters from Working Women 7, 77, 106, 111, 156
Women's Labour League 105
Women's Social and Political Union (WSPU) 139
Woodward, Kathleen 87, 108

Woolf, Virginia 45
woollen industry 252–65
Working Class Wives (Margery Spring Rice) 224–5, 228, 230, 239, 240
World War I 19, 88, 141, 233
World War II 6, 233
Wright, Helena 155

York 102, 224, 229, 240, 242